Wild Places, Wild Encounters
Exploring Edinburgh's Living Landscape

Glen Cousquer

WHITTLES PUBLISHING

Published by
Whittles Publishing Ltd,
Dunbeath,
Caithness, KW6 6EG,
Scotland, UK

www.whittlespublishing.com

© **2024 Glen Cousquer**
ISBN 978-184995-571-3

Printed and bound in Great Britain by
TJ Books Limited, Padstow, Cornwall

Contents

Preface

As a child growing up, I felt the call of the wild, and of Scotland's wild landscapes in particular, deep within my soul and the marrow of my bones. It is perhaps this same primordial call that has led you to pick up this book and alight on these words. This call is something we can all relate to. It animates our very being, for we are of the world, a part of nature, and yet we are increasingly aware of how estranged we have become. We carry a sadness and a profound sense of loss that we are unsure how to interpret. Every time we experience a sense of awe at the wonder of creation that is nature, we touch that which is beautiful and wholesome beyond words. These are the horizons that call us to venture beyond ourselves and to seek a sense and experience of connection and connectedness.

I spent my childhood and grew up in the city of Bristol, in south-west England, and my beckoning horizons were the nearest green spaces. I lived in Downend, which had been fully absorbed into the city of Bristol, making it harder to find those green spaces. The cricketer W.G. Grace (1848–1915) had himself been born in Downend, and could so easily have been an inspiration for a young lad such as myself, for he was both one of the greatest players of the game and a doctor. He played first-class cricket for a record-equalling 44 seasons (1865–1908), during which he captained Gloucestershire, England and the Marylebone Cricket Club (MCC), scoring England's first test century against Australia in 1880.

He could have been my inspiration – but he was not. Growing up in the late 19th century at a time when Downend was 4 miles from the city boundary, Grace had been blessed with the freedom of a country life, roaming freely with other village boys. It is said that one of his regular activities was throwing stones at birds in the fields, and that he later claimed that this led to his becoming such a skilled bowler and outfielder.[1] Whenever I hear the phrase 'killing two birds with one stone' I feel a sense of sadness and repulsion. The songs of the blackbird and the song thrush have always lifted my spirits, calling me out into the green spaces beyond the overly manicured and sterile village greens and cricket pitches. I am more interested in how we might bring two stones to life with one bird. Discovering a thrush's anvil and watching them breaking open snails on their chosen stone has always fired my curiosity. When I then discovered how the bird poop left behind on a perching stone provides nutrients for other life forms to integrate into their own growth and development, I found myself starting to experience the flux and flow of the ecosystem we call nature.

It was not long before my wanderings allowed me to discover the River Frome, which passes through Downend and Frenchay on its way to mysteriously join the River Avon

---

1 Grace's outstanding fielding was largely founded on his being such a strong thrower of the ball. He, himself, attributed this skill to his country-bred childhood in which stone-throwing at crows was a daily exercise. In later life, Grace, commenting on a decline in English fielding standards, blamed it on 'the falling numbers of country-bred boys who strengthen their arms by throwing stones at birds in the fields'. Rae (1998, p.21).

in the centre of Bristol. I say 'mysteriously', because this blue corridor literally disappears under the city, such is our habit of concreting over nature and papering over our cracks. Nature will, however, always find its way up through the cracks, and this was something I was slowly coming to appreciate and become fascinated by. My explorations of the Frome Valley Walkway, and the Oldbury Court Estate in particular, soon led to my first encounter with the swans, dippers and kingfishers that were to become a lifelong fascination. I also came face to face with the thundering weirs left behind by the industrial mills powered by the water flowing over these man-made structures, and the equally deafening mindlessness of our species in the form of shopping trolleys stranded in the river and sewage outfalls spilling into the water. This was the 1980s, and I was hungry to learn how to make a difference. As a member of the Cubs and the junior sections of the Royal Society for the Protection of Birds (RSPB) and the Royal Society for Nature Conservation (RSNC),[2] I took up every opportunity available to engage with nature conservation. One such opportunity took the form of the RSNC's Gold Award for Nature Conservation, providing a series of challenges to be completed. For me the final challenge involved organising an initiative to make a difference. What better way to do this than to organise a river clean-up? And that was the vision I set about realising, bringing together members of my local Cub pack and Wildlife Watch group and their parents to help retrieve some of those trolleys and other rubbish from the river. Over the years that followed I sought to pursue this vision of exploring and caring for our wild spaces and wildlife. It was this ambition that was to take me from the south-west

of England to the south-east of Scotland. It was the same ambition that saw me survive the bleak and very dark years of my veterinary studies without losing sight of my nature connection, despite the very best attempts of a scientific training to desensitise me to all that matters in this world. It was this ambition that saw me return to the south-west of England to work as a wildlife vet for the RSPCA and that subsequently saw me retrain in outdoor and environmental education.

When I was offered a place to study veterinary medicine at the University of Edinburgh, I leapt at the chance to discover and explore the Scotland I had read so much about through the works of Robert Louis Stevenson, Walter Scott, John Buchan, Samuel Boswell and Gavin Maxwell. That was in 1991, and over the last 30 years I have continued to nurture and deepen a reciprocal relationship between my own wild heart and passion for nature and the wild places of Scotland and her capital city. Every walk I have taken both within and beyond the city has contributed to the development of a rich understanding and appreciation of the nature and wildlife living alongside us and our own neglected nature, whose wellbeing is entangled with and dependent on the natural processes of the living world.

Robert Louis Stevenson (1850–1894) spent his own childhood exploring Edinburgh's wild places, and treasured the times he spent with his maternal grandparents in Colinton Village, exploring the wooded banks bordering the Water of Leith. His grandfather, Lewis Balfour, was minister of the parish of Colinton from around 1823. In the garden of the Colinton Manse stood a yew tree that had at 100 cm from the ground a girth of some 357 cm, and from whose branches hung a swing. The young Robert's imagination would

---

2   In 1995 the RSNC was renamed the Wildlife Trusts: https://www.wildlifetrusts.org/about-us/our-history

have been inspired by the uplifting experience of swinging backwards and forwards from that branch. That this inspiration is suffused with an appreciative and affectionate quality is suggested by the tribute paid to that tree in 'To Minnie', from *A Child's Garden of Verses* (1885), in which he writes:

"And the old manse is changed to-day;
It wears an altered face
And shields a stranger race.
The river on from mill to mill,
Flows past our childhood garden still;
But ah! we children never more
Shall watch it from the water-door!
Below the yew – it is still there –
Our phantom voices haunt the air
As we were still at play,
And I can hear them call and say,
How far is it to Babylon?"

In 'The Manse' which appears in Memories and Portraits (1895, p.108), he speaks of the "great yew making elsewhere a pleasing horror of shade", a theme that is further reflected in this quote, attributed to Stevenson:

A yew, which is one of the glories of the village. Under the circuit of its wide, black branches, it was always dark and cool, and there was a green scurf over all the trunk among which glistened the round, bright drops of resin.

Balfour, 1901, p.42.

Stevenson was a courageous character who remained true to his heart's passion and his calling. He could easily have allowed himself to follow in the footsteps of his successful family of lighthouse engineers, a family who for three generations were responsible for pioneering and building over half of Scotland's lighthouses. It is suggested that Fidra Island was the inspiration for Stevenson's classic *Treasure*

Figure P.1: The lighthouse on the Island of Fidra provides a useful navigational aid to those navigating the Firth of Forth. The light of the sun, our planet's life-giving star, accompanies us through our own lives, and at sunrise and sundown seems to speak to us with particular force. Such moments of awe remind us of the mysterious wonder and sacredness of life, a miracle we seem to keep losing sight of. Walking in search of awe lies at the heart of this book, and my hope is that you will be gifted moment after moment of wonder and grace.

Island (Figure P.1), and it is probably fair to say that the light that shone out and helped guide Stevenson was his ability to bring the richness of lived experience to life on the page.

Stevenson knew how to travel and explore the world. His travels with a donkey inspired my own research into the welfare of working equines on expedition. The central question at the heart of my work is one of relationality. We are born in relation. We are relational beings and yet in our western society our skill in crafting relationships receives little attention. That is partly because our society has become so materialistic and individualistic. We seek to consume before we seek to commune, and therein lies a clue as to the fundamental root cause of the mental health pandemic we are living through. Our patterns of consumption are a sign of numbing. We are suffering from a loss of meaning, of connection, of joyfulness and of wonder. And this suffering leads us to seek distraction. We seek to control what we are afraid of, and this leads us to exert power over. But no matter how many relationships are initiated by power and strength, none have ever been deepened by these 'qualities'. To deepen our relationships requires us to recognise our mutual vulnerabilities and interdependence. This is true whether we are seeking to deepen our relationship with our selves – with our deepest nature, with our friends and family – or with the natural world that lies beyond our ken. To explore such territory is an act of befriending.

In this book, I attempt to facilitate a little of this exploration. I don't pretend to have any definitive answers, and I recognise that the step from the page into lived reality feels more like a leap than a measured step. I hope my words and imagery stay true to the experiences I am seeking to share, and that these may inspire you to cultivate your own. In his essay on the American naturalist, Henry David Thoreau, Stevenson writes:

> The seeming significance of nature's appearances, their unchanging strangeness to the senses, and the thrilling response which they awaken in the mind of man … If we could only write near enough to the facts, and yet with no pedestrian calm, but ardently, we might transfer the glamour of reality direct upon our pages.

Stevenson, 1895, pp.148–149.

I hope my own ardour and passion remains pedestrian in its steady, patient and appreciative attentiveness whilst retaining the urgency needed to awaken not just your mind, but your heart and spirit. To do this, I have paid careful ethnographic attention to the unexpected depths of my own encounters and experiences as I have repeatedly explored a collection of my favourite wild places in and around Edinburgh. This has therefore been a co-creative and collaborative exercise, with nature very much co-authoring the narrative, providing me with material, questions and inspiration.

◾ References

Rae, S. (1998). *W. G. Grace: A life*. London: Faber and Faber.

Stevenson, R.L. (1895). 'Henry David Thoreau: His character and opinions'. In: *The Novels and Tales of Robert Louis Stevenson: Miscellanies Volume 2*. London: Scribner.

Stevenson, R.L. (1895). *Memories and portraits*. New York: Scribners.

Stevenson, R.L. (1885). *A child's garden of verses*. London: Longman Green and Co.

Balfour, G. (1901). *The life of Robert Louis Stevenson*. London: Methuen and Co.

Acknowledgements

The crafting of this text would not have been possible without the wild places and wild encounters that have written their way onto the page. I owe nature the deepest debt of gratitude. When I look deeper, though, my gratitude extends to those who have accompanied me on these walks and on my journey through life.

In particular, I want to thank my partner, Kirsty, for accompanying me on all these walks and for helping me to develop my gratitude practice through our shared review of our days spent out in the field. Kirsty has patiently afforded me the time and space to photograph and to write, and has gently told me off whenever my desire for a photograph led me to ignore the signs that my presence was intrusive and causing discomfort. Kirsty has also reread my narrative and helped in its development, whilst helping me sustain my belief that this was a narrative worth sharing. Thank you, Kirsty.

Several other people were not physically present on the walks, but were very much there in spirit. My mentors in fieldcraft and eco-literacy were ever present; in particular Dan Puplett – you are a legend and an inspiration. I thank, too, Dr Avinash Bansode, with whom I have trained as a mindfulness teacher; we have delivered wonderfully rich nature and mindfulness retreats together that have helped me learn to bridge the worlds of outdoor education and mindfulness.

Several other mentors and spiritual guides have made very significant and inspiring contributions to my journey, including Geoffrey Baines, Ali and John Philip Newell, Hamish Brown, Robbie Nicol and Jonathan Baxter. The list of thinkers I owe a debt of thanks to is immense, and would start with John O'Donohue, David Whyte and Mary Oliver – thank you all. I thank very appreciatively my mother and father who encouraged me to pursue my passion for wildlife and writing and all the teachers who fed my curiosity. This gift will be treasured forever.

I would like to thank Caroline Petherick for her incredibly attentive editing skills and for helping to refine the manuscript, and the team at Whittles for everything they have contributed to ensure this work brings to life Edinburgh's Living Landscape.

And, finally, looking ahead to the future, I thank all those who pick up this book, find inspiration in its pages and are inspired to contribute to the restoration of our ecosystems, whether locally, nationally or globally.

Foreword

There are two key reasons why I'm excited to write a foreword for *Wild Places, Wild Encounters*. One is that Edinburgh is my favourite city in these islands. My mother-in-law, Christine, although she has lived in Orkney for six decades, has a flat just off the Meadows. With my partner Mary I have been visiting for 40 years, and what Glen Cousquer has captured here is something that I have long surmised; Edinburgh is wonderful for wildlife, and his important book now gives me an opportunity to say thank you to the place …

… for the moment, for example, when I heard the trilling notes of waxwings in a park near Portobello. And there suddenly were the beautiful little winter nomads, their thick, lax cinnamon-ginger plumage more fur overcoat than feathers, tricked out in details that have the precision of human cosmetics – the Egyptian mascara over the eye, the curving lemon ends to tail and wings, and the red blobs of wax on their coverts. Waxwings are like birds-of-paradise but adapted to the northern winter.

On another occasion I watched, just off one of the city's seawalls, a big flock of velvet scoters and long-tailed ducks. The birds rode the slap and swell of the Firth of Forth on an ice-cold January morn, yet that fierce weather was no more to those wildfowl than a Sunday spin on a merry-go-round. Down they'd go into the troughs and up they would rise, suddenly winking into view, the black and white of their plumage crisp against the water's steel-grey.

Carrion Crows - The Keepers of the Castle. Image: Mark Cocker

I'm struck by the manner in which Edinburgh allows the very urban to slip effortlessly into the entirely wild. The smell of fresh-brewing beer can mingle with the coconut scents from the best display of flowering gorse in any European capital. I'm thinking of the yellow walls of blossom climbing the slopes of Holyrood Park in near-tropical abundance.

I was once heading down by the Water of Leith (an area outlined in superb detail in Glen's landscape walk number 12) to see an exhibition on the Belford Road. Suddenly I was upended by the vision of a fleck-throated predator snaking through the weed on the opposite bank. There was a mink hunting darkly in broad daylight, and it occurred to me: which other major capital could blend a creature so savage to a spot so civilised as Edinburgh's Gallery of Modern Art?

I am not surprised to learn that the city around which the author has woven this volume of wild encounters boasts more green space than any other large urban area in Britain. Most striking is that the figure of 49 per cent is more than three times that of Liverpool and more than double that in London. In this matter Edinburgh stands head and shoulders over others, and this book capture it all brilliantly.

Yet there is a real head and shoulders to this city, towering above its very heart. It forms part of a skyline visible from almost any street. It is called Arthur's Seat and it is my default destination on every visit. Robert Louis Stevenson called it 'a mountain in virtue of its bold design', but truthfully it is an extinct volcano formed 350 million years ago, and it means that the very essence of the other erupts into Edinburgh's urban centre. As Glen himself points out, as you wander about the area it allows you to forget that you are within a large city at all.

One of the things I love is to skirt the low cliffs called the Salisbury Crags and watch the carrion crows riding the rising bluffs of air as they blast off the Firth of Forth. These birds are such masters of the breeze. Then they land and saunter casually among the joggers and passers-by, gazing down on the skyline with an almost proprietorial air. At times you feel the crows have as much of a sense of belonging as you and me.

And this really touches on the part of this guide that most moves and delights me. Glen isn't only interested in Edinburgh as a dwelling for our kind. He is concerned for the rights of all other species that call the city home. They are integral to the sense of vitality, health and beauty in this place.

We are deeply familiar with books that tell us how we can go there, see this and do that. They sometimes explain how contact with nature is good for us. The problem with this approach is that it continues to look upon nature as a resource, and as a set of organisms and conditions delivering benefits for us.

Glen Cousquer is keen to break through these anthropocentric assumptions: to assert that relationships cut both ways; that if we feel better because of encounters with nature, then all those flowers, trees, fungi, insects, birds and mammals should also benefit from our presence and our attention. Glen bids us to attend to *their* well-being. That we feel connected and that these positive emotions lead to reciprocal action. On this issue he is way ahead of the curve.

So this book is as much a guide on to how we should live within nature, and acknowledge our deep obligations as a guide to a city's wildlife riches. In this regard it is groundbreaking. It is my kind of guide to my kind of city, and I'm absolutely sure that you will open its pages and feel the same.

Mark Cocker

Introduction

This chapter has been written to help you find inspiration and wonder as your eyes wander across the pages of this guidebook, and to help you carry this aliveness out beyond the leaves of this book, into the walks themselves. The intention here is to help you deepen your sense of connection with, and appreciation of, the natural world. This deepening is something that develops with time, practice and a gentle patient attitude. So you may find it can help to revisit elements of this chapter, dipping into them to help you reflect on your experiences and how your explorations of wild places can become more attentive, receptive and responsive.

The following overview summarises what is provided over the next few pages.

Overview

- Aims and objectives
- How to use this guide
- Wild walks, wild places
- Wild encounters
- Ethics and ethos
- Fieldcraft
- Ecology and ecological pilgrimage.

Aims and objectives

This guidebook has been written to help us all learn to slow down, wake up to and appreciate the green spaces and wildlife we can still encounter in and around Scotland's capital city.

In doing so, we also find ourselves waking up to and recognising the extent to which the UK has become one of the most nature-depleted and impoverished countries in Europe. It is well recognised that this perilous state has arisen largely as a result of the ravages of the industrial revolution, and the rampant growth of both the human population and the consumerism that followed it. This devastation has unfolded over several generations, and we have lost sight of what a healthy environment and fully functional ecosystem might look like. This guidebook therefore also sets out to help us to recognise this damage and what we have lost; in doing so it honours the profound grief and pain felt by a growing number of us.

All is not gloom and doom, however, for in honouring our pain we can also find it within us to notice the glimmers of a life-sustaining future trying to break through from this blanket of darkness and despair. There is a new dawn calling to us, and we can sweep the threshold clear and prepare to welcome it in. This guidebook seeks to balance a concerned outlook with a more hopeful one, for this is the threshold we stand on. Behind us lies a past in which our western colonialist and industrialist society became rich at the expense of the natural world, its indigenous peoples and its future generations. This is a past we must consign to history and take responsibility for. Ahead of us lies a field of possibility in which the relationships we nurture with our deepest selves, with others, and with the natural world can be re-imagined. We have an opportunity to reconnect and to become master artisans of connection, relationality, relationship, kinship and community. This may allow us to forge new understandings of ourselves as inter- and intra-connected beings. This can perhaps best be summarised as a shift from ego to eco.

In looking forward, in surveying this field of possibility, this guidebook recognises and pays tribute to the incredible work being undertaken by nature herself as she seeks to heal the damage we have inflicted on her. It also recognises the growing number of conservation organisations and other members of civil society who are mobilising and working together to restore natural ecosystems and embed them in a healthier societal web of interconnection and interdependency. We are still a long way from creating a future where we are living in harmony with nature, but we have greater clarity about the course we need to set and the response-abilities[1] we need to nurture.

The recent pandemic has helped us all pause and pay more attention to our local environment. This slowing down was largely imposed upon us and we now recognise the need for a slow counterculture to balance the draining effects of the hamster-wheel of modern society. We have also started to recognise the myriad connections between human health and wellbeing and the health of the ecosystem that sustains life on Planet Earth.

The principle aims of this guidebook are to encourage you to:

1. Walk with curiosity, and cultivate a sense of awe and wonder.
2. Develop your ability to read your environment, to recognise plant and animal species, and to see beyond their names to the entangled stories they are part of and contribute to.
3. Develop your understanding of ecosystems and how they function.
4. Develop your awareness of the human history, priorities and choices that have impacted on the lived environment we see today.
5. Nurture a sense of gratitude for the gift of life and an awareness of its sacredness.
6. Play your part in caring for and restoring Edinburgh's landscape and in ensuring the next generation inherit a living landscape rather than a dying one.
7. Cultivate an ability to imagine a future where nature is valued, respected and cared for.
8. Promote an awareness of our interdependence and interconnection with nature.
9. Recognise how important a flourishing natural environment is to our own health and wellbeing.
10. Contribute to an awakening to life and an appreciation of its sacred nature.

---

1   Response-ability is to be distinguished from responsibility. The term has been developed and popularised by Donna Haraway, who argues that rather than imposing ready-made, defined-in-advance frameworks (such as rights, social justice or vegan ethics), we need to respond in situated ways to our existing, irreducibly entangled, relations with other-than-human-animals. In particular, we need to create spaces and places in which we can be affected by animals in ways that attune us to their requirements. This requires us to nurture our ability to be responsive to these needs in ways that move beyond anthropomorphism. Response-abilities are potentiated 'by sensibilities and practices such as *attentiveness, politeness and curiosity, rendering each other capable, openness to encounter*, and *iteration or ongoingness*' (Bozalek and Zembylas, 2023, p.63), and are there for us to nurture and develop.

How to use this guide

This book presents 14 different walking routes carefully chosen from across the Edinburgh area to provide you, whether an armchair reader or a walker yourself, with a rich variety of seasonally flavoured and opportune encounters with nature. This will mean you can visit a range of habitats and explore a rich tapestry of socio-cultural and natural history.

The guide serves, in the first instance, to inspire you and to develop this flame of interest into a slow-burning, glowingly appealing fire that keeps drawing you back, again and again. Such fires need to be fed and nurtured beyond the magical transformation of a spark into a flame. This guide therefore seeks to keep the embers burning by providing a series of examples of surprising encounters that are then deepened through patient, kind and loving attentiveness.

You may wish to read the guide in one sitting, or to dip in and out of it as the fancy takes you. You may find it helpful to read, and even re-read, a particular chapter as part of your planning and preparation for a particular walk. It is worth bearing in mind, however, that many of the themes and encounters may cut across walks, so I would encourage you to stay open to these surprises. For example, whereas skylarks are considered in detail as part of the visits to Holyrood Park in the centre of Edinburgh and to Aberlady Bay Local Nature Reserve, in East Lothian, you may encounter them elsewhere.

The seasonal changes that make walking such a delight in this country are also woven into the account of each walk, and this provides you with an opportunity to attune yourself to the rhythm of nature and the behaviour of our flora and fauna. Other rhythms presented within the guidebook have a human quality to them and reflect the perverse relationship our species has developed with time. This interplay between hurrying and slowing down is therefore a background theme to the walks and a principal reason for my recurring invitation to slow down and pay attention. It is hoped that this helps to unveil the magic and spaciousness of each moment which we can learn to more fully live, experience and savour.

For each walk, the overview provides a description of the route, together with an account of the highlights of the walk. A map and details of the distance and terrain covered, as well as the habitat types encountered, are also provided. The historical sections are intended to help you develop a rich sense of the history of place that is ever-present, elements of which we may need to put to bed as we seek to embrace nature restoration in the years ahead. An indication of potential refreshment stops, access points and transport options are also included. The emphasis on buses and cycle routes as a way to access the start points of each walk reflects the need to promote more sustainable, carbon-neutral travel in this era of unravelling planetary ecological health. If you explore these travel options, you will find the quiet cycle route maps provided by Edinburgh Council very helpful. These can be downloaded from the council website,[2] or you can request printed copies by emailing the Active Travel team.[3]

The account of the walk that follows the Transport Links section moves beyond a traditional series of directions and into a more attentive and suggestive narrative. This is intended to help your experience become ripe with happening, as the spirit of walking with patience and presence brings forth the fullness of possibility lying latent in any walk.

2   https://www.edinburgh.gov.uk/downloads/download/14188/quietroutes-maps
3   activetravel@edinburgh.gov.uk

Wild walks wild places

The walks presented in this guidebook are listed below, together with some selected highlights and a summary of the distances covered and habitats explored. There then follows a short discussion of what makes for a wild walk and what may constitute a wild place where wild encounters become possible.

The walks

1. Blackford Pond, Blackford Hill and the Hermitage of Braid
2. Corstorphine Hill Nature Reserve
3. The River Almond from Cramond
4. London Road Gardens, Calton Hill and New Calton Burial Ground
5. Salisbury Crags, Hunter's Bog and St Margaret's Loch
6. St Mark's Park and Warriston Cemetery
7. Aberlady Bay Local Nature Reserve
8. Hewan Bank, Roslin Glen and Roslin Castle
9. Duddingston Orchard, Meadowfield Park, Dunsapie and Duddingston Loch
10. A Pentland walk: Flotterstone, Turnhouse and Carnethy Hills, and Glencorse Reservoir
11. Craigie Hill Wood, Fort and Quarries
12. The Water of Leith: from Canonmills to the Gallery of Modern Art
13. River Esk, Levenhall Links and Musselburgh Lagoons
14. The woods, shore and parkland of Dalmeny Estate.

Selected highlights

The walks listed above provide you with an opportunity to discover some of the secret gems of wild Edinburgh. These include visits to and explorations of:

- A selection of Local Nature Reserves including Aberlady Bay, the Hermitage of Braid and Blackford Hill, and Corstorphine Hill.
- Several watercourses running through Edinburgh and the Lothians on their way to the Firth of Forth, including the Water of Leith, the River Almond and the Braid Burn.
- Some of Edinburgh's most famous parks and landmarks, including Calton Hill and Holyrood Park, with a particular focus on how they support the needs of our local wildlife.
- A few secluded and all too easily overlooked Edinburgh cemeteries, including Warriston Cemetery and New Calton Burial Ground.
- Several estates where parkland and woodland have been preserved, including Dalmeny Estate.
- The coast of the Firth of Forth and the moorland of the Pentland Hills.

For each walk I have presented a series of walk-specific highlights, to provide you with some idea of what you may be able to look forward to whilst remaining open to the possibilities that may take you by surprise.

Distances and habitats

1. **City of Edinburgh (South)**   **4.6km**
   Woodland dell and stream, grass and
   scrubland, pond
2. **City of Edinburgh (West)**   **3.6km**
   Wood and scrubland
3. **City of Edinburgh (West)**   **7.1km**
   Woodland dell and river, coastal estuary
4. **City of Edinburgh (Centre)**   **2.9km**
   Mature woodland in urban park,
   grassland, cemetery
5. **City of Edinburgh (Centre)**   **4.4km**
   Grassland, pond, scrub and woodland,
   old quarries
6. **City of Edinburgh (Centre)**   **4.7km**
   Urban park, river, cycle path, old railway
   line and cemetery
7. **East Lothian**   **9.0km**
   Coastal sand dunes, river and coastal
   estuary, scrubland
8. **Midlothian**   **7.3km**
   Mature woodland, woodland dell and
   river, old railway line
9. **City of Edinburgh (South)**   **2.4km**
   Community orchard, woodland,
   parkland, loch, cemetery
10. **Midlothian**   **11.7km**
    Moorland, woodland, grouse moor,
    reservoir
11. **City of Edinburgh (West)**   **3.5km**
    Deciduous woodland and
    disused quarry
12. **City of Edinburgh (Centre)**   **7.9km**
    Urban streets, river, urban park
13. **East Lothian**   **5.3km**
    Urban street, river and coastal estuary,
    pond, woodland, scrapes
14. **City of Edinburgh (West)**   **7.8km**
    Parkland, deciduous woodland, estuary
    and cockle beach

Exploring wild places

An aerial or bird's-eye view of Edinburgh suggests that Scotland's capital city has retained a considerable area of green space. A report in *The Guardian*[4] showed the extent to which the amount of green space varies across British cities, with some of them three times greener than others. Analysis of satellite images taken in the spring of 2016 for the ten cities with the largest human populations showed that whilst Liverpool (16.4 per cent) and Bradford (18.4 per cent) had less than 20 per cent green space, and Manchester (20.4 per cent), Leeds (21.7 per cent), Sheffield (22.1 per cent), Greater London (23 per cent), Birmingham (24.6 per cent) and Bristol (29 per cent) had less than 30 per cent green space, with Glasgow registering 32 per cent, Edinburgh was leading the pack with an impressive 49.2 per cent of green space.

Closer scrutiny of Edinburgh's green spaces highlights that much of this is in the form of golf courses (and other sports grounds) plus a collection of private gardens, many of which only local residents have keys for. There are, however, plenty of parks and other green spaces that are open to the public. Many of these are characterised by wide open grassed areas that can hardly be described as wild. But there are areas that feel more alive and peaceful. In many instances, we have the foresight and generosity of the city's philanthropic burghers to thank for these accessible spaces where we can stretch our legs. Calton Hill, for example, was developed as one of the first public recreation spaces when in 1775 the philosopher David Hume petitioned the town council to provide a walkway for the benefit of the population; the first public walk in what was becoming a crowded and polluted city was duly opened. The Geddes Garden in the Grassmarket is

---

4   https://www.theguardian.com/cities/gallery/2017/jan/05/green-space-uk-largest-cities-mapped

another example of philanthropic foresight: it was created in 1910 having been inspired by the pioneering ecologist Patrick Geddes, whose vision was to create green spaces among the Old Town slums where children could play safely and experience the natural world through gardening. Geddes' daughter Norah, a talented landscape designer, together with several other committed women, created a series of terraces on the steeply sloping site that rises from the pavement and the busy thoroughfare of the West Port. Today, the West Port Gardening Group of the local residents' association[5] is working hard to revive Geddes' vision by creating a green space for everyone to enjoy. Nearby, on Johnson's Terrace at the foot of the Patrick Geddes Steps, is the Scottish Wildlife Trust's smallest wildlife reserve: Johnson Terrace Garden.[6] This little hidden gem demonstrates how a neglected urban area can be converted into a refuge for wildlife and provide inspiration for visitors seeking a calm refuge from the hustle and bustle of the surrounding streets – but, sadly, the trust has been forced to limit access to the reserve following repeated instances of vandalism and antisocial behaviour. A key to the gate can be obtained by trust members, who need to apply and pay a deposit to secure access. These are just a few examples of the green lungs breathing life into the heart of Scotland's capital city. In the next few paragraphs, we explore some of the challenges involved in discovering and then getting to know these precious emeralds.

When seeking out the reassuring and revitalising presence and company of nature, especially in an urban environment, one must learn to see past the concrete, beyond the tarmac, through the gaps in the built environment. Only then can one hope to find entry points into hidden green oases. This can feel like finding light at the end of the tunnel, like entering the afterlife, for in these spaces time slows and life makes itself felt. In some respects, this is a little bit like discovering a reassuring pulse under the skin of an unresponsive casualty. You need to know where to look for it and how to feel for it. Edinburgh's cemeteries are a particularly good example of the elfish otherworldliness that you can find when stepping through a gateway and into a place of moss- and lichen-covered gravestones, memorials, memories, vying with the creeping confidence of ivy and the nodding reassurance of daffodils.

The architectural heritage that has made Edinburgh's Old and New Towns a World Heritage Site is not all the work of architects and stone masons. The landowners who commissioned such grand castles and country houses as Dalmeny House, Inverleith House, Hermitage House, Inch House, Lauriston Castle, Craigcrook Castle and Craigmillar Castle have also bequeathed us some fine estates with many mature trees and stretches of continuous habitat. Many of these grand houses have passed into public ownership, whilst others, such as Dalmeny House on the Dalmeny Estate, remain in private ownership. This history of appropriation and enclosure is relevant to our evolving relationship with and access to green spaces.

Hermitage House, for example, was originally built in 1788 as a private residence; it sits within the Hermitage of Braid, one of Edinburgh's finest wooded dells. The deep river valley through which flows the Braid Burn was part of a parcel of 4 acres of land purchased in 1775 by Charles Gordon of

5   https://www.grassmarketresidents.org/
6   https://scottishwildlifetrust.org.uk/reserve/johnston-terrace-garden/

Cluny. He employed architect Robert Burn to design the mansion house that you can see today and will discover in Walk 1. In 1937 the then owner, John McDougal, presented the Hermitage to the city as a public park. The adjacent Blackford Hill had been purchased as a public park in 1884. This combined area was designated a Local Nature Reserve in 1993, and is now protected in perpetuity as a Queen Elizabeth Field. This is one of several designations established by the Fields In Trust charity, which since its creation in 1925 has been working to ensure that our parks and green spaces are not lost, recognising that once lost they are lost forever. The charity recognises the extent to which our green spaces are under threat and that it is up to all of us to stem and perhaps even reverse this cycle of disappearance and decline. To do this, they work in partnership with local authorities, town, parish and community councils and private landowners.

Another example of a property that has passed into public ownership is Edinburgh's 'other castle'. Craigmillar Castle was built in the 15th century by Sir John Preston, passing from the Preston family to Sir John Gilmour, a distant relative, in 1660. The castle and grounds remained within that family until 1946, when it passed to the State and subsequently to Historic Scotland, which manages it today. This massive baronial structure sits on the edge of Craigmillar Park Woods, which date back to the 19th century but also include a sycamore supposedly planted by Mary Queen of Scots and known as Queen Mary's Tree. Of greater note are the 40,000 trees planted here in 1997 as part of the Millennium Forest for Scotland project. According to Jan Bondeson (2018), there are as many as ten Queen Mary's Trees spread

across Scotland – but no evidence whatsoever that Mary planted any of these trees:

> It would have taken a frenzied effort from Scotland's tragic queen to pull off such an arboricultural tour de force, whereas in real life, she is not recorded as planting as much as a tulip. In Victorian times, there was a wish to associate large and ancient trees with some attractive historical character, to bring history alive from purposes of nostalgia, and to provide a living link from the present time to the historical past. The many Queen Mary's Trees in Scotland are the most striking instances of this, and the one at Craigmillar was the most famous of them all.

The sycamore in question was provided with a protective set of iron railings during the Victorian era, and over the years succumbed to decay. In 1953, there was only a 10-foot-high stump remaining, and in 1975 the tree was finally removed. This story highlights the extent to which our reverence for nature had become distorted by an individualistic culture in which protection amounted to impounding behind bars rather than nurturing a thriving forest ecosystem both above and under the ground. The significance of planting 40,000 trees should not be underestimated; indeed, it is immense, especially when compared to misguidedly worshipping and preserving a single tree in aspic. Such planting projects are an example of ecological restoration, and are often designated as community wood-lands. In 2003 the Community Woodlands Association[7] was established as the represent-ative body of Scotland's community woodland groups. With some 200 groups involved in, and/or responsible for, the management of

7   https://www.communitywoods.org/

thousands of hectares of woodland and open space, this represents a significant phenomenon, and one that is creating wild places for us to enjoy and explore.

There are community woodlands springing up across the Edinburgh area. One particularly notable flagship example is that of the Field Group in Duddingston. This was formed in order to take over the management of a field on the slopes of Arthur's Seat. Members of the local community have been working with volunteers from the Woodland Trust to create a diverse range of habitats, including woodland, managed grassland and a community orchard. This remarkable initiative is explored in Walk 9, which provides opportunities to see and better understand how habitat fragmentation has been addressed through work undertaken to provide richer biodiverse corridors linking Holyrood Park, Meadowfield Woods and Duddingston Village Community Land.

Patterns of landownership and land management have been heavily influenced by a feudal and hierarchical social structure and exploitative culture that extracted and sought to accumulate without giving back. Within one large, unified property, ecosystems might be connected, and to a certain extent preserved – but across a wider area there is fragmentation. This is particularly so in a densely populated urban area. As our human population continues to grow and impose itself on the living earth without listening carefully to the feedback provided, we find ourselves making decisions without a clear overview of the whole. We exist in bubbles, siloed off from other bubbles. In simple terms, there is a lack of joined-up thinking, and this way of thinking fragments everything, including the living environment that not just the rest of nature but *all* of nature (ourselves included),

depends on. We are only just waking up to this realisation.

When thinking about wild places, there is an urgent need to see not just the pieces but the whole of the jigsaw. We need to see the linkages and link up habitats so that wildlife can more easily move across our living landscape. Try to bear this in mind when you visit any one site described in this guidebook. Try to think about how you would move between wild places. How would you do this if you were a sparrowhawk, a butterfly, a bat, a toad, a fox or even a mole? Such movements can be particularly challenging for terrestrial creatures who are not able to fly or drift through the air.

Currently our landscape provides very narrow green and blue corridors. Somewhat fortuitously, in Edinburgh we still have a few green corridors running across the city. The green corridor of parks running south from the centre of the city into the hills is one such example. Bizarrely, it includes the Grange Cemetery and the grounds of the Astley Ainslie Hospital. The hospital and grounds were taken over by the NHS in 1948, and many are the patients who can attribute some of their recovery to the quiet tranquillity of the garden and grounds. The land has three rights of way cutting through it, so has wider interest and value to the community. When the NHS started exploring the possibility of selling the land, the community established the Astley Ainslie Community Trust (AACT)[8] in order to keep the land in public ownership. The Astley Ainslie Institute's history is fascinating, and provides yet another example of the nexus of reasons why we all need wild places to be preserved and are increasingly willing to coordinate campaigns to protect them. The institute owes its name to David

8   www.aact.scot

Ainslie of Costerton in East Lothian, who died in 1900. In his will he asked for his wealth be used to found a convalescent hospital in memory of his nephew John Astley Ainslie. John had been orphaned as a child and been brought up as David's own son, only to die at the tender age of 26. The institution that evolved from this wonderful gift was based on the gardens of several Victorian houses that were thus recovered from private ownership for the public good. The Royal Botanic Garden of Edinburgh helped to stock the gardens with an international collection of trees and Himalayan plants, and those convalescing here came to experience the healing and restorative properties of nature connection. The institution became known for its expertise in occupational therapy.

With the creation of the NHS, in 1948, the hospital came under the ownership and management of the government. Its announcement that it was intending to dispose of the hospital to fund more concentrated hospital sites represents a betrayal of the common good and a failure to recognise that healing and curing are not the same, for healing requires us to be made whole again at some deeper, natural level. It is of profound significance that the AACT was created in 2018 to try to persuade the Scottish government, who retained authority over the land, to keep it in public ownership. The AACT believes in a future where the intentions of David Ainslie to provide a significant natural resource within a crowded city for the health and happiness of all will be honoured. This example illustrates how inextricably entangled our wellbeing is with that of the natural environment. It also illustrates the crucial work we must all engage in to ensure that prioritising money over nature will not continue to drive the planetary crises we see today. Patrick Geddes summed this up beautifully when he wrote:

How many people think twice about a leaf? Yet the leaf is the chief product and phenomenon of life: this is a green world, with animals comparatively few and small and all dependent upon the leaves. By leaves we live. Some people have strange ideas that they live by money. They think energy is generated by the circulation of coins. But the world is mainly a vast leaf-colony, growing on and forming a leafy soil, not a mere mineral mass: and we live not by the jingling of our coins but by the fullness of our harvests.

(quoted in Defries, 1928, p.175)

There is considerable work to be done to reconnect the pockets of green spaces we can see on a map of Edinburgh. There are tiny Local Nature Reserves (LNRs) and parks dotted across the city. Meadows Yard, beside the busy Seafield Road, was designated as a LNR in 2002; it is a small, 1.45 ha, patch of land – stranded, it would seem, between a collection of busy roads, and opposite Edinburgh Council's Seafield Waste Recycling Centre. Those of us who have taken household waste to the dump will have driven right past it – but how many of us will have paused and taken the time to explore and discover this tiny reserve? In the past, Meadows Yard was a grazing meadow for dairy cows, hosted allotments, and was used as a railway siding for trains to rest in. Now it offers a quiet resting place for people and wildlife. It has thus been saved from being built on, but this is not enough, for there is a need to integrate it into a living landscape stretching across Edinburgh. This requires a different way of thinking about our shared environment. Fortunately, the reserve lies close to Craigentinny Golf Course, and immediately next to a railway line which, because it is one of the few parts of the city where humans are excluded for health and safety reasons, represents a functioning wildlife corridor. These railway lines are part of what Hugh Warwick (2017) has described as our 'linescapes' – essential connections that help link up our parks, reserves, golf courses and other green spaces, and which can be used by wildlife when moving across the city.

These green corridors are there by accident, however, rather than by design, and much needs to be done to link them up and make it easier for wildlife to live alongside us. The hedgehog is a great example of a terrestrial mammal needing our help. Our housing estates have been created in such a way that this low-to-the-ground prickly creature can no longer move from garden to garden in search of invertebrate dinners. As gardeners, we have excluded one of the gardener's potential allies. It is now recognised that housing developments need to be designed with hedgehog highways built in, so that such movement is possible. This is just one example of how we need to move from a self-centred, egocentric mindset that fragments and makes an enemy of the living world to an ecocentric mindset that seeks to befriend and restore the living world.

Blue corridors are a little different from green corridors. They are where water gathers, and are therefore also some of our best green corridors. For far too long they have simply been viewed by us as the low points through which water moves as it travels from high to low ground on its way to the sea. The reason we have wild places along our streams and rivers is because they are unsuitable for us to build on. These blue ribbons running through our cities are the relics of a landscape that was once vibrant and pulsating with life. Part of this book's exploration of wild places will consider how these last remnants of

nature came to be viewed and treated by us as sewers. The French word for 'sewer', *égout*, has a common root with *dégout*, 'disgust'. The challenge facing us as we wake up to the devastating impact our culture, behaviour and choices have had on the ecosystem that makes life on earth possible is to think and act less selfishly and more selflessly. The good news is that there is ample evidence that we *are* waking up, that we *are* seeking to care for and restore our remaining wild places. And it is because of this that we can still enjoy and look forward to wild encounters.

Wild encounters

If there is one thing that has given me cause for hope it is that on any given day I am blessed with a wild encounter, sometimes a generous scattering of them. These are the highlights of my days, the glowworms that keep shining in the darkness, the stars to navigate by. It is these encounters that remind me that whilst we may be lost, not all is lost.

When we let go of our desire to determine the way things will be and open ourselves up to possibility, our path becomes one of surprise, wonder and happiness. This is the conversational nature of reality.

What do I mean by this? Well, this is about humility. Our realities are not solely within our remit to determine, but arise through a conversational encounter with something beyond who we think we are, something larger than ourselves, something that helps connect us to our extended interconnected selves and to the eternal. To quote David Whyte (2001, p.180) has written evocatively of how deluded we are to think we make our own reality. Our part in such makings is modest and depends very much on how present we are to the swirling eddies and currents of time. He emphasises that reality is conversational and that this conversation arises between ourselves and the eternal unfolding productions of time. The challenge we face on any given day and in any given moment is to remain awake and responsive to the currents we are caught up in and must navigate on.

This essentially means that the attitude we carry into our walk has an important role to play in how we show up in any given moment. An encounter is a meeting, and how we meet is therefore predicated on how we are entering the field of possibility that is a walk in a wild place. If we are preoccupied, anxious, fearful even, so much that is there will never break through and register on our consciousness. Our noticing is thus stunted. The seeds that fall on the barren ground that we offer them simply blow away. So we must be willing to offer up fertile ground for those seeds, so that they can germinate, take root, grow and blossom.

When out on a walk, it helps to be willing rather than wilful. The clamour of alarm calls rippling through an area of woodland can prime you to the sudden appearance and disappearance of a sparrowhawk. Similarly, the excited buzz of a throng of bees can alert

you to the tiny flowers of an ivy tree when all is cold, when other flowers are a distant memory or a distant and dimly anticipated future promise.

A wild encounter is thus spontaneous and unpredictable. It can also be fleeting or sustained, and part of this is dependent on the energy we bring to the moment. I remember a remarkable moment when I happened to see a sparrowhawk drop down into the bed of a shallow brook. Something told me that this was not a dive onto an unsuspecting prey but something quite different. I approached very carefully and found myself watching this usually unapproachable and very flighty bird enjoying his daily ablutions (Figure P.2). We watched each other for what seemed like an hour. Time had slowed, perhaps even stopped. In such moments it is possible to be completely present to see every detail, hear every sound, and experience the fullness of each moment. This is awe. This is also pure and unadulterated joy, for we are experiencing a deep connection. In some respects we are seeing each other taking a bath, exposed

Figure P.2: I watched calmly as the sparrowhawk fanned his tail, flicked his wing feathers and took his time completing his ablutions. The ripples fanned out across the waters of the burn, droplets of water sprayed out into the air. And I savoured the ripples of this encounter.

and vulnerable. The scientist of awe, Dacher Keltner, says[9] that 'when we feel awe in the moment, we suddenly feel like we're part of an integrated community'. And the significance of such sacred moments is that they invariably lead us to want to do things that are good for the community – and in this case that means the more-than-human community.

The ornithologist Drew Lanham articulates very beautifully the depths we can sound when absorbed in a wild encounter. The brown of the sparrow becomes not ordinary but extraordinary; there is no mundane, there is nothing simple, no such thing as ordinary.

> There's so much that's simple out there or that appears simple, but that's really complex. It's sort of like the sparrow that appears brown from far away and hard to identify, but if you just take the time to get to know that sparrow, then you see all of these hues. You see five, six, seven shades of brown on this bird. And you see little splashes of ochre or yellow or gray, and black and white, and all of these things on this bird that at first glance just appeared to be brown. And so in taking that time to delve into, not just what that bird is, but who that bird is, and to understand to get from some egg in a nest to where it is to grace you with its presence, that it's taken, for this bird, trials and tribulations and escaping all of these hazards.

For me, this interview[10] excerpt captures the challenge we face in staying present to and throughout our wild encounters. For me every sparrow is like Jack Sparrow, a pirate who constantly surprises me and reminds me to look again and never to underesti-

mate. When we fail to look and look again, to respect, to re-spect[11] to pay due regard, we are failing to see what is in front of us. We are flattening our gaze rather than deepening it, and we are letting ourselves down, denying ourselves the wonder and joyfulness of a moment fully lived. This is not limited to seeing colours in all their glory; it is about being graced with the presence of another, and treasuring that opportunity as if it were a gift. For each encounter is a gift, a miracle of nature and of creation. Here creation is to be understood to extend beyond the generative process that has allowed this miracle of nature to evolve to the point at which you encounter it. Beyond here recognises that in the encounter a coming together occurs that gives rise to new possibilities of interconnection, understanding and appreciation. Anyone who has been changed by such an encounter, who thereafter sees the world differently, will know what I mean when I say that what evolves from such encounters is profoundly significant and meaningful.

The encounters we enjoy in the wild can be asynchronous; there does not have to be a wild creature immediately in front of you. It can be enough for one's senses to detect their presence and to tune into the rhythm of a place. This form of attunement allows you to read the unwritten script of the natural world. You might find yourself reading a path across a field and knowing that it was made by a badger by the breadth of the trail and way the grass was flattened, then confirming this on detecting the characteristic hairs snagged on a low hanging strip of barbed wire. Or you might find a smooth bit of sandy beach on a riverbank and read who has passed through since last that recording device was wiped clean (Figure P.3).

---

9 https://onbeing.org/programs/dacher-keltner-the-thrilling-new-science-of-awe/
10 https://onbeing.org/programs/j-drew-lanham-pathfinding-through-the-improbable/
11 To look again, and more fully.

Figure P.3: The deep linear tracks immediately above the leaves and grasses of the tideline bear testimony to the passage of a fox. The front two digits are level and there is a clear cross (X) between the pads. Immediately, above and much fainter are the prints of a squirrel. And above this the elongated palm pad and five toes of an otter.

Encounters, if truth be told, can take many forms, and their significance cannot be predicted. On one memorable evening I was walking across Calton Hill in the darkness after taking my mother out for dinner. There against the night sky was not a Milky Way of stars but the silhouette of a tawny owl. When I was working as a wildlife vet the tawny owl was one of my favourite species, so to meet a healthy owl on an evening walk felt very special indeed, especially as we have never seen each other since. Other encounters are more familiar. During the winter months, if I am out in the park of a morning I enjoy listening to the exuberant swoop of the score or so of jackdaws dropping down the scarp of Winnie's Hill as they return from their evening roosts on the southside of the park. As they pass overhead, heading for the tenements on the north side of the park, I am reminded that they too enjoy a night out socialising with their kind … but how many of us are aware of this rich corvid conviviality? And there is a warts-and-all character to encounters: During the toad migration season, there is something magical about coming upon the thousands of young toads as they leave their ponds and try to cross a road. On the far side of the road there is an expanse of ground where their ancestors have always overwintered. The pavement edges of our roads present a real barrier to the baby toads, and helping them find their way out of this deathtrap feels a little bit like a lollipop lady must feel when stopping the traffic and safely seeing children across a potentially dangerous road crossing.

And then there are encounters with ladybirds, spiders, spider webs, flies, dragonflies, snowdrops, flowers of every description, mosses, lichens, fungi and of course trees. So many of the members of our natural community are there waiting for us to pay attention to them. And an encounter can be all the more meaningful for not knowing anything about who we encounter. That can come in time. The scientific names and observations can all wait. In the field we just need to breathe, to relax our nervous systems and become one with the scene. It never ceases to amaze me how when we are calm and fully absorbed we blend in and are made to feel welcome again. Being made to feel welcome and at home is the essence of a wild encounter. And, remarkably, one of the most wonderful encounters we can have is with our own wild mind and true nature. Discovering these deeper connections between the natural world and our own inner nature is why we keep seeking moments of awe and wonder and connection. It is then that we know that we truly belong, for our being and our longing come together as we experience the sacred and transformational character of what Martin Buber describes as 'genuine meeting'.

A genuine encounter involves a turning to the sacred. My own work on deep listening draws on a crucially important shift in our source of attention. This is described by Buber as a shift from the I-It mode of attending to the world, where we conceive of the world out there as external to ourselves and therefore objective, to an I-Thou mode, where we recognise our mutuality and interconnectedness. The I-Thou is a mode of being that we experience as 'living dialogue' – we are in communion with and open to a richer interchange and exchange of energy and meaning. Every encounter characterised by an I-Thou moment can be carried back into our daily actions in the I-It world.

If there is to be any hope for the survival of life on Planet Earth, it is rooted in our reconnection with nature, with the life-sustaining processes that we are made of and contribute to. We need to see life as a dynamic relationship and our life-making as a practice of relating – relating to ourselves, to others and to the natural world. Buber's life work helps us to distinguish between two primal life strands:

When we interact with the world through the mode of I-It we create I-It relations. When we interact with the world through the mode of I-Thou we co-create I-Thou relationships. The relations we create and experience through using and knowing are very different from the relationships we create together, in partnership. This is because relations are one-sided and controlling, whilst relationships are two-sided and demonstrate mutuality. A relationship is open and yielding, and it is this reciprocity that gives rises to its beautiful emergent properties. Western science has failed miserably to understand that its objective tradition is predicated on a subject–object duality that is deeply damaging to the world. But science is also waking up to the fact it has been complicit in the colonialist project that has exploited the world. There are a growing number of academics who recognise that dualistic reductive thinking needs to be brought into conversation with a non-dualistic holistic ecological way of thinking. This shift will allow us to embrace our whole selves and to become better partners and collaborators.

In genuine encounter, a wholeness emerges from genuine listening (through the I-Thou mode of attending) and responsive, responsible responding. This, I have argued, is as true of the relationships that arise between humans as it is of the other relationships we co-create with the more-than-human world (Cousquer, 2022; 2023). Our relational practices can be evolved, and will allow us to enjoy deeply meaningful wild encounters. But how can we experience and become proficient in the encounter? To answer that we need to understand how to navigate the threshold between an I-It and an I-Thou way of attending to the world. This is described as a turning. We literally need to turn toward, and open our hearts to, the other. The cognitive scientist Francisco Varela has highlighted the significant role played in this process by the twin steps of suspending and redirecting.

Varela describes 'suspension' as the first basic gesture in enhancing awareness. It allows us to pause our habitual ways of thinking and perceiving. As the physicist David

Bohm used to say, 'normally our thoughts have us, rather than we having them'. Suspending does not require us to push away or deny our thoughts, but rather to observe them. In doing so, we become aware of our habits of thought. In essence, suspension allows us to see our seeing. And as we create the spaciousness that allows us to become conscious of our thinking, we start to notice the fear and judgement and relentless stream of thinking that our minds produce.

We might notice our fears – the reaction we have when we find ourselves face to face with a spider, a bat or a rat. We may also see how hate creeps in. Suspending is an essential step that allows us to see the creature we are encountering rather than our picture of the creature. This allows us to stay present to the experience of our wild encounters, and to notice the incredible beauty of an orb spider's painted body, the remarkable precision of a bat's flying in the darkness, and the intelligence of Ratty. Without knowing it, we have started redirecting and getting curious. When we suspend repeatedly, we may also find ourselves listening with an open heart as well as an open mind. Witnessing the care a mother spider, bat or rat bestows on her offspring reminds us of the common threads we share, and how we are all invested in nurturing life.

The magic really happens when two individuals open to each other at the same moment. When we meet and we are both willing to suspend our fear and to meet without judgement, when we allow curiosity to animate the encounter, and when we deepen this by suspending our cynicism and opening to compassionate concern … remarkable things happen. There is a growing body of evidence that multi-species communication is possible, and that we can achieve a remarkable quality of respect and understanding. This is especially true of the species who know how to tune into our wavelength. Equines are particularly remarkable at this. Dolphins, dogs and even rabbits have demonstrated time and again that they are able to create close bonds with us humans. And, this is also true of free-living wildlife. When they learn they have nothing to fear from us, they open towards us and invite us to meet with them. Martin Buber describes such encounters as taking place 'on a narrow ridge'. We have to turn onto and walk along this narrow ridge towards those we want to meet, and demonstrate our commitment and earn their trust. This is the path we must become familiar with if we are to earn the magical wild encounters that are there to be realised.

> The narrow ridge is the meeting place of the We. This is where man can meet man in community. And only men who are capable of truly saying 'Thou' to one another can truly say 'We' with one another. If each guards the narrow ridge within himself and keeps it intact, this meeting can take place.
>
> Buber, quoted in Hodes 1972, p.70.

If this is true of humans, and making a deliberate move to transcend and move beyond the patriarchal and anthropocentric world view, it is becoming increasingly clear that we are members of an ecological community. And our full membership of this community suffers for our failure to recognise our interconnectedness and interdependence. It is this ethical dimension that we explore next as we consider what an ethic of reconnection and healing might consist of.

Ethics and ethos

In this section I expand a little on the ethos of walking into wild places, of seeking wild encounters, of finding our home in the wilderness. There is an ethic to such encounters and homecomings, a practice of the wild. It helps to approach our practice with a clear understanding of the reciprocal, give and take, nature of the encounter. We then see this as an exchange. One of the most powerful ways of thinking about this is in terms of a gift economy.

Gary Snyder, in his essay *Etiquette of Freedom*, reminds us how our stinginess of spirit leads to carelessness and wastefulness. He describes this as an unwillingness to complete the gift-exchange transaction. An ethical life he writes, remains mindful of this, proposing (2020, p.22) that stinginess is the worst of character flaws and moral failings, and emphasising how our opportunities for interspecies communication and for conviviality suffer when our thoughts and deeds towards nature and towards others become rude. Such rudeness threatens our physical and spiritual survival because it prevents us appreciating and respecting the vivifying essence common to us all. In short we are being unwittingly rude to our selves.

To better appreciate this, we need to recognise that knowing is not a smash-and-grab raid on the objectified other. Such reductive and objectivist practices are fundamentally flawed for this is not science, this is pillaging. Knowing is what Heidegger (1996) describes as a *being-with* for our being (*Dasein*) is fundamentally entangled with the world (1996, p.170). We are in relationship with the world, not independent from it. Knowing is fundamentally a relational practice for –we are a gift to each other.

Trusting in the reciprocal nature of the gift-exchange is not an obvious move for the selfish, defended ego to make. We have to let go of expectation and the desire to control the outcome, opening instead to the emergent possibility of the wild encounter.

Robin Wall Kimmerer draws on the indigenous wisdom of her ancestors to articulate why the shift from a deficit mindset into an abundance mindset is crucial for nurturing our wellbeing and mental health. When, for example, we choose to view and speak of nature's gifts, whether these be the wild strawberries we savour on a walk (see Walk 13) or the bilberries we pick in a woodland glade (see Walk 8), not as commodities, products or things but as gifts. When what we hold before us is seen as a gift, the whole relationship changes. The relationship that arises between the grateful person and the gift is radically different. This is, in part, because it flows. When we view things as commodities, we seek to accumulate, and this creates a block that stunts and harms us because it denies us the flourishing of life that comes of flow.

In the presence of such gifts, gratitude is the intuitive first response. The gratitude flows toward our plant elders and radiates to the rain, to the sunshine, to the improbability of bushes spangled with morsels of sweetness in a world that can be bitter.

> Gratitude is so much more than a polite "thank you." It is the thread that connects us in a deep relationship, simultaneously physical and spiritual, as our bodies are fed and spirits nourished by the sense of belonging, which is the most vital of foods. Gratitude creates a sense of abundance, the knowing that you have what you need. In that climate of sufficiency, our hunger for more abates and we take only what we need, in respect for the generosity of the giver.
>
> Wall Kimmerer, 2022.

An ethic of the wild rooted in wholeheartedness recognises that a grateful first response encourages us to give a gift in return. When we open to reciprocity in this way, we know that a meaningful connection is forming.

This, then, is the spirit or ethos we can try to cultivate. In very practical terms, this ethos has been over recent years translated into various codes that help guide us as to how we should walk. These are presented below for completeness's sake and because they are a useful benchmark. The key for me, though, is that we deepen our familiarity of the underlying ethos that ideally will inform and animate such 'rules'. This next section will therefore explore the principles of the Leave No Trace practice and the responsibilities enshrined in the Scottish Outdoor Access Code.

Leave No Trace and responsible walking

However we choose to walk, whether as walkers or as pilgrims, our right of access is not absolute, and we must conduct ourselves respectfully and responsibly. There are several sets of guidelines that we would do well to be familiar with in seeking to understand the duty of care we owe in exercising our access rights. The Scottish Outdoor Access Code is one of the most forward thinking in the world; south of the border, the Countryside Code applies. The principles of respect that lie behind these codes are far more important, however, and it is for this reason that I first make mention of the Leave No Trace principles.

The seven **Leave No Trace** principles are applied worldwide as best practice when visiting the outdoors. I strongly recommend them to you, and indeed all walkers, as the tried and tested approach for ensuring you minimise your impact. Perhaps most importantly, they provide you with an invitation to carefully consider how you will prepare for and execute your walk.

The seven principles are:

- Plan ahead and prepare
- Travel and camp on durable surfaces
- Dispose of waste properly
- Leave what you find
- Minimise campfire impacts
- Respect wildlife
- Be considerate of other visitors.

Please do visit the website and familiarise yourselves with the seven principles and how to apply them: https://lnt.org/why/7-principles/.

The **Scottish Outdoor Access Code** provides everyone with the right to be on most land and inland water for the purpose of recreation and education, and to move from place to place, providing they do so responsibly. The basis of access rights in Scotland is thus one of shared reciprocal responsibilities between landowners / managers and the public. Please do download the code and take it with you; the more familiar you are with how to walk responsibly the better: https://www.outdooraccess-scotland.scot/

In a nutshell, the three key principles of the code are:

- To respect the interests of other people
- To care for the environment
- To take responsibility for your own actions.

There are clearly tensions between our competing responsibilities. We also need to be cognisant of the damage we unwittingly cause. In an age of climate collapse and rising temperatures, the impact of a campfire can be devastating as stray sparks or hidden embers allow a fire to spread. The ripple effect of our passage along a trail should not be underestimated, either. Some disturbance is easily managed because it does not exceed the ability of the environment concerned to return to an undisturbed state. But when wildlife is living on the margins, squeezed into smaller and smaller spaces, the impact of disturbing a roosting, feeding or nesting area can be catastrophic. These concerns are explored at different points in this guidebook, especially with regards to ground-nesting birds.

Fieldcraft

In this section I have provided some advice on field equipment and fieldcraft. Some of the equipment items listed below may seem a little obvious, but the idea is to provide a checklist that will help you to remember essential items, together with some suggestions that may make your experience more enjoyable. An insulated sit mat and a flask of warm soup and/or a hot drink can help to make sitting still more comfortable.

To wear while walking

- walking socks
- walking boots
- gaiters (if the ground is wet)
- shorts – or, better, trousers, to help manage the risk presented by ticks
- a shirt or t-shirt (avoid cotton, as this soaks up sweat, is slow to dry and can lead to chilling, as well as being uncomfortable)
- a warm layer (depending on time of year and walking pace)
- a baseball cap or sunhat
- a smile!

Carry in your backpack (or pockets)

- a map with notes from the guidebook about the route
- wallet (including bank cards, cash, bus tickets, etc)
- your phone (on silent!)
- water bladder / bottle (1 litre)
- food and a warm drink
- waterproof liner
- a folding insulated sit mat
- spare clothing (extra layers)
- waterproof jacket and overtrousers
- sunglasses, sun cream and lip balm
- emergency equipment (including whistle and survival bag) – optional
- first aid kit
- notebook and pen / pencil
- camera and binoculars
- a hand lens (see Walk 12)
- head torch (if you are likely to be out in the evening and risk benightment)
- penknife
- hand sanitiser
- walking poles
- gloves
- rubbish bag.

A good pair of binoculars represents a really good investment. For longer walks, of half a day or more, I tend to take a light pair, but for the walks presented here something heavier, with good optics that enhance the watching experience and perform well in low light, is essential. There are opportunities to try out a range of binoculars at specialist shops and fayres, and the Scottish Ornithology Club's visitor centre at Aberlady[12] provides opportunities to try out some different pairs. I also recommend the SOC centre as a really good place to go in search of both new and second-hand guidebooks.

12 https://www.the-soc.org.uk/about-us/shop

Weather forecasts and tide timetables: There is a saying that seems especially appropriate for those heading out into the wilds of Scotland: there is no such thing as bad weather, only inappropriate clothing. As part of your planning and preparation, it pays to check the weather forecast and build this into your plans. In addition, knowing where the weather is going to be coming in from will help you identify where you are most likely to find birds, especially if the weather is sufficiently poor for them to be seeking shelter. Checking the tide times will also allow you to factor in whether feeding areas will be exposed. As you frequent and become familiar with a place, you will start to develop an attunement for it and for the interactions between the place itself and the wildlife living there and/or moving through it.

Integrating the forecast into the planning of an outing is a small example of how we develop and hone our craft. This takes patience and practice. It benefits from the development of a rich familiarity with a place over the seasons and the years. I like to see it as a jigsaw or a patchwork, where new pieces are offered to us and are then integrated into our approach. What I am describing here is a philosophy of learning that constantly integrates the wonder and curiosity arising from new encounters. It may be that you see an unusual insect or mushroom, that you hear a snatch of birdsong that you don't recognise, or see a fascinating bit of behaviour. These are worth recording in some way so that you can follow up on them afterwards. There are shortcuts to such recording made possible by our mobile phones and the apps we can upload

to them, but this is no substitute for careful patient observation, for the latter will allow the details to register within our nervous system and help us train that system in a responsive way that retains its connection with the environment.

Courses and apps: A good place to start learning is with a skilled and experienced wildlife guide. There are a growing number of courses that can help us learn to explore the natural world. The Field Studies Council[13] (FSC) is one of the leading providers of such courses and it is worth scanning their programmes of short and longer courses. The British Trust for Ornithology[14] offers several courses that can help us to become more proficient at bird identification, and this can in time lead us to become valued contributors of data, for there is an urgent need for citizen science to contribute to the way we know and understand the world. Some of this involves data collection, but there are a growing number of ways of becoming engaged in the larger project of caring for nature.

Having over the years attended several weekend courses on bird identification, I heartily recommend signing up for one. I still remember the time that, on one such course I first learnt to recognise the call of the bullfinch and of the stock dove, and it is this step-by-step apprenticeship that has fed into the special features on these birds in Walks 4 and 5. Whenever I make an unusual observation or collect a whole list of species seen on a walk, I upload these to the BTO's Birdtrack website. This also provides me with the opportunity to report a range of other species, including amphibians, butterflies, dragonflies and damselflies,

13 https://www.field-studies-council.org/courses-and-experiences/
14 https://bto.org/develop-your-skills/training-courses

mammals, orchids and reptiles. And if your curiosity takes you out beyond this short list of life forms, there is almost certainly a way of contributing your data as a citizen scientist. There is, for example, a website on which glowworm[15] sightings can be reported, and another where you can report sightings of stag beetles.[16] This is not meant to be a comprehensive list of reporting opportunities, but rather encouragement to explore and get involved.

Among the various apps that we promote at the University of Edinburgh and that I have found helpful, I particularly recommend i-Naturalist.[17] It allows me to take a series of photos whenever I encounter an unusual flower, and there is then a good chance I will receive an identification over the next few days whilst also contributing the report to a body of data available to researchers. The BTO has produced an app version of Birdtrack[18] that is also worth downloading. There are a growing number of other applications provided by specialist charities such as your local wildlife trust and the SOC.[19] There are also more unusual apps, including the bug splatter[20] provided by Buglife, which allows us to report the bugs hitting our number plate after a car journey.

The importance of such work should not be underestimated. It has, for example, allowed the bordered brown lacewing to be rediscovered at Holyrood Park and the pond mud snail to be rediscovered at the Red Moss of Balerno. Some other apps are suggested below.

- **UK Pollinator Monitoring Scheme (UKPoMS)**
  UKPoMS is the first scheme in the world to have begun (since 2017) generating systematic data on the abundance of bees, hoverflies and other flower-visiting insects at a national scale. • https://ukpoms.org.uk/
- **Big Butterfly Count**
  The Big Butterfly Count is a UK-wide survey aimed at helping us assess the health of our environment simply by counting the amount and type of butterflies (and some day-flying moths) we see. • https://bigbutterflycount. butterfly-conservation.org/
- **Ladybird Survey**
  The UK Ladybird Survey aims to encourage the recording of all species of ladybird found within the UK. • https://www.coleoptera.org.uk/ coccinellidae/home/
- **Mammal Mapper**
  This free app that has been designed by the Mammal Society to enable you to record signs and sightings of mammals in the UK. • https://www.mammal.org. uk/volunteering/mammal-mapper/

Gandhian boxing: I am closing this section with something unusual to intrigue you and invite you into reciprocal thinking. It is inspired by Arene Naess's passion for non-violence and his interest in Gandhi's philosophy.

In Gandhian tennis, if you hit the ball in a way that makes it impossible for your partner to return it, then it's you who loses the point.

15 https://www.glowworms.org.uk/
16 https://stagbeetles.ptes.org/take-part-in-the-great-stag-hunt/
17 https://www.inaturalist.org/
18 https://www.bto.org/our-science/projects/birdtrack/about-birdtrack-app
19 https://www.the-soc.org.uk/about-us/app
20 https://www.buglife.org.uk/news/new-bug-splatter-app-to-reveal-more-about-insect-populations/

Similarly, in Gandhian boxing the idea is to go forward with insane speed but with no weight or power. You also try to move in such a way that you are never where you might be thought to be. This makes the activity both playful and curious. It is a questing, a questioning; a non-violent way of listening and being listened to. Anyone who has watched hares boxing or other creatures play-fighting will have some understanding of how attentive and respectful the interplay is. There is an awareness of one's responsibility not to abuse one's strength and power over another but to seek instead the co-creative synergy of generative dialogue.

This, then, is the art of fieldcraft. If you are listening to the wild you will learn to probe and quest without scaring off your interlocutor. Time and again I have pushed this too far in seeking to approach or take a photograph. I have missed the signs that are there to be read which tell us that we are creating stress. If we provide a creature with reason to become alarmed, they close off. The essence of fieldcraft is openness. If we invite curiosity and are curious, genuine meeting can occur… It is said of Arne Naess (2008, p.9) that he became aware of his responsiveness to nature when he would wade into, and play in, the waters of the fjords around Oslo. He experienced a spontaneous and 'intense sense of belonging and connection' as he came to realise that even the tiniest of creatures 'can respond to us, depending on how we act and feel about them'. He noticed how creatures would explore his body if he remained very still but would move away when he moved. This essentially taught him to view our presence in the world as a question we live into. Life is born in relation; we are made in relation, and any sense we make of life is a relational one. This, therefore, is the fieldcraft we need to develop.

Ecology and ecological pilgrimage

Whilst there is a persistent tale that Henry David Thoreau (1817–1862) may have been the first person to use the word 'ecology' (Serres, 2006), this remains contested. It would make for a neat history of the term's origins, for Thoreau was the American philosopher, poet, environmental scientist who, as the author of *Walden* gifted us one of the most influential meditations on the problems of living in the world as a human being. Schwartz and Jax (2011, p.145) argue that the word ecology can be traced back to the 1866 book *Generelle morphologie der organismen* by the German zoologist Ernst Haeckel. The term's Greek roots are significant for the word derives from the Greek *oikos* meaning house, household, dwelling place, family and the Greek logos meaning language, word, reason. Ecology thus came to mean the 'whole science of the relations of the organism to its surrounding outside world' or 'the science of the household of nature or the economy of organisms'. Definitions are clearly problematic, for they are always open to interpretation and can suffer from a lack of precision. Part of the problem here is that science is an imprecise art that always fails to do justice to nature because of a tendency to open up a space between nature itself and how we think about nature. Our thinking can then take us away from nature, creating distance and separation, without us even realising it. We may have a strange feeling of discomfort, that we are not at home, lost perhaps, that there is a stone in our shoe or even a wedge somehow holding apart the parts of ourselves that want to reconnect. We can find our way back home, though. Our journeying out into the world can allow us to find ourselves and our place in the world, for it teaches us to pay attention to both the outer landscape and the landscape we carry within.

David Whyte articulates this beautifully when he writes (2009, p.75) of being smitten by the unfolding direction of a path's intuited possibilities. Whether understood as one's path through life or into a landscape or both, there are always thresholds we encounter where intuiting becomes essential. At such times, a fierce attention is required, a focused attentional practice that allows us to discern what it is we belong to. Such discernment helps us become serious about what we desire and clearer about the difficult paths we are called to start out on.

Much of this guidebook seeks to explore how we bridge the gaping gulf that has opened up around and within us. This is about how we come home to the body, to experience and to the world. Home, after all, is as large as we choose to make it. The question is whether we are dwelling fully in that home, whether we are fully present in the moment, in our bodies, and in the 'weather-world'[21] beyond our 'skinned bodies'. This therefore is a pilgrimage of reconnection that allows us to reconnect with nature and to dwell more wholeheartedly and comprehensively in the world. A good starting place is to develop our ability to walk less mindlessly. The invitation is to walk mindfully and carefully, and for this openness of mind and heart to enhance your life's journey.

The life work of the deep ecologist Arne Naess has been primarily concerned with exploring the depth of wisdom needed to live well in our complex and ever-changing world. He challenges us to develop an ecology of wisdom that is primarily concerned with the development of insights into how we can improve our quality of life whilst lowering the demands and impacts we place on others. This is about understanding our footprint. In concerning ourselves with our footprint on the world as we explore with compassion the great emptiness, we find that, as the Tibetan saying goes, 'the experience of emptiness engenders compassion'. Through opening, we discover what we care about.

Walking mindfully

To walk mindfully can mean so many things, for within every step we take we can be paying attention such that we are present to all that offers itself to us in that moment. To be mindful is thus to be present.

- To walk mindfully can be to walk with joy in our hearts, to enjoy our walking.
- To walk mindfully is to feel alive and attentive.
- To walk mindfully is to surrender into the moment and forget about the next.
- To walk mindfully is to forget about the destination.
- To walk mindfully is to shake off our worries and anxieties.

The great teacher Thich Nhat Hanh suggests we can find peace in every step, and invites us to consider our footprints, and what our each and every step prints upon the world. What is our footprint? What traces do we leave behind? How does our stepping shape our footprints? Hanh (1991, p.28) helps us see that if our walking is more akin to running we will tend to print sorrow and anxiety on the world. But if, by contrast, we walk as if we were kissing the Earth, we bring our peace and calm to that on which we tread. We can

---

21 Anthropologist Tim Ingold, writes of the many ways we come to know the world as we move through it: 'Breathing with every step they take, wayfarers walk at once in the air and on the ground. This walking is itself a process of thinking and knowing. Thus knowledge is formed along paths of movement in the weather-world" (Ingold, 2010, p.S121).

therefore choose to print peace and serenity on the Earth. We can choose to tread lightly, lovingly and mindfully.

> To walk mindfully is thus an invitation to consider how we move through life.

We can choose whether to seek to be present through our breath, or alternatively through our bodies and, perhaps most specifically, our feet. We can do so simply by directing our attention. There will be moments when we notice that our mind has wandered away from our feet, away from the present moment. The thinking butterfly mind can then be asked to land again and continue walking. Like a butterfly, it may flutter off again. And again, it can be invited to land and to walk.

> Walking mindfully is a practice that connects us to ourselves, to nature, to each other and to all life.

The following practices are offered as ways of walking mindfully:

Walking mindfully Practice 1

- Breathe in for three steps, perhaps saying 'In, In, In' with each step.
- Breathe out for three steps, perhaps saying 'Out, Out, Out' with each step.
- Remind yourself as you breathe: 'As I breathe in I calm my body; as I breathe out I smile.'

Walking mindfully Practice 2

- Choose a suitable area of ground and allow your bare feet to kiss the ground.
- You may want to stand with your eyes closed, listening to your feet.
- With each step, form a new kiss and feel the ground reciprocate.

Walking mindfully Practice 3

- Standing in bare feet on a suitable area of ground, lift your heels up and bring your weight onto your toes.
- Then lower your heels and rock backwards, lifting your toes.
- As you come onto your toes you may want to flex your hands at the wrist, extending them again as you come back onto your heels.

Walking mindfully Practice 4

- Walk into the weather.
- Pay attention.
- Welcome whoever comes to meet you: the wind, the rain, the sun.
- They are all friends, whose invigorating, cooling, watering, drying, warming awaken us to the moment.

Walking mindfully Practice 5

- Pay attention to the purpose of your walking.
- Watch yourself choosing your path. Observe, smile and enjoy.
- Why rush? Our final destination is not worth thinking about. Getting there is not our purpose. Observe, smile and enjoy.
- Walk in the direction of life and enjoy peace in every step.

Walking mindfully Practice 6

- Immerse yourself in your sense world as you walk, by paying attention to what your senses contribute to your experience. Keep coming back to this anchor.
- If listening, pay attention to the sounds in front, to the sides and behind you.

The Japanese Buddhist priest, writer, poet, philosopher we know as Dōgen, who founded the Sōtō school of Zen in Japan, famously wrote that 'when you find your place where you are, practice occurs'. My own experience of coming into a deeper felt sense of presence through mindful walking at the start of any of my walks has taught me that this is when I become more attentive and observant. I start to become aware of the significance of insignificant things, and to realise that we can find something amazing in places that seem rather ordinary. I like to think of this as an *Awe-walk*. I am literally cultivating my ability to walk and wander in wonder.

Walking and wandering in wonder

When we walk in wonder, the world is wonderful. 'What a Wonderful World' is thus far more than the title of the song made famous by Louis Armstrong; it is also an invitation to pay attention, to notice and to get curious. We are thus invited not to judge but rather to explore, to ask questions and to do so without expectation. Free of judgement and expectation, we are open to so much more, and will be blessed with many wonders. As mentioned earlier, this is why suspending and redirecting is such an important skill.

This is particularly so when we think of our journey as one that sees us moving toward a distant horizon whilst recognising that that horizon is also moving with us. We are constantly breaking new ground, crossing thresholds, becoming more who we really are. And this process is what allows us to enjoy the novelty and vitality of each step and of each moment.

In trying to understand the role of wonder in each moment, it is perhaps worth considering how much more exciting the world of possibility is than the world of facts. Imagination allows us to explore beyond the threshold of what we know. And this concept of the threshold is so very powerful, for we are invited to step into the new

with each breath we take, each stride, and each new day. Where we have in the past, perhaps, been trapped by habits of thought or inattention, we can find ourselves noticing new possibilities and opportunities.

The Celtic poet and philosopher John O'Donohue expresses the power of wonder beautifully when he says that:

> a question is really one of the forms in which wonder expresses itself. One of the reasons that we wonder is because we are limited and that limitation is one of our great gateways of wonder. ... All thinking that is imbued with wonder is graceful and gracious thinking. Thought is the heart of reality. All of the things that we do, the things that we see, touch, feel, are all constructions of thought. ... And thought if it's not open to wonder, can be very limiting, destructive and very very dangerous. If you look at thought as a circle, and if half the arc of the circle is the infusion of wonder, then the thought will be kind, it will be gracious, and it will also be compassionate, because wonder and compassion are sisters.

> O'Donohue, 2018, pp.6–7.

One of the things that walking with wonder can present us with is the offering of surprising ways to move forward in life. We are all moving forwards through life – but what of our unchosen lives, what of those unrealised possibilities? Which of these are summoning us? Allow yourself to find your stillness as you move through the faithful landscape, open to wonder and to listen to your inner wisdom as it reaches out to you.

- What are you wondering?
- Where does your curiosity take you?
- What do you find yourself drawn to?

Pilgrimages and *peregrinati*

The origins of the term 'pilgrim' and 'pilgrimage' can be traced back to the French word *pélerin* and Latin *peregrinus*. These terms are typically taken to refer to a foreigner or traveller from another country. But as with all terms and practices steeped in history and tradition, there lies a wealth of meaning that extends far beyond this simple definition.

Our contemporary and somewhat unfortunate unfamiliarity with the term says much about how modern society has become sedentary and disconnected from the wider world. There are, however, a few reminders of the profound relationship that exists between freedom and pilgrimage. One such is particularly surprising, for whilst we may rarely talk of pilgrimages and peregrinations, we do talk of peregrines. It is therefore heart-warming to note that Richard Treleaven once wrote of the peregrine falcon that 'of all wild creatures, they are the most symbolic of freedom'. The peregrine falcon, whose scientific name is *Falco peregrinus*, is thus named because they were thought at one point to be migratory birds; quite literally, birds without a home, whose lot it was to journey through life. You may meet them when out and about around the city of Edinburgh, for we have several breeding pairs (see Walk 5) gracing our skies and livening things up for those who are paying careful attention.

At its simplest, the term 'pilgrim' can perhaps be understood as defining a person who travels through life toward an unknown destination. That destination has often been interpreted, whether literally or metaphorically, to be a particular, often holy, place. Examples of holy places that have for centuries attracted pilgrims include Santiago de Compostela, Lourdes and Mecca. The journeys to these places, whose spiritual purpose became associated with specific religious traditions, came to be known as pilgrimages.

Sadly, the rich and diverse cultures that grew up around pilgrimages have largely slipped, with a few notable exceptions, from our modern consciousness. How many of us are aware that one of the key social roles of monasteries was to receive the exhausted, footsore pilgrim? Hospitality is thus rooted in this receiving. The original hospice, or *hospitalet*, was destined to receive weary pilgrims; indeed, the very terms 'hostel' and 'hotel' can be traced back to the emergence of monasteries and hospices, and the welcome they offered to travellers. Bede's life of St Cuthbert tells of how one such visitor was received by Cuthbert when he was given the role of guest master (Webb, 2016, p.41). This account tells of how Cuthbert welcomed his guest without hesitation and with his customary kindness, providing him with water with which to wash his hands, whilst he himself washed the guest's feet. Wiping the man's feet with a towel, Cuthbert then humbly warmed these feet against his own chest and proceeded to rub them with his own hands.

Such kindness is unexpected, and all the more welcome for that. This is perhaps part of the mystery of the pilgrim's path. At every step we are moving into unknown territory, breaking new ground and discovering a little more about ourselves and how we construct the world, and could construct it differently. It also begs a question – will we receive our own selves, and greet those we meet, with kindness? Each step along the way crosses a line in the sand, a threshold. And that line is oriented at some usually subconscious level. It is for us to intuit and to discover what it is that draws us and to take greater ownership of our direction of travel. This demands that we pay attention.

David Whyte articulates this beautifully when he writes:

> Being smitten by a path, a direction, an intuited possibility, no matter the territory it crosses, we can feel in youth or at any threshold, as if life has found us at last. Beginning a courtship with a work, like beginning a courtship with a love, demands a fierce attention to understand what it is we belong to in the world. But to start the difficult path to what we want, we also have to be serious about what we want.

Whyte, 2009, p.75

It is therefore worth emphasising that a pilgrim's progress is neither careless nor aimless. The pilgrim may leave much to providence and will, in consequence, be appreciative for that which they receive.

A *peregrinato* is thus, perhaps, one who knows how to journey and who travels well. Perhaps this deeper understanding of what it takes to fare well on the road, as in life, is one of the gifts that a pilgrimage bestows upon us.

Long distance walking

What meaning are we to find in a long walk and in long distance walking? In this book I have mainly included short walks, but at least one is more than 10 kilometres. All of them could be extended on any given day, and you will also find yourself crossing long distance walking routes such as the John Muir Way. This section therefore encourages you to consider taking longer walks and perhaps even undertaking a multi-day walk.

It is for each of us to seek answers to questions about the meaning we find in any walk, and indeed in life. A long walk can literally take a lifetime and can be incredibly,

profoundly liberating … as it was for Nelson Mandela, whose autobiography is titled *A Long Walk to Freedom*. Mandela found freedom in his prison cell. Perhaps we can therefore see a long walk as an opportunity to free ourselves from the walls that we and others have built, and that imprison us.

The Norwegian explorer, Erling Kagge, who was the first man to reach the North Pole, South Pole and the summit of Everest writes in his wonderful book on walking that what he most likes is to walk until near-collapse; at this collapsing-point the absurdity of walking and of exhaustion blend together to such a degree that they can no longer be distinguished. For Kagge (2018, pp.135-136), such experiences are transformative; they change his head. The longer he walks, the less he is able to differentiate between mind and body and the surrounding environment. His internal and external worlds inform each other and this intra-dependency means that he is no longer an observer of nature but an observer whose involvement is so invested and entirely engaged that the word "overlap" starts to feel inadequate.

Perhaps this is what Nan Shepherd is referring to when she suggests we walk into the mountains. I suggest that we can walk into a deeper awareness of who we are by walking in this way. We can walk into, sit and contemplate the mountains, and both lose and find ourselves. As Li Po wrote: 'The birds have vanished into the sky and now the last cloud drains away. We sit together, the mountain and me, until only the mountain remains.'

In seeking oneness through the immersion and deep connection born of a walk, whether long or short, we can glimpse and tap into that deep awareness, the freedom that Mandela is referring to. Our walking can always, therefore, be long and sustained. It is a process in which every step counts and we cease to be able to distinguish the A from the B, and the A-to-B from the I. In moving from A to B, it is worth pondering whether we find or lose the I.

May you carry curiosity and joy, compassion and courage in your heart and may you share these on your way.

◨ References

Bozalek, V. and Zembylas, M. (2023). *Responsibility, Privileged Irresponsibility and Response-ability: Higher education, coloniality and ecological damage*. London: Routledge.

Bondeson, J. (2018). *Phillimore's Edinburgh*. Stroud, Gloucestershire: Amberley Publishing.

Cousquer, G. (2023). 'From domination to dialogue and the ethics of the between: Transforming human-working equine relationships in mountain tourism'. *Austral Journal of Veterinary Sciences*, 55 (1), pp.35–60.

Cousquer, G. and Haounati, A. (2022). 'Action research with and for pack mules: Transforming the welfare of working equines in international mountain tourism'. *Journal of Awareness-Based Systems Change*, 2 (2), pp.109–139.

Defries, A. (2028). *The Interpreter Geddes: The man and his gospel*. London: Routledge.

Hanh, T.N. (1995). *Peace is Every Step*. London: Rider.

Heidegger, M. (1996). *Being and time : a translation of Sein und Zeit* (J. Stambaugh, Trans.). State University Of New York Press.

Hodes, A. (1972). *Encounter with Martin Buber*. London: Allen Lane/Penguin.

Ingold, T. (2010). 'Footprints through the weather-world: walking, breathing, knowing'. *Journal of the Royal Anthropological Institute*, S121–S139.

Kagge, E. (2019). *Walking: One step at a time*. London: Penguin Random Press.

Naess, A. (2008). *Ecology of Wisdom*. London: Penguin.

O'Donohue, J. (1997). *Anam Cara: Spiritual wisdom from the Celtic World*. London: Bantam Press.

O'Donohue, J. and Quinn, J. (2018). *Walking in Wonder: Eternal wisdom for a modern world*. New York: Penguin.

Schwarz, A. and Jax, K. (2011). *Ecology Revisited: Reflecting on concepts, advancing science*. London: Springer.

Serres, M. (2006). *The Natural Contract*. Trans. by E. MacArthur and W. Paulson. Michigan: University of Michigan Press.

Snyder, G. (2020). *The Practice of the Wild: Essays*, 30th anniversary edition. Berkeley: Counterpoint.

Wall Kimmerer, R. (2022). 'The serviceberry'. Available from: *Emergence Magazine*: https://emergencemagazine.org/essay/the-serviceberry/

Warwick, H. (2017). *Linescapes: Remapping and reconnecting Britain's fragmented wildlife*. London: Penguin Random House.

Webb, S. (2016). *Bede's Life of St Cuthbert: In a modern English version*. Durham: Langley Press.

Whyte, D. (2009). *The Three Marriages: Reimagining work, self and relationships*. London: Riverhead Books.

Whyte, D. (2001). *Crossing the Unknown Sea: Work as a pilgrimage of identity*. New York: Riverhead Books.

Walk 1

Blackford Pond, Blackford Hill and the Hermitage of Braid

This exquisite walk explores one of Edinburgh's best-preserved woodland dells, through which the Braid Burn gurgles. This small river rises in the Pentland Hills and runs for some 32 kilometres, to reach Duddingston Loch on its way to the Firth of Forth at Portobello. The Hermitage of Braid lies more or less halfway along the burn's course, by which point the watercourse is approximately 5 metres wide and 20 centimetres deep. Your walk thus explores an important blue corridor that twists and turns through the city, changing its name after leaving Duddingston Loch, to become the Figgate Burn. The varied nature of this walk is in some part due to the contrasting nature of the sunny heights of Blackford Hill, from where you can enjoy fine views across the city on a clear day (Figure 1.1). This walk could be said to offer you almost everything that a walk within a city might be asked to provide:

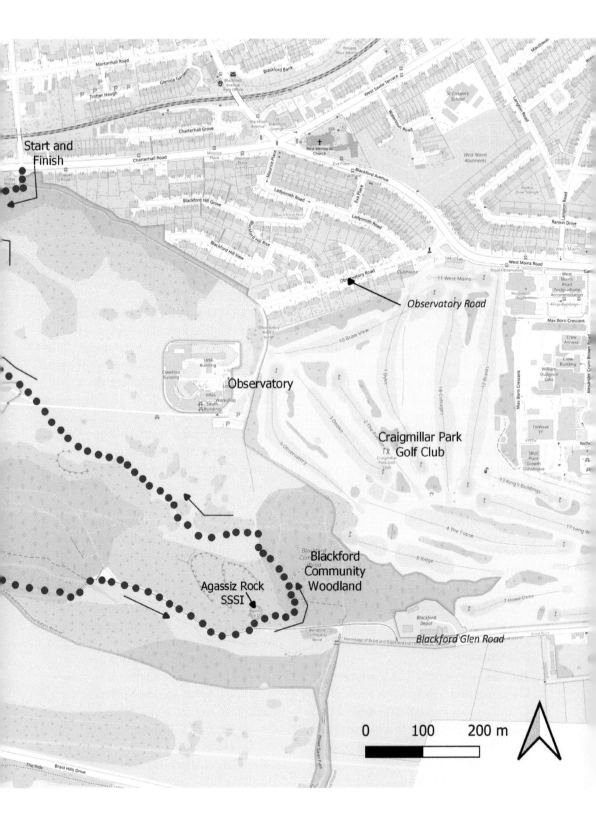

Start and Finish

Observatory Road

Observatory

Craigmillar Park Golf Club

Blackford Community Woodland

Agassiz Rock SSSI

Blackford Glen Road

0 100 200 m

Figure 1.1: Blackford Hill offers an exquisite and unique viewpoint from which your eye can take in the south side of the city of Edinburgh and Holyrood Park. The Fife coastline is also visible in the far distance, as is the island of Inchkeith, out in the Firth of Forth.

This walk's highlights include:

- Incredible views across the city; the distant Forth Estuary and Lomond Hills can hold you spellbound as you look out from the vantage point that is Blackford Hill.
- A fantastic opportunity to discover the Local Nature Reserve (LNR) made up of Blackford Hill (a Scheduled Ancient Monument) and the Hermitage of Braid, and to explore a number of habitats, including a large freshwater pond, an area of open heathland, a delightful river valley and one of Edinburgh's last and best vestiges of ancient woodland.
- The significant geological discovery and wonder that is the Agassiz Rock, a designated Site of Special Scientific Interest (SSSI).

👣 Summary

The walk, as described here, starts at Blackford Pond, which can be accessed from Cluny Gardens. Parking is available at the entrance to the park at the foot of Oswald Road, where it meets Cluny Gardens. Alternative access points are possible from Braid Road and Blackford Glen Road.

Start with a circuit around Blackford Pond, before climbing a flight of steps to access a balcony path that runs around the hill. Then follow a delightful path through woodland, to reach the Hermitage Doocot, the second largest dovecot in Scotland. After descending to the valley floor, go uphill again to reach the southern rim of the Hermitage and a path with majestic views down across the wooded valley and the Old Hermitage House. The river is then regained and followed towards Blackford Glen Road until you reach a path up and over Blackford Hill. Finally, drop down again, to regain Blackford Pond and the start, completing this circular walk.

🏛 History

Here I provide a historical overview of the site with an emphasis on the socio-cultural elements that contribute to and impinge on the site's natural history. Part of this involves developing an understanding of land ownership and land management practices, for it is these that determine how nature is impacted by the presence of humans.

The Hermitage of Braid's name may be traced back to the first recorded owner of the land, the 12th-century Sheriff of Edinburgh

(1165–1214), Henri de Brade. The family name is of Flemish origin, for Henri was the son of a Belgian knight, Richard De Brad. Another possible explanation for the Hermitage's name suggests that it may derive from *Am Braghad*, meaning the 'upper part' or 'high ground', as in Breadalbane (*Am Braghad Alba*) – the high ground of Scotland. Harris (2002), in his book on place names of Scotland, meanwhile suggests that the name may derive from *bràghaid*, a Gaelic word meaning 'throat' or 'gorge'. This could well describe the deep-cut nature of the Braid Burn. In the absence of clear records that capture the appearance of a name and how it came to capture the popular imagination, we shall move past the name, and see and experience the real place behind the name.

The oldest tree in the Hermitage is a 500-year-old oak, whose girth is nearing 5 metres in circumference. The age of many of the trees we can still see in this wooded valley speak of their being spared the axe. There may be various reasons for this, including the value placed on the woodland as a hunting forest by its owners. What is known is that as its ownership did not change hands often, this would bring with it a certain level of stability and conservation. The de Brad family owned the lands of Braid until 1305. Ownership thereafter was uncertain, but by 1485 the area found itself the property of the Fairlie family. The Fairlies retained ownership until 1631, when Sir Robert Fairlie sold Braid to Sir William Dick, who later styled himself Sir William Dick of Braid. On his death – in a debtors' prison in Westminster – the lands were subsequently sold by the Exchequer to a John Brown of Gorgie Mill. In 1695 Braid was leased by Nicholas Dupyne, who replaced the existing corn mill with a paper mill. In 1772, less than three quarters of a century later, Charles Gordon Cluny bought 4 acres of land. In 1785 Cluny commissioned Robert Burn to build a new house, the Hermitage of Braid House. The building was completed in three years, and as part of this development the mill was demolished, the avenues of trees and the lawns were created, and the walled garden, stables and ice house constructed.

The Hermitage is shown on a 1735 version of John Adair's map,[21] where it is shown to the south-east of an older building referred to as 'Braid'. On this map both houses are depicted as being surrounded by trees. The 1682 Adair map[22] of Midlothian, however, shows this older building, calling it 'Bread' and situating it beside the 'Breadburn' and what is almost certainly Blackford Hill but is referred to as 'Bread Craig'. The dovecot (or 'doocot' in Scots) predates Hermitage House, having been built in the late 17th century, most probably as part of the older building.

The Hermitage of Braid Estate remained in the Gordon family until 1937, when the final owner, a John McDougal, gifted the estate to the City of Edinburgh. This was a significant acquisition, connecting as it did sites of value for their natural history; Blackford Hill was already in public ownership, having been purchased in 1884 for a sum of £8,000 by the then Edinburgh Corporation. There are a number of adjacent green spaces that make this area of Edinburgh particularly well connected and valuable as an oasis and green lung in an urban sprawl. Whilst savouring this green oasis, we must also understand the extent to which it is ecologically impoverished – it is what conservationists refer to as an ecological desert.

21 https://maps.nls.uk/view/216390004
22 https://maps.nls.uk/view/00001013

This green desert is made up of:

1. Midmar Allotments, on the north-west sides of Blackford Hill. These are owned by the City of Edinburgh Council.
2. Midmar Field, a field on the northwest of Blackford Hill, owned by the A.J. Laing Trust.
3. Craigmillar Park Golf Course, a privately owned property to the east of the LNR.
4. A Millennium Forest Community Woodland to the east of the LNR, where a forest was planted in the late 1990s over a reclaimed quarry and dump site.
5. Braid Golf Course and fields to the south of the LNR (privately owned).

As mentioned in the Introduction to this book, the Hermitage of Braid and Blackford Hill were accorded protected status as a Local Nature Reserve in 1993. The year before that, the area had been identified as an Area of Great Landscape Value, and of specific nature conservation interest within the Local Plan for South-east Edinburgh. These designations were effectively superseded by the site's identifica- tion as an Urban Wildlife Site in the City of Edinburgh Council's Urban Conservation Strategy for Edinburgh (1992). That was over 20 years ago. It is sobering to recognise that these designations have not led to dramatic improvements in the natural capital of the site; the designation is largely a way of stemming the tide. This is reflected in the lack of ambition of the reserve's recently published Management Plan,[23] which recognises the pressures placed on the reserve by certain recreational practices:

> Despite its designation as a 'Local Nature Reserve', the site is managed equally to meet the needs of nature conservation, recreation

and access. Several formal and informal recreational activities occur on site, including: walking, picnics, dog exercising, running, orienteering, climbing, natural history studies, art and photography and cycling, and potentially horse riding.

Of these activities, the most impactful and del- eterious is almost certainly dog walking. The Management Plan acknowledges the various impacts of dog walking quite unambiguously:

> Despite the creation of signage, and the provision of litter bins across the site, there is an excessive degree of dog fouling. The thoughtlessness of some dog owners presents a very real health hazard and inhibits other users from visiting the site. The high incidence of dog usage in areas of the LNR is also seen as detrimental to wildlife, with species of former ground- and scrub- nesting birds, e.g. skylark (*Alauda arvensis*) and meadow pipit (*Anthus pratensis*), no longer nesting on site. In addition, several 'desire lines' within the woodlands are the consequence of dog activity, in certain cases these tracks running through areas of locally important ground flora, e.g. bluebell (*Hyacithoides non-scripta*). Erosion of the banks of the Braid Burn is also a result of excessive dog activity, with some areas, including just outside the Hermitage House, showing large areas of scouring earth and mud. An examination of how this can be countered or repaired should be undertaken and actioned as resources permit.

This represents a very real and common chal- lenge for wild spaces in and around a city, and one that we need to approach with compassion and creativity. Dog ownership brings com-

---

23 https://www.edinburgh.gov.uk/downloads/file/22587/hermitage-of-braid-local-nature-reserve-management-plan

panionship and a means of connection to the more-than-human world. It is also however, a product of our crowded living, and a symptom and reflection of our disconnection from nature, which has its own history. With the increased public access to this area has come a growing desire to protect and care for it. This is reflected in the creation of the Friends of the Hermitage of Braid group[24] in 1999, which became a registered charity in 2001 (SC031776), and in 2010 had members in 200 households.

This historical section has provided an overview of the shifts in land ownership and use that the area covered by the Hermitage of Braid and Blackford Hill, and visited by this walk, have been subject to. It has also highlighted the tensions that arise when access is made available to a larger number of people, and we are challenged with understanding how to balance the health and wellbeing of local human residents with the health of the environment.

🍃 Habitats

Woodland, scrub and grassland, wetland (river), rock outcrops.

🚌 Transport links

The starting point for the walk on Cluny Gardens is well served by the Number 38 Lothian Buses[25] service that runs along this road as it heads from Morningside to Blackford Avenue. The George Square to King's Buildings quiet cycle route provides cyclists with access from King's Buildings. There is also a good cycle path running through the Hermitage itself, which links with the Braid Burn Path. For details of these cycle routes, visit the Edinburgh Council website.[26]

☕ Refreshments

There is a converted police box serving coffee at the car park on Cluny Gardens. A good range of cafés are also to be found in Morningside. For those wanting to extend their walk as far as the entrance on Braid Road, you will find the Lodge Coffee House there.[27]

🔖 References

Harris, S. (2002). *The Place Names of Edinburgh: Their origins and history*. Glasgow: Steve Savage Publishers.

Land, D. (2001). The international significance of Agassiz Rock. *The Edinburgh Geologist*, 37, 3–5.

Directions

1 A circuit of Blackford Pond

Enter the park and proceed to the right, to reach a set of gates that provide access to the path that skirts Blackford Pond. This artificial pond was created during the 19th century in a glacial hollow, and is now home to a rich variety of birdlife who appreciate the refuge and safety provided by the pond's island, reedbeds and vegetation (Figure 1.2).

The pond measures some 60 × 225 metres, and whilst sizeable is vulnerable to several threats. In particular it is subject to an excessive build-up of nutrients. This is termed a eutrophic state, and arises because the pond receives runoff from the allotments to the west, from food thrown into the pond to feed waterfowl, and from the large quantity of bird faeces deposited by birds attracted to this site by humans. The pond's margins have also suffered considerable erosion.

---

24 https://fohb.org/2018/index.htm
25 For network maps for each numbered bus service visit: https://www.lothianbuses.com/maps-and-times/network-maps/
26 https://www.edinburgh.gov.uk/cycling-walking/explore-quietroutes/1
27 https://www.facebook.com/thelodgecoffeehouse/

Figure 1.2: The pond edge is well vegetated and provides rich habitat for wildlife. The moss-covered willow pictured here can be a good place to observe chiffchaff and other birds in early spring.

The build-up of nutrients leads to algal blooms and addressing this issue will require a coordinated community approach. Addressing the erosion is easier, as demonstrated by the restoration project that in 2010 saw the banks reinforced with barriers of elm cuttings anchored by larch posts. These barriers have helped retain organic material, and this has been further consolidated by the roots of the plant life that has since established itself, including the marsh marigold (*Caltha palustris*) whose yellow flowers are easily recognised along the shoreline and among the bulrushes.

The pond is an excellent place to observe many of the birds commonly found on freshwater ponds, including mallard, coot, moorhen and mute swan. A breeding pair of mute swans can often be seen nesting on the island, illustrating the value of such moated and vegetated sanctuaries. The more secretive little grebe or dabchick can also, with care, be observed here – moving in and out of the reedbeds, whose reflections in the still waters (Figure 1.3) are rewarding to observe. Heron, pochard and tufted duck may also be seen when they choose to visit.

Moorhens are particularly appreciative of this pond, whose hospitality to this secretive and easily overlooked bird is recognised by the special feature on moorhens presented as part of this walk.

2 Balcony path

On reaching the far end of the pond turn right, leaving the pond behind you. After a short distance, turn left to head up a flight of steps. On reaching the top of the steps, look out for a broad path contouring round the hill. Below you, a view opens up across the Midmar allotments that run along Midmar Road to the south-west of the pond. These represent a potential source of nutrient rich run-off that can make the pond vulnerable to eutrophication and algal blooms.

The balcony path runs through a delightful stretch of gorse (Figure 1.5), whose scent can be a real delight on warm days, and whose pods can even be heard popping and crackling towards the end of the summer as the warm air helps them burst open and release their seeds. Should you choose to pause and look back, you may find yourself rewarded with a delightful view across the city towards Edinburgh Castle, whose silhouette can be made out in the distance.

3 Entering the Hermitage of Braid

The path descends gently to reach an open space and rejoin the lower path that here runs along the boundary wall. Follow this to the left for a short distance until you reach a gap in the wall, through which you pass, entering an area of woodland.

Turn to the right and follow the path that now runs back along the wall. Here the wall is to your right, whilst to your left a rich area of woodland falls gently downhill. A mix of trees are in evidence here, including ash, beech, Scots pine and holly. Look out for finches, including greenfinch (Figure 1.6a) and bullfinch, as well as great spotted woodpecker (Figure 1.6b) who all appreciate the rich feeding grounds provided by this area of mature woodland. Whilst the call of the finches may be somewhat discreet, the same cannot be said of the blackcap, whose call is a rich harbinger of spring (Figure 1.6c).

Soon the wall and the path both make a right-angled turn to the left and you start descending, to gradually reach the old dovecot (Figure 1.7), Edinburgh's second largest structure of that type. It has close to 2,000 sandstone nest boxes (1,965 to be precise) so is likely to have been able to accommodate several thousand pigeons. These were kept for meat by the then owners of the mansion house that stands a little lower down, beside the Braid Burn.

Figure 1.3: The calm and tranquil waters provide a perfect mirror for the vegetation at the west end of the pond.

★ Special Feature – the moorhen

For many of us, the moorhen (*Gallinula chloropus*) may be a nondescript black-and-white bird commonly seen skulking along the margins of ponds and other wetland areas. Indeed, together with the mallard duck, they are probably one of Britain's most common and widespread water birds.

A closer look can be revealing, however, for there is always so much more to see. This special feature will help you to hone your eye and pay attention to the moorhen so that you start noticing and appreciating them that little bit more.

To start with, it is worth considering whether this truly is a black-and-white bird. By sitting quietly, you might be treated to a view of them stretching out those long limbs, and can then observe just how rich those colours are; the dark blue-grey (some would say slate grey) of the chest, contrasts with the hints of browns and greens of the back and wings. These very different blacks are enhanced by a series of broken white lines running along the bird's flank. The legs, meanwhile, are a delightful lime green. Close attention to those legs might also allow you to spot a small area of red pigmentation on the upper leg. The beak is tipped with yellow, which gives way to a rich cherry red that also colours the frontal shield. And what of the iris? Observing such details requires a little patience and a more sympathetic surveying of the bird. Then, when moving away, you may be able to catch the flash of the underside of the tail, revealing the white panels that sit either side of central set of black tail feathers.

Figure 1.4a–4b: The moorhen, here seen stretching both right wing and right leg, is in many ways an unassuming and oft-overlooked bird. Careful study can prove very rewarding, especially in the good light which is often available at Blackford Pond.

Close observation of the moorhen's movement will draw your attention to their characteristic tail twitch that allows you to spot this bird at a distance even when moving through vegetation. A similar jerking movement is evident when swimming. When out of the water, you may notice that they lack webbed feet, and you might be forgiven for wondering how they manage to propel themselves when swimming. Those remarkably long legs and toes are not designed for swimming, however, for the moorhen is exquisitely able to high-step his or her way through (and/or over) the vegetation and other obstacles they encounter in the shallows. A similar lower-limb dexterity seems to help them navigate the similarly complex terrain found on riverbanks. The moorhen is here by design, so to speak, and fully deserves its alternative name of water hen, or *poule d'eau*, in French.

Visiting ponds such as that at Blackford will afford you the opportunity to befriend this magical water hen. Soon the telltale signs of their presence will become clear to you. You may, for example, come to recognise the alarm call – the *krrrrruk* that reverberates through the air and accompanies their quick return to water.

★ Special Feature – common gorse

Figure 1.5: Take a moment to appreciate the gorse in flower, particularly on a clear sunny day. Close your eyes and breathe deeply, and allow your senses to make the acquaintance of this member of the pea family and its remarkable fragrance. What does it remind you of?

Blackford Hill is justifiably famous for its gorse bushes. This special feature celebrates this wonderful shrub, and the joy and perhaps even hope (for it is said to be a remedy for hopelessness) that it brings to our lives.

There are three forms of gorse that between them flower through the year, hence the expression: 'when gorse is out of flower, kissing's out of fashion'. Perhaps this may be one of the reasons why, as a flower remedy, it is said to embody hope. The larger *Ulex europaeus* species grows to about 2 metres, is known as common gorse, and flowers between January and June. Western gorse and dwarf gorse are smaller, are more common in southern parts of the UK, and flower between July and November. These long flowering periods mean that gorse is particularly valuable as a food source for invertebrates, especially in early spring and winter, when little else is in flower. Sitting among gorse with your eyes closed can thus be a feast for the senses, as you soak in the scent and listen to the hum of insects. You may also hear the calls of the many birds who favour this dense shrub. If you are lucky these may include stonechat, whitethroat and blackcap as well as the more commonly heard wren and dunnock.

4 Hermitage House

Follow the path down through the garden, which has been painstakingly laid out in front of the dovecot and, after studying the signs, follow the path towards the main house.

The house (Figure 1.8) is surrounded by ancient woodland, and it is thought that woods have been present on this site for over 300 years. The older trees in the valley, meanwhile, probably date back to the 19th century, and include a mix of species, including Scots pine, beech, ash, chestnut and oak. You may want to visit the house before climbing up the hillside ahead of you to reach the southern rim of the valley. The house is now home to a visitor centre with some excellent displays.

A detour down the drive to your right will take you to the Old Lodge Coffee House. This is housed in an old tollhouse on Braid Road, beside the gated entry to the Hermitage.

Figure 1.6a: The buds and seeds of wych elm (Ulmus glabra) offer up a veritable feast for finches, including this handsome greenfinch, whose golden wing edgings are particularly striking and recognisable.

Figure 1.6b: High up in the ash tree, a great spotted woodpecker is finding something to feast on among the ash buds. Insects perhaps? Or the fresh buds themselves? You will have to pay careful attention to determine definitively what they are eating.

Figure 1.6c: In early spring listen out for the melodious and very throaty-rich song of the blackcap. They typically arrive during the first part of April, as the buds are just starting to burst open. Their song makes it a little easier to spot them, discreetly perched in the higher branches above your head.

Figure 1.7: The woodland path descends gently towards a large building which, when it comes into view, turns out to be what is thought to be the second largest dovecot in Scotland.

5 The southern rim of the valley

Your route takes you up a series of steps on the other side of the tarmac road. You will see these steps rising to your left as you walk back from the main house towards the doocot. Climb these to find a path running along the edge of the valley rim. Turn left along this and follow it as it more or less parallels the Braid Burn below. In doing so, you will be treated to fine views over the valley as it plunges 50 metres or more – with, through the trees, some tantalising glimpses of Old Hermitage House.

In addition to taking in the views, pay attention to what lies at your feet, for this is one of the best areas to see wood anemone (Figure 1.9), whose presence is a sure indicator of old woodland. Continue pursuing the path you are on; it will eventually start descending to Scout Bridge. Here, give yourself time to take in the tranquillity of the gurgling stream whilst keeping an ear open for the flight call of the grey wagtail.

Cross the bridge to reach the trail on the north side. This you then follow to reach Blackford Quarry and the Agassiz Rock. As you do so, look out for some delightful tree life, particularly in spring when the beech leaves are at their vivid best (Figures 1.10a–1.10b).

Figure 1.8: The Old Hermitage House now houses a visitor centre and is well worth a visit. It can also, and perhaps best, be viewed from the woodland on the southern rim of the valley, high above the Braid Burn.

Figure 1.9: Wood anemones (Anemone nemorosa) are beautiful flowers, and one of the first to emerge in spring to take full advantage of the light falling through the still leafless canopy. They are reliant on rhizomes, rather than seed dispersal, to spread, and this means they are slow to colonise the woodland floor. Their presence is thus a good indicator of ancient woodlands providing suitable conditions for slow growth. The petals are white with a pinkish tinge, whilst the leaves have a characteristic three-lobed shape.

6 The Agassiz Rock

As you follow the track eastwards towards Blackford Glen Road, keep an eye on the fields to your right for signs of roe deer (Figure 1.11a). These fields and the stables ahead of you commonly attract starling, who are always entertaining to watch and listen to as they bathe, forage and chatter away. In the spring you may also see the sudden and impressive appearance of butterbur (Figure 1.11b). Before reaching the stables, however, you will see on your left a much-overgrown quarry. This site is particularly significant to geologists, for it was here in 1840 that Louis Agassiz, the Swiss biologist and geologist, declared to have found conclusive evidence that the marks on the rocks had been produced by glacial action.

To understand the significance of this declaration, you need to realise that this was the first time that anyone had publicly proposed that Scotland had once been covered by ice sheets, and that it was the action of these glaciers that had produced various local geological features.

Agassiz's early work on fish and fish fossils brought him to the attention of William Buckland (1784–1856) who in 1813 was appointed Professor of Mineralogy and then of Geology at Oxford University. In 1838 Agassiz shared with Buckland his observations of the action of Swiss glaciers on rocks when Buckland visited Switzerland. On learning from Buckland that he had seen similar marks in ice-free Scotland, Agassiz drew a remarkable conclusion, for he was able to make the intellectual leap from mere valley glaciers to ice sheets on a completely different scale, stretching across vast swathes of countryside and even across continents.

Figures 1.10a–1.10b:
One of the early leaves to emerge in spring is that of the beech. These thin hairy leaves are translucent and have a magical ability to flicker in the sunlight. They can also grace salads and are much appreciated by browsing creatures such as deer. They can be admired one by one, close up or at a distance, as they dance and shimmer in the breeze.

Figure 1.11a: The fields adjoining the track that leads to Blackford Glen Road are a good place to watch roe deer. This young individual is demonstrating just how tasty young bramble leaves are – and how vegetation might become overgrazed when deer populations are left unchecked.

Figure 1.11b: These impressive-looking plants with their clumps of tiny purply-pink flowers are very striking, and provide a great source of nectar early in the year. The flower spikes appear before the leaves, and have tiny flowers arranged down the stems, which can reach 10–40cm in height. The leaves are very large, sometimes almost 1 metre wide, and are downy-grey underneath. The common name, butterbur, derives from the historical use of these enormous heart-shaped leaves to wrap butter.

This prompted him to make his 1840 visit to Scotland, culminating in his visit to Blackford Quarry. As David Land concludes, in his excellent account of the international significance of this rock:

> 'this spot is not … yet another … example of ice-scratched and smoothed rock, … it marks the first recognition in the world of the reality of former ice sheets where now there is no ice'.

> (2001, p.5)

7 Blackford Hill and the Observatory

From the rock (Figure 1.12), there are several paths that lead off to the right-hand side. These head uphill and eventually gain a broad area of heathland above the quarry. Ahead of you, the towers of the Royal Observatory peek out from above the gorse, broom and other shrubs.

In seeking to return to the start, you may pass to one side or other of the Observatory. The left side takes you towards the trig point (NT 254 706) at the top of Blackford Hill from whence you can enjoy a particularly good view across much of Edinburgh. A well-traced path then descends the north-facing hillside ahead of you, allowing you to regain the stairs you ascended at the start of the walk.

Figure 1.12: The Agassiz Rock, esteemed by geologists and boulderers of all persuasions.

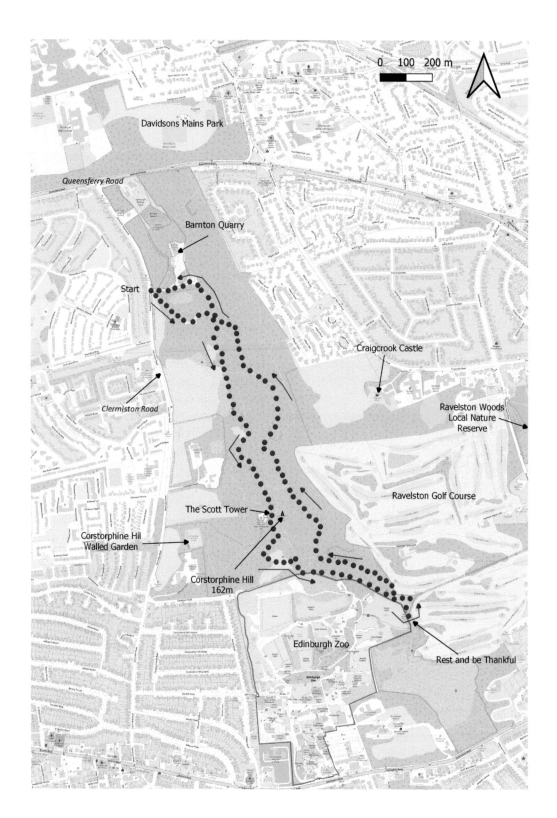

Davidsons Mains Park

Queensferry Road

Barnton Quarry

Start

Craigcrook Castle

Ravelston Woods
Local Nature
Reserve

Clermiston Road

Ravelston Golf Course

The Scott Tower

Corstorphine Hil
Walled Garden

Corstorphine Hill
162m

Edinburgh Zoo

Rest and be Thankful

0   100   200 m

Walk 2

Corstorphine Hill Nature Reserve

'By leaves we live', wrote the eminent poly-math Patrick Geddes. This timeless and uni-versal truth sums up how crucially important the trees in our cities are to sustaining our wellbeing, and indeed life itself. They are constantly giving. Any visit to Corstorphine Hill is rewarded with whatever seasonal gifts one of Edinburgh's best remaining woodlands cares to offer. The emphasis in this walk is therefore on the gifts not just of oxygen and clean air, but of surprising encounters.

This heavily quarried whin outcrop runs in a north-to-south direction, rising to a height of 161 metres. It is the westernmost of Edinburgh's seven hills[28] and provides fine views that can extend as far as Ben Lomond on a fine day. This protected area is signifi-cant, for it has resisted the encroachment of the city and those who would build on this green site, becoming Edinburgh's first Local Nature Reserve in 1993, having been a designated public park since 1924. Today the hill finds itself hemmed in by urban develop-ments that have fragmented the habitats that once provided for wildlife. The tiny nearby Ravelston Wood Local Nature Reserve, which miraculously still hosts badgers, feels even more marooned in the urban sprawl. Fortunately, the Ravelston Golf Course helps to link up these habitats, although there is much that could be done to ensure safer and freer movement across and through the inter-vening barriers posed by the busy Ravelston Dykes Road and its stone walls.

The Edinburgh City Local Plan lists Corstorphine Hill both as a Local Biodiversity Site and as a Local Geodiversity Site. The

Figure 2.1: A fine view towards the bridges and the distant hills from an opening in the woodland on the western edge of the hill.

28 This is a reference to the seven hills of Rome, and is a way of recognising the principal high points that dot the Edinburgh landscape. In addition to Corstorphine Hill, the list includes Castle Rock, Calton Hill, Arthur's Seat, Blackford Hill, the Braid Hills and Craiglockhart Hill.

former listing recognises the value of the mixed and pure woodland and developed scrub spread over the 217.6 hectares of Corstorphine and Ravelston, whilst the latter listing recognises the combination of geomorphological landforms and geological outcrops that the biodiversity grows on and from. Corstorphine Hill itself hosts 49 of the 887 hectares of mature woodland that the Nature Conservancy Council identified across Edinburgh in its Inventory of Ancient, Long-Established and Semi-Natural Woodland. Much of this is classed as Long-established Plantation, which means that it has been wooded for at least 130 years.

This walk's highlights include:

- Incredible views north-westwards to the Forth bridges (Figure 2.1) and the distant Ochil Hills.
- Fine views across Scotland's capital city from the Rest and be Thankful.
- An opportunity to discover this delightful Local Nature Reserve and explore Edinburgh's largest area of woodland, to encounter individual trees who are members of this semi-natural broadleaf woodland community, and to discover the incredible biodiversity this woodland supports.
- The opportunity to observe specialist woodland creatures, including the nuthatch, jay and badger.
- The discovery of the John Muir Way, which passes through Edinburgh on its way from Dunbar to Helensburgh.

🛥 Summary

The walk starts at the car park on Clermiston Road North. Parking is also available on the road itself. Alternative access points are possible from Ravelston Dykes Lane and from Queensferry Road.

This walk loops along the western edge of the woodland, heading in a broadly southerly direction to reach the historically significant viewpoint known as the Rest and Be Thankful before returning along the paths running along the eastern edge; you can take one of a variety of paths to complete the loop. The eastern slopes enjoy the sun in the first half of the day and can find themselves in the shade once the sun passes its zenith.

🏛 History

Corstorphine Hill has a fascinating and deeply entangled geological, natural and social history. The following is a brief overview of some of this history.

The crystalline igneous rock that characterises Corstorphine Hill is called dolerite. It was formed as molten magma intruded between the existing beds of sandstone and mudstone. The resulting sheets of hard, resistant rock were left behind as glacial ice moved across this part of Scotland in a west-to-east direction. The glacial erosion is still very much in evidence today, as demonstrated on the exposed surface of the dolerite by the grooves cut by stones into the ice-smoothed rock. The stones were carried within the ice as it flowed over the rock. These are not the only historical marks left within the rock, for there are also cup markings on the western slopes of the hill. It is thought that these were produced during the Neolithic or Bronze Age (c. 3600–1500 BCE), but their precise purpose remains unknown. The possibility that they may have played a role in sacred traditions is suggested by the cup clusters potentially aligning with the setting summer sun during the summer solstice.

Much later, these rocks were extensively quarried for dolerite and sandstone, as well as pavement stone. The latter stone was so named because the slabs, produced as sedimentary siltstone, were hardened by the heat of the magma flowing over them, were suitable for paving. In the late 17th century, both George Heriot's School and Parliament House were built from Corstorphine Hill stone. According to MacKintosh (2014), an 1855 map shows ten quarries on the hill, six being actively exploited. It is likely that the geology and quarrying of these areas helped to save Corstorphine Hill from being consumed by the post-World War II urban housing development.

World War II saw the defensive merits of the local geology being further exploited, with Barnton Quarry Command Centre being built as a secret operations room for RAF Fighter Command based at Turnhouse Airport. In 1952, during the Cold War, the facility was expanded into a central coordination facility for radar stations throughout Scotland, housed in a bunker which comprised three underground levels and a large surface building. In the early 1960s, it was redesignated as a Regional Seat of Government and kept ready to accommodate 400 politicians and civil servants for up to 30 days in the event of a nuclear attack. The site closed in 1983 and ownership was transferred to the local council. It was subsequently sold to James Mitchell, owner of Scotland's Secret Bunker, near Anstruther, in Fife. Since 2011, a team of volunteers have been helping with renovation efforts with a view to creating a local Cold War Museum and education centre.

Today, the Barnton Quarry areas at the northern end of the hill are fenced off and excluded from the LNR. In addition to the nuclear bunker, another of these areas is actively used by the council's Roads Department as a depot. But what of the history of the rest of Corstorphine Hill? What of the life-sustaining wonders we really care about once we have managed to let go of the paralysis imposed by our fears of a nuclear or other anthropogenic Armageddon?

Corstorphine Hill was acquired by Edinburgh City Council in 1924. The hill was designated as a Local Nature Reserve in 1993 and as a Regionally Important Geological Site (RIGS) in 2000. Today the park is managed by the council's Ranger Service with the support of a local friend's group[29] that was instrumental in restoring the area's historical walled garden and in opposing the zoo's plans to encroach on this wild space. The walled garden originally belonged to Hillwood House.[30] but has been in council ownership since 1927, during which time it was disused and had become overgrown. It has now been restored by volunteers from the Friends of Corstorphine Hill, a charity who are also responsible for maintaining the Corstorphine Tower. Also known as the Scott or Clermiston Tower, this impressive building, located close to the hill's summit, was built in 1871 to commemorate the centenary of the birth of Sir Walter Scott. In 1932 it was gifted to the city, to mark the centenary of Scott's death.

🍃 Habitats

Deciduous woodland, scrubland, grassland.

🚌 Transport links

The Corstorphine Hill LNR is well served by the local bus routes, particularly along Queensferry Road, Clermiston Road and Corstorphine Road. The site also has one of Edinburgh's Core Paths (CEC 14) running through, and this makes it easy to access the area sustainably.

---

29 https://www.corstorphinehill.org.uk/

30 Hillwood House was home to the MacKinnon family, who owned the Drambuie blend of whisky, honey, herbs and spices for more than 100 years before selling it to William Grant & Sons in 2014.

There is only a small amount of car parking available at the car park on Clermiston Road North, and I would suggest that where possible this be prioritised for those with accessibility needs.

☕ Refreshments

Several cafés can be found along Corstorphine Road, which can be reached by following the John Muir Way as it drops down from the Rest and be Thankful to Corstorphine High Street.

🔖 References and further reading

Cousquer, G. (2021). 'Nuthatches feeding on birch sap'. *Scottish Birds*, 41(3), 234–235.

MacKintosh, A. (2014). *The Corstorphine Story*. Edinburgh: The Corstorphine Trust.

The management plan (2017–2026) for this Local Nature Reserve can be viewed on the Edinburgh Council website: https://tinyurl.com/4z4y5jyc

🌐 Weblinks

Tree map: http://corstorphinehill.org.uk/documents/FoCH_Trees_page_2.pdf

🪧 Directions

1 Entering the woodland

From the car park, pass through the gateway and turn right to pick up a path that wends over the roots and rocks, passing several mature beech trees, together with a collection of birch, wych elm, sycamore and even a surprise yew tree. See if you can spot it! The path that runs along the western edge of the woods can be delightfully sunny, particularly later in the day, when the light plays on the steely silver bark of the beech trees. These trees seem to attract the attentions of graffitists who leave their arguably less-than-appreciated marks declaiming their passage for posterity. The older

beech trees somehow draw the fire of those who like to cut bark and, in doing so, perhaps help protect their neighbours. Grandfatherly beeches they certainly are, extending their protective canopy over quite some area.

2 Follow the edge of the woodland

As you pass along this path in spring, look out for clumps of wood sorrel, whose delightful not just white, but mesmerisingly white, flowers light up the woodland floor hereabouts (Figure 2.2a). In April new life can be seen bursting out everywhere – the bracken uncurls gracefully (Figure 2.2b) and fresh green leaves spring from every bud.

If you are able to revisit this wonderful stretch of woodland regularly, try to identify a 'tree-friend' who you can check in on through the seasons. This might be an old granny tree (Figures 2.3a–2.3c) or a younger tree with a different energy and story to tell. It can be quite rewarding to enquire as to

Figure 2.2a: The delicate flower of wood sorrel (Oxalis acetosella) is best observed by crouching down to within inches of the woodland floor. The trifoliate leaves have been used to represent the holy trinity, and have earnt this delicate little plant its association with St Patrick. Wood sorrel is thus one of the shamrocks that have come to represent Ireland. The leaves are edible and are often described as having a slight lemony flavour, and can be seen to fold up before and during rain and at dusk.

Figure 2.2b: Watching young bracken uncurl in spring can be quite magical, particularly if you revisit the same plant and capture 'its unfurling and unfolding. How do you unfold in spring?

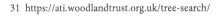

their story. Try to learn to listen to them by spending time underneath their canopy, listening to the movement of their boughs and leaves. Pay attention to where the first new leaves spring forth.

Encounters with trees are often best allowed to unfold without any expectations, as this helps us stay open to possibility and surprise. At the same time, you may from time to time want to seek out specific trees purposefully. The Woodland Trust's Ancient Tree Inventory[31] shows, at the time of writing, three trees having been registered across this site. The first is a yew whose girth at 0.5 metres from the ground has been measured at 2.83 metres (location NT 206 742). The other two are both sycamores. The largest of these has a girth at 1.5 metres above the ground measures over 6 metres; its location is at NT 208 736. The Friends Group has a tree map for Corstorphine Hill that may be worth consulting.

Listen out too for the calls of blue, great, long-tailed and coal tits, as well as wren, blackcap, robin, chaffinch, goldfinch and bullfinch. These feathered creatures clearly value

Figure 2.3a: Choosing your tree-friend invites you to feel yourself drawn to a particular tree, one that you will want to revisit, perhaps touch, caress, sit under and come to know. This old rowan has many a story to tell, and an extended family whose lives have been touched by this tree's contributions. What might his family tree look like?

Figure 2.3b: Pay attention to the old rowan tree, and you may notice surprising signs of new growth from old wounds.

31 https://ati.woodlandtrust.org.uk/tree-search/

Figure 2.3c: Alternatively, you may want to befriend an old beech tree and immerse yourself in its story. Pay attention to the dead wood that has been broken off by the wind's ravages, and the vestiges of last year's leaves who clung on despite the wind. An old beech tree has many a tall tale to tell.

Figure 2.4: An officer and a gentleman: the mistle thrush seems to have perfected the parade ground moves. Whether standing to attention or marching with purpose, he carries himself differently. Pay attention to the steelier grey of his coat and tails if you can. What do you see?

this habitat, and challenge us to consider what it takes to know and appreciate it as they do …

Where did we take a wrong turn and lose our appreciation and connection? A good question to carry through the woods, perhaps.

It is often tempting to name and to move on, thereby creating a list of names. How is it that some of us seem to reduce the birds we meet to a collection of squiggles on paper, a sequence of names? If you indulge in this habit, it can be helpful to notice it and how you respond to it. Are you ticking off – or are you ticking yourself off for not being more present?

We have choices: instead of moving on, try moving in.

Pay attention to the birds themselves, their distinctive features and character. What is it about the character of the mistle thrush (*Turdus viscivorus*) that marks them (Figure 2.4) out from the song thrush and the blackbird?

For me, this creature has something of the upright gentleman out to dinner in his coat tails. He is confident! So confident that he of-

ten drives off bigger birds, including magpies and crows, and even buzzards and sparrowhawks. Mistle thrushes have been known to take possession of a whole tree of berries in autumn and fend off all comers right through the winter.

He seems to respond to the attention he attracts with a grating growl; a call some have compared to the sound made by one of those old football rattles. This call is imbued with aggressive overtones that seem to be consistent with his outward confidence. The mistle thrush also sings and, indeed, is one of the first birds to develop a full voice as the days start to lengthen, doing so as early as late January. Most other bird species will still be singing fragments of song (often termed subsong) whilst waiting for winter to loosen its grip on the land. Not the mistle thrush! The same disdain shown to larger birds is typically shown to the winter weather, and this thrush's indifference to wind and rain has earnt him the widespread name of storm cock. A forgotten but equally apt name for his

Figure 2.5: The smooth rocky surfaces that you cross on your way to the high point of the walk have been polished by the action of glacial ice during the last ice age. The rock you are walking over is dolerite, and was produced by magma that rose upwards before encountering thick blankets of sedimentary rock that acted as a stopper, impeding the eruption of the magma and forcing it to spread laterally. These deposits are now exposed following the erosion of the overlying sedimentary rock.

operatics is Jeremy Joy, a corruption perhaps of January Joy.

Try observing the woodland birds who cross your path and, in observing them closely, try to concoct your own names for them. Soon enough you may have ceased to list them by name, preferring instead to meet genuinely and exchange a knowing glance.

Another question to ponder is the following: Why is it these birds choose to be part of woodland life? Why is it they are at home here? What are they up to? The special feature on the nuthatch that accompanies this walk explores some of these questions.

3 Ascent to Clermiston Tower

As you make your way along the woodland paths, look out for an area of polished dolerite that bears testimony to the hill's volcanic past and the subsequent passage of glacial ice during the last ice age (Figure 2.5). This stone was quarried in and around the hill. The stone produced was called *whin* by the quarrymen, no doubt in recognition of the widespread presence of gorse, or whin, flourishing on the thin stony dolerite soil.

You soon climb up to the high point of the walk, which stands at 162 metres above sea level. In truth, there are a succession of three bumps, all at about 160 metres. On the third of these, you will pass on your right a fenced enclosure, surrounding a mast. A little

beyond that you will reach Clermiston Tower (NT 206 738).

Also known as the Corstorphine Hill Tower, or the Scott Tower, this monument (Figure 2.6) was erected to mark the centenary of the birth of the author Sir Walter Scott on 15 August, 1771. It stands 20 metres tall and, during the summer months, you may take advantage of planned openings to climb the 101 steps to the cap-house and viewing gallery, where you can take in the panoramic views from the top. If you observe the masonry closely, you will notice two distinct stone types. The stonework of the tower is largely coursed whinstone, almost certainly drawn from quarries on the hill, whereas the lighter stone surrounding the openings and parapets is sandstone.

Figure 2.6: The Scott Tower can perhaps best be seen before the surrounding trees have come into leaf.

★ Special Feature – the nuthatch

Where we humans are made for walking, having long forsaken the sanctuary of trees, the nuthatch is made for a mesmerising array of arboreal moves. If you should spy a bird moving confidently headfirst down a tree trunk, it is almost certainly going to be a nuthatch (*Sitta europaea*). Should you spot that characteristic movement and get it in your sights, you will recognise it by his powerful dagger of a beak, the long black bandana of an eye stripe, his silver-blue back and orangey belly (Figure 2.7a). The jaunty pose that sees him raise his short upper body away from the trunk to survey his domain whilst holding expertly fast to the bark under his feet is straight out of elite climber school. To stand a chance of making it into and then graduating from this academy you have to be either a nuthatch or a squirrel.

Figure 2.7a: From below, peer up though the buds and branches and try to feel understand what it takes to hold a position so well on a vertical surface. Pay attention, too, to the interplay of colours: the white throat, the buff orange undercarriage, the chocolate brown of the iris and the not-quite-so-black-as-I'd-expected underside of that powerful chisel of a bill.

This most remarkable creature is unique as tree birds go for, unlike treecreepers and woodpeckers, nuthatches do not rely on a cleverly stiffened tail for support and are not limited to moving skywards. The nuthatch is the consummate climber, capable of moving in any direction.

They have developed a poise and balance when moving that never ceases to stimulate the curiosity and admiration of anyone who spends time studying their movements. Their acrobatic abilities stem in part from their short legs, wide-based stance and needle-sharp claws. Their assuredness is, however, best appreciated not by trying to understand how they achieve it but by watching them from an inconspicuous and comfortable vantage point.

Comfortably settled, perhaps even lying on your back, you can peer skywards without twisting or craning your neck, and start paying attention to how this masked bandit commits daylight robbery on the nuts that he wedges into suitable cracks before breaking open. It is this habit that has earnt them the name of nuthatch or nuthack. Nuts, however, are not the only food item appearing on these creatures' menu, for they are largely insectivorous; when insects become available they will seek them out throughout the tree, and even take them in flight or from the ground. The nuthatch can break open the bark of trees to reach insects under the bark, and will also use this ability to access and feed from the sap of acer, birch, poplar and ash during spring (Cousquer, 2021), when the sap of these trees is rushing up towards the leaves (Figure 2.7b). It can be a joy to watch the questing, skilful, purposeful foraging of a specialist bird such as the nuthatch, and to try to appreciate how they exploit the food resources available to them at different times of year.

Figure 2.7b: This nuthatch has used his beak to groove the bark of a young birch tree in order to access the sap coursing through the tree in spring, helping support the production of chlorophyll in the leaves that are preparing to burst from their buds. Later in the year, the sugar-rich phloem sap can similarly be accessed. It is, of course possible that sap released in this way will attract insects, and that the nuthatch will be feeding on these. Only by watching carefully will you be able to discern how the nuthatch is being rewarded ... every meal is different.

It can be invaluable to familiarise yourself with the call of the nuthatch as this can alert you to his presence and location, long before you set eyes on him. Bill Oddie presented the nuthatch's calls on BBC Radio 4's Tweet of the Day; this represents an excellent opportunity for those wishing to familiarise themselves with what to listen for: https://www.bbc.co.uk/programmes/b03ws7gc.

Perhaps the most distinctive call is a loud and explosive '*chwittt!*' that was likened to a pebble skittering obliquely off a piece of ice by the naturalist and author of *The Natural History and Antiquities of Selborn*, Gilbert White (1720–1793). I prefer to think of this as the sound made by the skates of an accelerating speed skater. This 'excitement call' can be repeated, usually as three to four successive notes. The call may be heard throughout the year, for nuthatches maintain their territories year-long.

Hearing the nuthatch's call can prompt you to start scanning the trees and branches ahead of you for the nuthatch's signature movements. It is strange to reflect that Edinburgh's trees did not use to resound to these calls, and many of the older trees will have no historical memories of this bird rampaging up and down their trunks. In the 18th and 19th centuries the nuthatch's range was limited to southern England. In the 20th century, however, the nuthatch started spreading northwards, arriving in Northumberland in the 1980s, and breeding in Scotland for the first time nine years later. They are now well established, and you have a decent chance of encountering them wherever there are mature deciduous trees – particularly, but by no means exclusively, beech and oak.

4 Continuing to the Rest and be Thankful

The path from the tower heads off in a southerly distance, descending gradually to reach an area of open ground, where you will see signs for the John Muir Way coming in from your right, and heading on to make a short ascent towards a metal fence.

In spring you may be fortunate to see a rich carpet of lesser celandine beneath the trees as you make this ascent (Figure 2.8). William Wordsworth wrote an ode to the plant, and it even gets a mention in C.S. Lewis's *The Lion, the Witch and the Wardrobe*.

Celandine is an anglicised form of the Greek term for the swallow: *chelidon*, an entirely appropriate name for one of the early harbingers of spring. One of its folk names is, unsurprisingly, 'spring messenger'. When spying your first lesser celandine flower of the year, listen out to see who is singing. It might just be a mistle thrush!

With the fence on your right, follow this as the path contours round to reach a fine viewpoint with views across the golf course below you and out across the city (Figure 2.9). This is the famous Rest and Be Thankful viewpoint that greeted many a traveller as they made their final approach to Edinburgh. This spot lies at the eastern end of Corstorphine Hill, and has been immortalised in Robert Louis

Figure 2.8: Lesser celandine (Ficaria verna) is a member of the buttercup family, and a common plant associated with woodlands and hedgerows. It appears early in February, taking advantage of the light that makes it through the canopy at that time of year. Its heart-shaped leaves are distinctive, its eight-petalled yellow flowers even more so. These flowers appear through March and April and, in doing so, provides a valuable source of nectar to insects early in the season. The plant then dies back in May. In its raw state, like all buttercups, it contains a compound known as protoanemonin, which causes nausea, vomiting, dizziness and other symptoms in mammals. This toxin is neutralised when the plant is dried or cooked, and it is in this state that it continues to be used by some herbalists as a treatment for haemorrhoids. Indeed, one of the old names for this plant was pilewort. The lesser celandine's tuber root resembles a bunch of figs (hence the scientific name Ficaria), a somewhat archaic name for piles. According to the Doctrine of Signatures, this resemblance justified its use as a herbal remedy.

Figure 2.9: The Edinburgh skyline stands out clearly from the wonderful viewpoint of the Rest and Be Thankful. On a clear day you can pick out the distant Bass Rock, North Berwick Law and Traprain Law, and, closer to hand, Calton Hill, Edinburgh Castle and Arthur's Seat. Immediately below, the trees of Ravelston Golf Course are a delight in spring.

Stevenson's classic novel *Kidnapped* as the place where David Balfour and Alan Breck parted company.

5 The eastern edge of the hill

Retrace your steps to arrive at the mini col beyond the flight of steps. The ground drops steeply away to your right, whilst the John Muir Way heads off to your left. Look im-

mediately ahead to spy a clear path running round the eastern flank of Corstorphine Hill; you can follow this as it loops back round to the tower.

On your return to the car park, whence you started out, try to keep to the eastern flank of the hill. This can be shadier in the afternoon as the sun drops to the west, but will hold the sun through the morning. The

Figure 2.10a: There is evidence of fresh excavation at the opening to this sett. The badgers have been spring cleaning!

ground below drops off steeply into the woods, and it can be worth keeping your eyes peeled for roe deer passing secretly through the trees below.

The eastern flank of the hill is home to several setts (Figure 2.10a); the badger's presence has, in part, earnt the hill its status as a nature reserve. In spring, freshly dug soil can be in evidence, and you may be able to identify the footprints of this fascinating nocturnal creature (Figures 2.10b–2.10c). Remember to keep a respectful distance, however, and keep any disturbance to an absolute minimum. They will be sleeping, after all! It is generally recommended that visits to a sett be conducted only in the morning so that human smells have time to dissipate before dusk.

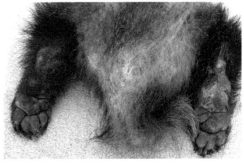

6 Returning to the car park

Having explored the many paths running the length of the eastern edge of the hill, but without following them downwards, you will find yourself with the quarry at the northern edge of the hill ahead of you. Ignore the path running along the right-hand edge of the quarry, unless you want to explore this. Instead turn left with the railings on your right, and return to the car park.

Figures 2.10b–2.10c: Close attention to the freshly dug earth may reveal footprints. That shown above is probably made by the pads of a badger's hind paw, for the hind claws are much shorter than those at the front, whose length reflects their role in digging. Note the rounded appearance of the foot, and the way the ventral pad extends in an even band across the complete width of the foot.

Walk 3

The River Almond from Cramond

This walk provides you with an opportunity to discover the mouth and lower reaches of the Almond River. This stretch offers many highlights, including:

- An opportunity to take in and enjoy the peaceful scene where the waters of the River Almond empty into the Firth of Forth (Figure 3.1).
- The opportunity of observing a host of waders and other birds, including eider (Figures 3.2a–3.2b), gathering to feed on the mud flats exposed at low tide on either side of the estuary.
- A succession of habitats that range from the tidal waters of the Forth Estuary and Cramond Harbour to the mature broad-leaved woodland beside the river valley, with its cliffs overlooking the river, and a post-industrial river that is now enjoying an ecologically healthier new chapter.

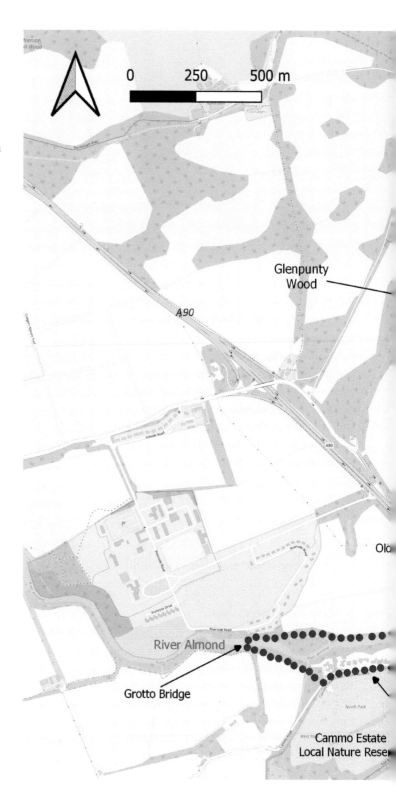

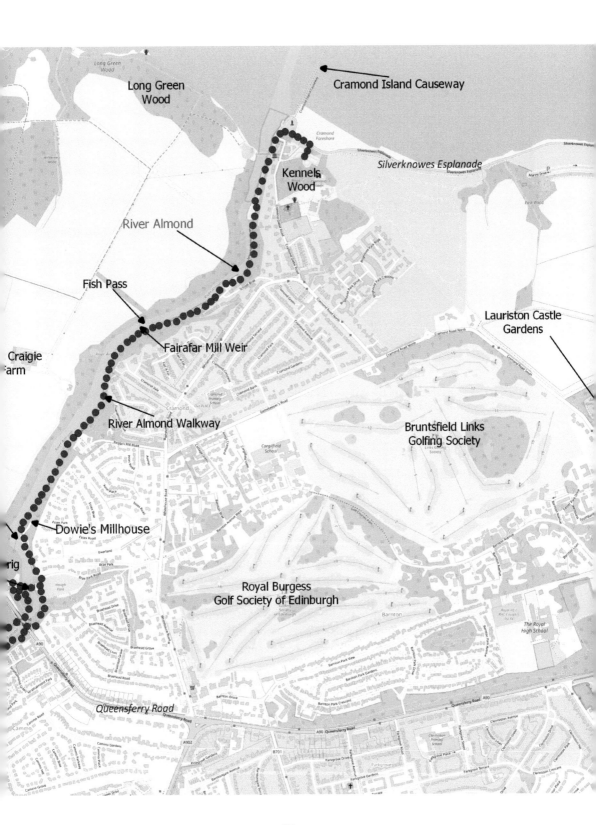

Cramond Island Causeway

Long Green
Wood

Silverknowes Esplanade

Kennels
Wood

River Almond

Lauriston Castle
Gardens

Fish Pass

Fairafar Mill Weir

Craigie
Farm

River Almond Walkway

Bruntsfield Links
Golfing Society

Dowie's Millhouse

rig

Royal Burgess
Golf Society of Edinburgh

The Royal
High School

Queensferry Road

Figure 3.1: A fine view across the sandbanks to the causeway leading out to Cramond Island can be obtained from Cramond foreshore.

- Encounters with riverine birds, including the grey heron, kingfisher, grey wagtail, dipper and goosander.

⮞ Summary

The walk starts at the Cramond Beach car park in Cramond village (NT 190 770), and takes in the foreshore and harbour before following the River Almond Walkway along the east bank of the river all the way to Old Cramond Brig. After crossing over the bridge to the west bank, follow the path upstream as far as the Grotto Bridge, then regain the east bank and follow it back to the start.

🏛 History

Cramond has a wonderfully rich archaeological history, reflecting the many ways this site has been valued from ancient times. The rich oyster and mussel beds offered a reliable food resource to nomadic hunter-gatherers whose Mesolithic encampments have been dated to approximately 8500 BCE, by analysing the discarded shells of the hazelnuts that would have formed one of their staple foods. Today humans rarely go foraging but these nuts continue to attract a number of wildlife species.

Cramond has undergone many changes over the intervening 10,000 years. Its hunter-gatherers used microlith tools made of flint and chert, as has been found from their recovery from the raised beach that sits back from the sea along the coast here. This fine example of a raised beach shows us how much higher the sea was during past ice ages; as the glaciers disappeared, the land bounced back, gaining height and creating an abandoned shoreline above the shoreline we see today.

In 208 CE the Roman Emperor Septimius Severus set out for Britain with a great army. For three years Severus ruled the empire from York, and was mistakenly thought by many

Figures 3.2a–3.2b: Male and female eider may be viewed together on the water at the mouth of the Almond during the early breeding season. At this time of year their plumages have two very different roles: one for camouflage, and the other to impress and attract attention.

in the medieval and early modern period to have built Hadrian's Wall. Modern archaeology has, however, disproven this, confirming that this great wall was begun in 122 CE under Emperor Hadrian, the Antonine Wall (between the Clyde and the Forth) being constructed some two decades later. In the years preceding Severus's campaign, his provincial governors had undertaken extensive renovations on Hadrian's Wall. It was during his campaign, however, that the Roman Fort at Cramond came to be built, as Severus campaigned beyond the wall, seeking to gain territory from the northern tribes.

Today, Cramond's name reflects the importance of this site to the Romans, who built a fort covering some six acres that could be supplied via the small port they had established at the mouth of the Almond. The river was called Amon as recently as the late 18th century (Wood, 1794) and it is suggested that Cramond derives from *Caer Amon*, meaning 'fort on the river'. According to Bruce Campbell (1904, p.119), a road is supposed to have led from Cramond over Mons Hill to reach the eastern end of the Antonine Wall, at Caerriden. The site of the fort has been extensively excavated and studied since its rediscovery in the 1950s. During this time, it has been subject to over 60 archaeological interventions, 12 of those undertaken by the amateur archaeologist Mr Charlie Hoy, working principally with the Edinburgh Archaeological Field Society. A detailed summary of this work is available from Hunter (2017).

Bringing this history closer to the present day, it is worth noting how significant the port was at the turn of the 19th/20th century. Written in 1904, Bruce Campbell's account of the natural history of Cramond highlighted the extent to which the area that had once sustained hunter-gatherer communities had been negatively impacted. One particularly poignant example concerns shellfish; at the time of writing he retained a faint memory of seeing boats dredging for oysters, but this industry had since collapsed and died. He contrasts this with the Cramond of 1740, which had 11 large boats 'dragging for this delicious bivalve' (Campbell, 1904, p.122). These were sold to Dutch vessels, meaning that the five-man crew of a Cramond fishing boat could earn 30 shillings a day. Campbell then goes on to tell of how a river that once abounded with fish is now so polluted that no fish of any kind can live in it. His account then tells of the whales that had been recorded beaching on this coastline. Perhaps

the most interesting part of this report is the list of 136 bird species, including nightjar, merlin and peregrine, that he reports as breeding. He elaborates on birds of note, bemoaning the crash in barn owl numbers and dippers, and the shooting of a waxwing in Cramond in 1904. He notes that capercaillie were first recorded in 1878 and several times since, and turtle dove seen in 1896. His account then summarises the mammals known to frequent the Almond, and he states that otters had not been seen for about 15 years (p.129).

Much of this devastation of the living world is likely to have arisen as a result of the industrialisation of the Almond. A number of industries, including quarrying and milling, sprang up along the river; they are explored in this walk, and described further in the special feature on Fairafar Mill and its weir.

In 1920 Cramond was absorbed into the City of Edinburgh, and it has since become a desirable suburb of Scotland's capital city. Today the River Almond Walkway is owned by the City of Edinburgh Council and managed by the Countryside Ranger Service. The 2011–2020 Management Plan for the area was the first ever specific management plan for the walkway, and sought to complement the five-year management plan written by the Cramond Angling Club (CAC) on behalf of the River Forth Fisheries Trust. This plan highlighted conservation objectives for both the woodland and the river that the walkway explores. It notes that the tree stock is associated with larger estate houses, which historically owned the lands running down to the riverbank, and recognises that there is a need over the longer term to promote diversity within the tree composition. This will involve addressing the natural regeneration of non-native tree species such as sycamore and the rhododendron, and the stands of laurel that the estates have left behind.

🍃 Habitats

Tidal estuary, river, deciduous woodland, small areas of semi-improved grassland.

🚌 Transport links

The starting point for the walk at Cramond Beach car park is a short (8-minute) walk from the bus stop on Cramond Road, near where it joins Cramond Glebe Road. This stop is served by the number 47 Lothian Bus[32] service to and from central Edinburgh and Penicuik. When arriving by bus, get off here and turn right down Cramond Glebe Road, passing Cramond Kirk and descending to the Cramond Inn and the shore.

The start of the walk can also be reached via the Silverknowes+ Esplanade, which now forms part of route 12 in Edinburgh's network of Quiet Routes.[33] It can be picked up in Granton, with access points on West Shore Road. This can be a nice way to access the walk, with a cycle ride along the sea front to warm you up. It should be noted, however, that whilst the esplanade offers excellent cycling on a broad hard surface, with no inclines and fine views over the Firth of Forth, the path can be busy with dog walkers, families and young children.

☕ Refreshments

The walk is well served with cafés in Cramond and at Cramond Brig, including the Cramond Falls Café and the Cramond Gallery Bistro.

📕 References and further reading

Campbell, B. (1904). 'Some notes on the antiquities and natural history of Cramond district'. *Transactions of the Edinburgh Field Naturalists and Microscopical Society*, 5, pp.116–129.

Dods, J., & Scholes, W. (2012). *Cramond Through Time*. Amberley Publishing Limited.

Hunter, F. (2017). 'Excavations and interventions in and around Cramond Roman fort and annexe, 1976 to 1990'. *Scottish Archaeological Internet Reports*, 74. https://doi.org/10.9750/issn.2056-7421.2017.74

Wood, J.P., & New York Public Library. (1794). *Antient and Modern State of the Parish of Cramond*. In Internet Archive. J. Paterson. https://archive.org/details/antientandmoder00woodgoog.

🪧 Directions

1 Exploring Cramond Harbour and the foreshore

From the car park, either head back to the road and follow this round to the right to reach Cramond's tiny harbour, or look for the path dropping down from the car park to the promenade. There is much to take in and observe on the foreshore itself, on the sandbanks and mudflats at the mouth of the river, and within the harbour.

The exposed intertidal zones stretching out into the main estuary are always worth scanning for redshank, oystercatcher, curlew and other waders, particularly in winter when large numbers of overwintering birds may gather there to feed. It is a site that is typically best viewed in the two to three hours before high tide, as the birds are pushed higher up, closer to you. The hours that follow the tide's turning may also attract birds up close. In the evening look out too for waders heading out to roost on Cramond Island.

Within the harbour, you are likely to see eider both during the breeding season and during the winter months. You may also see mute swans, shelduck, goldeneye and mallard, and then there is always the challenge

---

Figure 3.3 (left): Perhaps the most distinctive feature of the black-headed gull (Chroicocephalus ridibundus) *is the white leading edge to their wing. Look out for this when they take off, and note the black tips to the primaries. The black head is only seen during the breeding season; as the birds come into winter plumage, this is gradually lost, giving a banded appearance until they are left with a black ear-spot. The adults, shown here, all have reddish legs and bills.*

Figure 3.4 (right): The female goosander possesses something of a punk hairdo that extends down the back of the bird's head and onto the nape. There is a distinct line between the rich chocolaty colours of the head and the silvery-whites of the neck and body. This is worth looking out for when learning to distinguish goosander from their near relative, the red merganser whose colours merge ('merging mergansers' may help you remember this). When you focus on their feathers, try to appreciate how well they suit this incredible bird for life both in and on water and in the air. This is a feathered torpedo in full evening dress.

of identifying the resident and passage gulls (Figure 3.3). Given the challenges involved in identifying gulls, whose plumage evolves through several moults during their first two years of life, it can be useful to capture some photographs and to work through useful identification features at home with the image on a screen and a good bird identification guide in front of you.

The attempts to fence off small areas of the foreshore to provide shelter from trampling feet and other disturbances feel tokenistic. It is worth observing this area with a view to appreciating how it has been rendered inappropriate as a nesting site for ground-nesting birds. It is worth pondering, perhaps, how this might be transformed if the area was fenced to exclude dogs and people, and the vegetation allowed to grow in. Fortunately there are a few other, less accessible, sites that are able to accommodate wildlife.

2 Cramond Harbour to Cramond Falls Café

As you head upriver, pay attention both to the riverbank and water on your right and to the woodland on your left. With any luck you may see goosander and little grebe diving for fish, and you will be left wondering just how they hunt so adeptly under water. The goosander's bill (Figure 3.4) is clearly well equipped for securing and swallowing fish, and looks nothing like that of the dabbling mallard, whose diet does not include fish. Whilst the terminal hook at the end of the goosander's bill may look severe, what renders these bills so efficient is the array of tiny backward-pointing teeth that lie hidden inside, which allow them to grasp, manoeuvre and swallow fish. They share this 'secret weapon' with other members of the 'sawbill' family, including the red-breasted merganser and the smew. Without incredible underwater propulsion, however, these diving ducks would not be the efficient predators nature has intended them to be. Their talent is perhaps best observed by watching them propel themselves against the current and from pool to pool when in the pursuit of fish, whether on or below the water.

As you continue along the riverbank, try to move slowly and make use of the ample cover. There are many good places to sit and watch, and there are always surprises, providing you are open to them.

Among the trees, as the new spring growth daubs the branches in greenery, you may hear and see tits foraging away. If you pay careful attention, you may even be able to find clues as to their evolving diet, for this new greenery attracts a host of feeding insects, who themselves represent food for other creatures in the food web (Figure 3.5). The great and blue tits ably make use of their light weight and ability to hang upside down, for this allows them to access the underside of leaves and the treasures that may lurk there. Such feats would be beyond many other birds … you certainly won't see wrens, thrushes, robins or pigeons doing these acrobatics. These little differences can be a joy to pay attention to. And with joy comes deeper appreciation, for it is in observing such specialisms that we can start to understand just how well these birds occupy their ecological niche.

3 Cramond Falls Café to Cramond Falls

Having perhaps interrupted your walk for some refreshment at the excellent Cramond Falls Café, you can then continue up to the impressive weir for a taste of Cramond's industrial past and signs of the river's rejuvenation. You have a choice of following the more obvious roadway to reach the weir or of sticking more closely to the riverbank.

Figure 3.5: It is so easy to overlook our familiar birds, such as this great tit. Slowing down can allow us to absorb the little details of their daily lives, to observe what it is that they pay attention to. As the buds of this sycamore burst open and the fresh green leaves taste their freedom, they attract the attention of aphids, and these are soon spotted by observant birds. Not all such birds have the agility to reach these aphids where they hide on the underside of the leaves. The great tit, however, is perfectly suited to such exploits, and there is something exquisite about the poise they bring to this balancing act and the contribution they make to the balance between the tree and the hungry aphids.

Figure 3.6: Maidenhair spleenwort (Asplenium trichomanes) is a delightful fern who has managed to colonise many of the crevices on the sun-kissed walls of the mill. It occurs worldwide on rocky terrain, and the curious among you may well wonder how it manages to colonise such tiny cracks. The answer lies in the spores that are released and carried by the wind. Those that settle in a promising site can give rise to new growth.

As you approach the falls (also known as Fairafar Weir), the roofless edifice that is all that remains of Fairafar Mill invites exploration (see the special feature). It used to be the site of an iron foundry powered by the weir, but its walls, now open to the sun, are home to an attractive fern known as maidenhair spleenwort (Figure 3.6) as well as a few specimens of brittle bladder fern.

The water leading up to the weir is much favoured by mallards, and during the spring it can be very rewarding to watch them pairing up, breeding, raising their ducklings (Figures 3.7a–3.7c), and negotiating not just the rapids but also a surprising degree of intraspecific (i.e. within the same species) conflict (Figures 3.7d–3.7e).

Figures 3.7a–3.7c: There is something quite entrancing about watching young ducklings bravely keeping up with their mother from such a young age. They must learn fast, for they will have to navigate both slow (3.7a) and fast-moving water (3.7b). In the black-and-white picture the force of the water has actually displaced the mother duck's wing backwards; fortunately, the ducklings are somewhat sheltered in her wake and soon can break out into the shallows again.

Figures 3.7d–3.7e: The same mother duck pictured in Figures 3.7a–3.7c was twice hurried on by two different aggressive drakes. The second chose to attack her, seizing first her webbed foot in his beak as she tried to evade the attack and then, having pulled her back to the ground, her tail. All this while the ducklings watched on and tried to stay out of harm's way.

★ Special Feature – Fairafar Mill and Weir, and the River Almond Barriers Project

During the 18th and 19th centuries the River Almond's potential as a source of power led to Cramond's development as an important industrial centre. By 1799 the village boasted three iron forges and two steel furnaces as well as three water-powered rolling mills. The steel produced was shipped out as far away as India, which provides us with an indication of the global significance of this industry at the time, founded on the local availability of coal, water-power and iron ore. During the second half of the 19th century the iron industry started failing, and many of the local mills were converted to sawmills or pulp mills. Their survival was short-lived, however, and at the turn of the new century the mills largely disappeared.

A waulkmill[34] was first mentioned at Fairafar as early as 1676, but there is no evidence that it was developed for ironmaking before 1770. In 1773 the mill was turned into the works forge after the arrival of the Cadells at Cramond Mill, and it forged small items including files, plough socs[35] and girdles. The mills were supplied with coal from Grange, which allowed them to operate furnaces where the iron was smelted. The iron was turned into malleable bars by means of a prodigious hammer, weighing around hundredweight (50 kg). The hammer at Fairafar was operated by water power, for the purpose of which the weir had been constructed, with significant impact on the ecology of the river. A horse railway operated between the mills, and allowed both coal and iron to be moved, and the iron to be delivered to vessels on the river itself. The walkway between the boathouse slipway you see today and Cockle Mill was constructed at the end of the 18th century to serve as a towpath that allowed boats to be pulled up to the mill. When the Cadells' association with the mills came to an end in 1860, iron milling continued on a reduced scale for some 20 years. Then in 1935, following a flood, Fairafar Mill itself was largely demolished.

Perhaps the best way to travel back in time and gain an impression of the extent to which the Almond River was industrialised is to view the 1853 map of the area and to carry this image in your head as you walk. The map can be viewed online at the National Library of Scotland, and shows a series of mills, from the mouth of the river upstream:

- Cockle Mill at Cramond Bank – Iron Foundry
- Fairafar Mill – Iron Foundry
- Peggy's Mill – Paper
- Dowies Mill – Sawing.

It is hard to know what the impact of this industrial period may have been. We can, however, be sure that it was a negative one, for not only was the river catchment area contaminated, but also the weirs that were constructed interrupted the natural movement of fish from the river mouth to their spawning grounds. Among the weirs that continued to interfere with the ecology of the river following the disappearance of the mills is Fairafar Weir, built in 1790 as part of the iron works at the mill of the same name, whose ruins stand before the weir.

---

34 Cloth-fulling mill.
35 The soc (also known as sock or share), is the hardened blade dressed onto the mouldboard of a plough. It cuts into the earth and turns it over.

In 2003 the Water Environment and Water Services (Scotland) Act was passed into law. This Act is informed by the EU's Water Framework Directive (Directive 2000/60/EC) which commits member states to achieving good qualitative and quantitative status of all water bodies and provides a framework for achieving this. From today's vantage point it is sobering to look back on the time it took to appreciate the extent to which the ecology of our rivers had been devastated and then to repair the damage. It took a generation – and that represents a lot of water under the bridge!

Work on Fairafar Weir has already been completed. The fish pass built in the 1970s has been upgraded and the new Larinier fish pass is visible on the far bank (Figure 3.8). This construction allows the passage of fish, so the weir no longer represents the barrier to migration it once was. Attention will now turn to addressing the problem at Dowie's Weir, the second of seven barriers to fish movement on the River Almond.

In early 2019 Edinburgh Council undertook a consultation on how to pursue the next stage of the River Almond Barriers Project. Their preference for the removal of much of the weir, together with improvements to the riverbanks whilst retaining the mill pond below the old Cramond Brig, has however met with resistance from locals who see value in preserving the industrial heritage. This further highlights the various obstacles to ecological restoration. It may be that another generation will come and go before we see the devastation wrought by industry on this river fully healed.

Figures 3.8a–8b: Fairafar Weir represents an imposing obstacle to migrating fish, and is one of many such obstacles whose ecological impact is gradually being addressed by the construction of specially designed passes that allow fish to circumnavigate the weir. The fish pass was built between the autumn of 2017 and the spring of 2018. A time lapse video of its construction illustrates what is involved in this kind of ecological restoration.

Figure 3.9: A path high above the water upstream from Fairafar Weir provides you with fine views across the valley.

4 Cramond Falls to Old Cramond Bridge

From the falls, a steep set of stairs provides access to a wooded path that hugs the cliff top high above the river. This path provides you with a number of vantage points out across the river, together with some treetop vistas (Figure 3.9), before descending via another set of stairs to regain the path running beside the Almond.

The riverbank is then followed all the way to Dowie's Weir (NT 179 756) and then pursued to emerge onto a roadway, where you turn right to reach Old Cramond Bridge, a good view-point from which to gaze up- and downstream.

5 Old Cramond Bridge to the Grotto Bridge

Your route continues on the south bank of the river. To reach the footpath, return to the roadway that leads onto the bridge and look for an opening on your left where a path skirts the edge of a field where you may well see starlings, attracted by the invertebrates typically found in horses' fields.

A fine view of the Old Cramond Bridge can be had from the edge of the riverbank (Figure 3.10). As you follow it, take the opportunities that present themselves to descend to the bank. There are sections where the exposed mud beside the river are worth scrutinising carefully for otter tracks (Figure 3.11) for, with the river's

Figure 3.10: Old Cramond Bridge viewed from the south bank upstream of the bridge. It dates back in part at least to the late 15th century, circa 1487, when a new stone bridge is recorded as being constructed across the River Almond. Just under 100 years later, in circa 1587, the two eastern arches on the Edinburgh side collapsed. They were reconstructed in 1619, and the southern parapet on the bridge records subsequent repairs in 1687, 1761, 1776 and 1854.

Figure 3.11: The soft mud that can be found in places on the riverbank is worth inspecting for tracks, especially away from the areas regularly visited by dog walkers. If you keep looking, you will eventually find examples of clear prints where the faint imprint of the claws and the imprint of the webbing between the toes are discernible. It takes practice, though.

Figure 3.12a: The exquisite form of the snowdrop defies description in the same way that a snowflake does. They are miracles of nature and have a unique ability to take the breath away.

Figures 3.12b–12c: The path running from Cammo Road back into woodland that takes you back to the river hosts a succession of white flowers in early spring. First to emerge is the snowdrop (above) whose stems and leaves are a dark green. These are usually still around when the lighter green shoots of the few-flowered leek (Allium paradoxum) appear. The bell of this flower is exquisitely shaped in its own way, but its form wondrously different (below). As it is a member of the allium family it possesses that characteristic garlicky smell.

recovery and the return of insects and fish, the apex predator in the food chain has also been able to make a remarkable comeback.

The path crosses the Bughtlin Burn before moving away from the river, climbing up through two contour lines and then turning to the left to emerge on a track running between gardens. This leads you to Cammo Road. Turn to your right and follow this quiet road past a collection of houses until you reach another wooded area. There you will find a path heading off through the trees on your right (NT 173 750). In early spring, this path is a great place to pause and admire snowdrops (Figures 3.12a–12b). As the days lengthen these give way to another exquisitely shaped white flower: the few-flowered leek (Figure 3.12c).

6 The Grotto Bridge to Old Cramond Bridge (north bank)

Pursue the main path to reach the Grotto Bridge, and cross it to reach the north bank of the Almond.

The main path takes you away from the river and maintains height, with an area of dense woodland gradually appearing below

Figure 3.13: The river bed downstream of the Grotto Bridge is rocky and provides an exquisite place to sit and listen to the current surging past. The sound can soothe your mind in much the same way as the waters have, over the years, smoothed the rocky river bed.

Figure 3.14: Grey wagtail favour these little stones in the river, for they provide the perfect vantage point from which to spot insects flying over the water. Many of these insects will be emerging from the water as the days warm up and their lifecycles are completed. This seasonal increase in available food is exactly what brings the grey wagtail back to the rivers that during the winter they will have abandoned for warmer climes. When insects are spied, the grey wagtail makes short, agile feeding flights, taking the insects in mid-air. In between such feeding bouts, they can be seen bobbing their long tails rhythmically; a movement that has earnt them the name 'wagtail'. This bobbing action may be interrupted during preening, when the bird collects oil from the preen gland that sits at the base of the tail. This oil is applied as a conditioner to the feathers during preening, and helps realign and protect the feather's barbs.

you. For a particularly fine view of the river flowing under the Grotto Bridge (Figure 3.13), it is worth following one of the smaller paths down this bank. You will find yourself in an area of woodland that has been creatively developed as a park for mountain bikers. Providing there are no cyclists flying around, you can safely pass through the trees to gain the riverbank.

After taking in the view back up to the bridge, it is worth studying the pools of calmer water. Many of these may hold fish, and it is this secret larder that attracts the grey heron (see the special feature). Should you see the heron standing like a statue in the riverbed, you might be persuaded to sit down and watch this master fisher at work.

Your return to Old Cramond Bridge follows the riverbank and is quite delightful. Look out for grey wagtail (Figure 3.14) and dipper in the riverbed, and take your time considering how they too make use of the food sources provided by a river in recovery. As you approach the bridge, the path veers a little to the left, to emerge in the car park behind the Cramond Brig.

★ Special Feature – the grey heron

Figure 3.15a: There is much we could potentially learn from a heron, including perhaps: focus, patience and accuracy. Watching a heron working a fishing patch can be quite magical. Their reading of the river is born of countless hours of studious attention to the array of food available to them. Here, in this image, it is a small smolt* sheltering in the quiet water that lies in the lee of these rocks that has attracted the heron's focused attention and lightning-fast strike.

* *Two-year-old salmon or sea trout.*

The grey heron (*Ardea cinerea*) is, arguably, one of our most iconic and instantly recognisable avian species; one whose prowess as a hunter and sheer adaptability has led to their becoming the most widespread large predatory bird in the UK. You can therefore expect to encounter this striking ashen[36] bird on several of the walks in this book.

By paying attention to the heron and by realising just how well these master fishers have come to occupy a particular ecological niche – one in which their talents allow them to make the most of the opportunities nature provides – we can develop our eye and our sense of wonder. It is, after all, not just the plumes and garb of this majestic bird that are striking; their spearing of unsuspecting prey is equally so (Figures 3.15a–15d). The heron's diet is opportunistic, and encompasses everything from fish to amphibians, insects, water voles and rats, even birds as large as water rail. All of these are swallowed whole, and given to the powerful digestive juices of the heron's stomach to deal with.

36 *Cinerea* means 'grey' or 'ash-coloured', from the Latin for ashes: *cinis*.

The heron's stomach is able to separate out the indigestible fur, bones and scales of prey from the nutritious elements. The indigestible elements are then regurgitated in the form of pellets that are themselves worth looking out for, especially under heronries.

The heron is one of a number of fish-eating birds that can attract the ire and anger of fish farms and anglers. Fortunately, the heron is a protected species under the Wildlife and Countryside Act (1981); this means they can only be shot under licence. For a licence to be issued, significant economic loss has to be demonstrated, together with clear evidence that all other methods of addressing the issue have been exhausted. When we step back and consider the situation, however, it is clear that artificially high concentrations of fish are bound to attract predators, and we need to be much more imaginative when it comes to managing the interface between wildlife and farmed animals.

Figures 3.15b–15d: The strike: The heron's characteristic S-shaped neck is designed to strike and to do so at lightning speed. After a patient wait or cautious approach (b), the dagger-like bill is fired forwards to seize the prey (c). The opposite group of neck muscles then allow the head to be withdrawn (d) so that the heron can move on to the next task: swallowing its prey.

Whilst it may be true that herons do take their share of fish and can be seen as competition … it is also true that simply seeking to eliminate them creates a space that will inevitably be filled again. So the challenge lies in stepping out of the antagonistic relationship in order to transform it. The attitude and intent that informs how we relate to nature will shape the relationships we are able to enjoy with the heron and the natural world.

In contemplating how other creatures live alongside the heron, you may like to get curious as to who shares the fishing pools with our long-legged friend. Do you see goosander, grebes or kingfishers working the same pools? If not, what can you determine about their respective preferences? This might be about being able to see quarry before plunging into the water; it might be about the size of fish or the depth of the water. There is much to ponder and wonder at.

Figure 3.15e: The grey heron stands statuesque studying the river – unflappable, it would seem, if it weren't for the breeze gently lifting and flapping those wonderful plumes that adorn its head, throat and back.

7 Old Cramond Bridge to Cramond Harbour

Having made it back to Old Cramond Bridge, cross it and turn left to rejoin the River Almond Walkway that you followed earlier. This you can follow all the way back to Cramond Harbour.

Retracing your steps can easily lead you to switch off and walk just to get back. It is worth noting this, for this attitude can creep up on us, especially when tired, and make it easy for us to miss the delights that present themselves unexpectedly. I often have found that at the end of the walk the riverbank can be quieter, and I need to stay alert to surprises. Who knows what you might encounter?

Walk 4

London Road Gardens, Calton Hill and New Calton Burial Ground

This happens to be one of my favourite walks in this book. In part, this is because I have spent over a decade living nearby and have grown both familiar with and fond of the incredible gardens that run alongside London Road, and the fine views from Calton Hill. It is also because these haunts never cease to surprise me, no matter how often I return.

This walk's highlights include:

- London Road Gardens, which can yield some unusual and surprising birds, including tree creepers, and in winter redwings drawn by the offerings of a rich assortment of mature deciduous trees, including elm, chestnut, beech and ash.
- Incredible views down Prince's Street, across the city to the Forth bridges and the Fife coastline, and an opportunity to wander among and get to

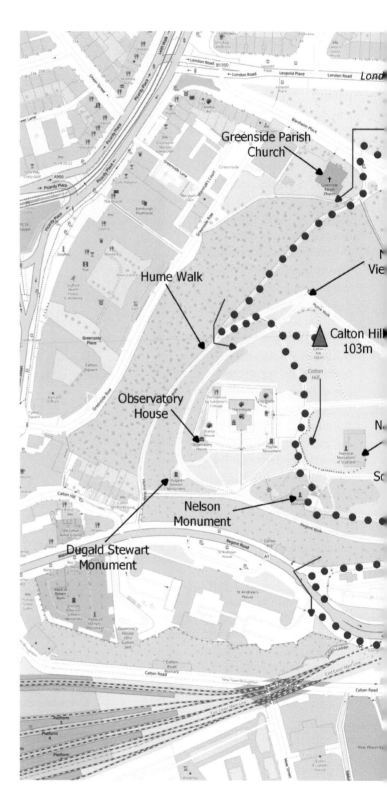

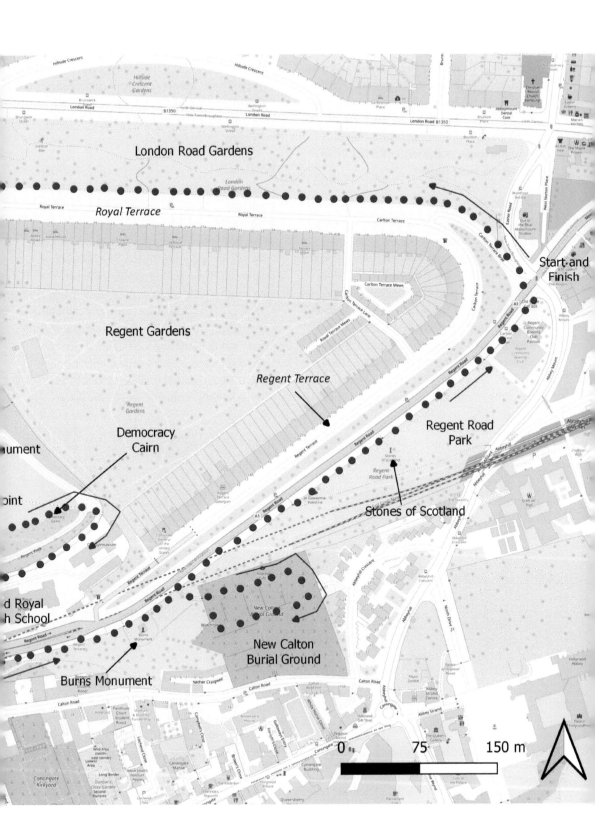

London Road Gardens

Royal Terrace

Carlton Terrace

Start and Finish

Regent Gardens

Regent Terrace

Regent Road Park

Democracy Cairn

Stones of Scotland

New Calton Burial Ground

Burns Monument

0   75   150 m

know some of Edinburgh's finest landmarks, including the Nelson Monument (Figure 4.1) and the National Monument.

- An unusual invitation to visit an old cemetery where many notable members of the family of the writer Robert Louis Stevenson are buried.

Summary

This walk starts from Carlton Terrace Brae and follows the high-level path that runs inside the hawthorn edge that shields London Road Gardens from Carlton Terrace. This delightful path provides excellent views down into the gardens below, and serves as a useful vantage point from which you can observe birdlife in the mature trees without craning your neck skywards. At the end of the gardens, cross over Blenheim Place and start the climb round and up onto Calton Hill. The

walk exits Calton Hill onto Regent Road to pass the Burns Monument. You will have an opportunity to explore the New Calton Burial Ground before you return to your start point via Regent Road Gardens.

🏛 History

London Road Gardens used to be a number of small quarries that were popular locations for duels. In the early 19th century, the quarries were filled in by William Playfair, the architect responsible for developing the New Town of Edinburgh. The resulting area was planted with trees in 1829, and it is quite possible that a number of the older trees in the gardens date back to this time. In 1830, when Charles X of France was deposed and took up residence at Holyrood Palace, a path was developed through the gardens to provide him with access to St Mary's Catholic Cathedral on Picardy Place.

Figure 4.1: The Nelson Monument caught in a snowstorm. This Edinburgh landmark commemorates Nelson's victory at the Battle of Trafalgar in 1805 and represents an upturned telescope. A mechanised time ball can be seen; it was added in 1852 as a signal for the shipping in Leith Harbour. It is synchronised with the firing of the one o'clock gun from Edinburgh Castle.

A Friends group for the Hillside and Calton Area was set up in May 2007 with the primary purpose of supporting the Council who hold the land in trust for the people, and the Parks Department in particular. Together they help to promote good stewardship of all the green spaces from Calton Hill to Montgomery Street Park.

🌿 Habitats

London Road Gardens is a mature wooded urban park with an impressive lime tree avenue running along London Road. The tree cover in London Road Gardens is relatively uniform in composition, comprising ash, beech, elm, lime, oak and sycamore of fairly even age, conforming to the original planting in 1829-30. Calton Hill is part of the Arthur's Seat Volcano Site of Special Scientific Interest (SSSI) and is one of three biodiversity sites in this area, including Calton Hill, Regent Gardens and the Union Canal. Its designation is due to the presence of species-rich grassland that supports wildlife including grayling butterfly (*Hipparchia semele*) and buff-tailed bumble-bee (*Bombus terrestris*). Calton Hill also has a number of areas of woodland, including an extensive area of mature woodland on Greenside slope, which includes ash, sycamore, maple, holly, rowan, cherry, elm and birch.

🚌 Transport links

The start of the walk on Carlton Terrace Brae is well served by several Lothian Bus and East Coast Services. The bus stop on Brunton Place is a two-minute walk from the start, and is served by bus services 1, 4, 5, 19 and 34. The bus stop where Regent Road meets Carlton Terrace Brae is served by services 26, 44, 113, 124 and X5. If you are cycling to the start, quiet route 20 allows you to leave the Edinburgh cycle path network and pick up a quiet cycling road along McDonald Road

and Brunswick Road to meet Easter Road. London Road itself also has designated cycle lanes that make cycling in traffic easier.

☕ Refreshments

The walk is well served with cafés at the start, including the excellent Little Fitzroy, and Art and Vintage, both within a few minutes of your start and finishing point.

📕 References and further reading

MacDiarmid, H. (2017). *Complete Poems* (M. Grieve & W. R. Aitken, Eds.; 2nd ed., Vol. 1). Manchester: Carcanet Press.

🪧 Directions

1 Carlton Terrace Brae to Blenheim Place

Starting on Carlton Terrace Brae, avoid the steps that drop down to your right into the gardens. Instead look ahead for the path that parallels the cobbled Carlton Terrace (Figure 4.2). This path runs inside the mature hawthorn hedge, which you will keep to your left so that you have the expanse of the gardens stretching out below your feet on your right.

Among the first trees you will encounter beside the path are the wych elm, sycamore and chestnut. If their buds, flowers and seeds and leaves are unfamiliar to you they will soon become instantly recognisable (Figures 4.3a–3d and 4.4a–4b).

Figure 4.2: Of the two paths leading into London Road Gardens from Carlton Terrace Brae, take the left one to maintain height above the gardens.

Figure 4.3a: The clumps of seeds of the wych elm are instantly recognisable, and are a valuable food crop for birds and other wildlife. The buds here are bursting open; in winter they can be identified by their dense coverage of orange hairs.

Figure 4.3b: The leaf of the elm tree is serrated and tapers to a distinct tip. Arguably, the most helpful identification feature is its asymmetric base.

Figures 4.3c–3d: The colour and form of the leaves and seeds of wych elm dance in the sunlight.

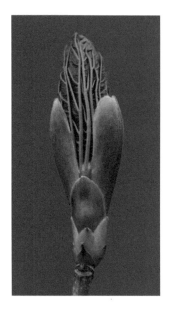

Figures 4.4a–4b: The exquisite bud of the sycamore has a rosy set of lips that swell as the leaves prepare to burst forth. It can be rewarding to visit the same tree over a series of successive days to watch the fresh green leaves erupting from the bud.

The wych elm (*Ulmus glabra*), also known as the Scotch or Scots elm, is one of Scotland's native trees. The term 'wych' derives from the suppleness of the wood (*wice* is Old English for 'pliable' or 'supple'). Widely planted in Edinburgh during the 19th century as a park and avenue tree, these trees may well account for the naming of nearby Elm Row. Despite the ravages of Dutch elm disease, this wonderful tree remains abundant in Edinburgh, where its ability to regenerate through seedlings is much in evidence.

Continue along the path. As you do so, slow down. Pay attention and allow yourself to be surprised. It might be that you spot some rampaging ladybirds (Figure 4.5a) or a cheeky wren singing from among the ivy and tree roots (Figure 4.5b).

*Figure 4.5a: A pair of mating cream-spotted ladybird (*Calvia quatuordecimguttata*) cling to an elm leaf despite a strong breeze. These beautiful creatures occur in a wide range of habitats, including parkland, and feed on aphids and other small insects. You can observe them more closely by using a magnifying glass or by inverting your binoculars.*

The gift of green

Sometimes, every now and again, it can be worth settling on a colour and developing one's appreciation of that colour. For the purpose of this exercise, I am proposing that as at the time of writing winter is giving way to summer, we pay attention to the 'gift of green'.

As you walk along the path, pay attention to the three tree species mentioned above – wych elm, sycamore and chestnut. Allow yourself to recognise not just the shapes of their leaves but their colours. The dense clusters of seeds on the elm tree can mean that two colours are present concurrently, that of the leaves and the seeds. Notice how this somehow sets the tree alight and how these greens dance in the sun and the wind.

The sycamore and chestnut trees' leaves are bigger and darker, and their canopies denser. Try to observe these differences and how the impression shifts when a breeze causes these leaves to dance and the light plays on them. Pay attention to how these greens change as leaves first open and the fresh greens of early spring mature into those of summer.

The leaf greens you are observing are a gift. How do you receive this gift? Do you find that they have an ability to calm the eye and soothe the spirit? Do you sense the many ways they also give us life as they expertly capture the sun's energy and feed it into the ecosystem that sustains us? This green literally provides us with energy. It also provides us with every molecule of oxygen that we breathe in and that our bodies rely on. It is sobering to think that oxygen cycles through us continuously. Indeed, it is not inconceivable that the molecules that constitute part of us today could well, perhaps as recently as yesterday, have constituted part of the very trees you are contemplating.

Figure 4.5b: Given their diminutive size, the wren packs more character than almost any other bird I know. The jaunty way they carry their tail cocked, together with a powerful call that any opera singer would be proud of, are all part of their persona. They are busy and vivacious, and in and out of the nooks and crannies that provide them with food and safety.

Figure 4.5c: This robin has taken on more than he can handle. Tempting as the earthworm might be, this wriggly creature needs to be swallowed whole, and this is a talent that blackbirds and other thrushes specialise in. A few moments after this image was taken, the robin was dispossessed of the worm by a hungry blackbird.

Figures 4.6a–6b: A nuthatch with nut flies from the trunk of a tree. Such views allow us to observe how the feathers fan out and provide a strong but light structure capable of providing them with lift.

Perhaps you might be surprised by the sight of an opportunistic robin trying to despatch an earthworm before the local blackbird, a wormer *par excellence*, appears on the scene and muscles in on the act (Figure 4.5c).

Before the emergence of the leaves, the trees are worth scanning for any of the trio of tree climbing-birds that frequent these gardens: the nuthatch, the great spotted woodpecker (Figures 4.6a–6c) and the treecreeper (see the special feature). These three birds can also be identified by their calls, and it is worth familiarising yourselves with these. This skill will become particularly helpful once the leaf coverage increases and it becomes harder to spot birds moving in the dense foliage.

- Nuthatch: https://www.bbc.co.uk/programmes/b03ws7gc.
- Great spotted woodpecker: https://www.bbc.co.uk/programmes/b03t02sk.
- Treecreeper: https://www.bbc.co.uk/programmes/b03x46sm.

Figure 4.6c: The great spotted woodpecker can be heard drumming in spring (typically January to April). This behaviour allows them to project a message that helps them establish breeding territories. Although the sound is produced by striking the surface of a resonant object such as this dead bough, as recently as the 1940s many people maintained that the sound was produced vocally. But in 1943 birdwatcher Norman Pullen placed a microphone inside a tree and was able to demonstrate exact correspondence between the woodpecker's bill hitting the wood and the resulting sound. The sound is worth listening out for and marvelling at, for it is another miracle of nature. Here we are seeing a creature that has evolved to exploit the instrumental and food-bearing potential of woodland.

Another woodland bird to listen out for – one that most of us would overlook if we did not know what to look and listen for – is the stock dove. This wonderful pigeon can be reliably be observed in the gardens, providing you know how to distinguish them from the wood and feral pigeons, in whose shadow the stock dove carries on in its own unobtrusive way. So easy is it to overlook this bird that I have chosen to dedicate a special feature here, for they are richly deserving of a special place in our attentions.

It is worth noting the red at the back of this woodpecker's head; this bird is an adult male, for the females only have red around the vent (under the tail).

Figure 4.7a: The correspondence between the treecreeper's long curved beak and the crevices of the tree are clear. These crevices are home to their own community of invertebrates, and the treecreeper knows how to seek them out. The tail feathers here can be seen tapering to a point that provides additional purchase against the tree. This is an anatomical adaptation shared with the woodpecker family but not the nuthatch.

★ Special Feature – the treecreeper

The tree creeper is one of my favourite woodland birds, for they challenge me to spot the characteristic movement they make as they move progressively up a tree trunk or along one of the upper branches. It is the movement that stands out, for these birds, with their mottling of browns and whites (Figures 4.7a–7b), are exquisitely camouflaged. Their white bellies may be more obvious, but this typically requires a side-on view.

The movement is made possible by a fantastic set of claws that allows this little bird to grip the bark and defy gravity. Progression is also aided by the rigid, pointed tail feathers that provide an extra and very supportive point of contact.

Then there is that curved probing beak, which can reach spiders and other invertebrates hidden in the deepest crevices of a tree trunk. This is what it takes to exploit a particular ecological niche and the feast that tree trunks offer the 'diner with the winkler'.

Figure 4.7b: The tree creeper race ... looks like the ivy has crept into the lead. A photo finish perhaps?

Figure 4.8a: The stock dove's name refers to their propensity for nesting in tree trunks (stocks). They particularly favour elm trees, which may account for their favouring those of London Road Gardens. Note the dabs of darker colouring crossing the wing.

★ Special Feature – the stock dove

The stock dove (*Columba oenas*) is possessed of a gentleness and a soft subtle beauty, yet somehow we manage time and again to overlook their presence. Their anonymity intrigues me. How is it that this exquisite creature should, like some secret agent, pass unnoticed? Unnoticed, that is, until you have learnt to notice certain features.

For a start, there is that dark iris (those of feral pigeons are often reddy-orange, whilst those of wood pigeons are a pale yellowy-green) and that perfectly rounded head (Figures 4.8a–8d). Then there are the faintest of bars on the wing (Figure 4.8a); where many feral pigeons have a strong brushstroke of a dark wing bar, the stock dove has delicate dabs rather than strokes – a real work of art (Figure 4.8b).

The stock dove's voice is also easily overlooked, for it is the gentlest of coos that for me is one of the soothing background noises I can enjoy when listening to the gardens on a quiet early morning in a spring weekend. The wood pigeon, by contrast, possesses a clear set of four notes that lack the comforting quality of the stock dove's cooing. Sorry, wood pigeon.

Figures 4.8b–8c: Note the round head, that dark iris and the way the green of the neck catches the light. In addition, there is no white on this dove's neck or wing, which further helps distinguish it from the wood pigeon.

Figure 4.8d: Everything about the stock dove is somehow … subtle; nothing is overstated.

Figure 4.9a: The wood forget-me-not provides a delightful splash of colour beside the path in London Road Gardens from April to June.

Figure 4.9b: The small blue flowers are best seen up close. They thrive in shady woodland, as here under a beech tree.

An unforgettable blue may also attract your attention during the months of spring, when the wood forget-me-nots (*Myosotis sylvatica*) carpet the side of the path (Figures 4.9a–9b). Flowering from April to June, this plant copes well with shady woodland, and you will see it thriving despite the dense tree cover.

Wood forget-me-not is easily recognisable thanks to its clusters of five-petalled azure flowers. The centre of these flowers varies between white and yellowy-orange. The stems are hairy, and the leaves narrow and oval-shaped.

As you continue along the path, you can enjoy some curving detours that pass under a series of old beech trees where your feet may crunch the beech mast that has accumulated on the woodland floor. The parkland is home to all the thrushes (blackbird, mistle thrush and song thrush) and in winter is a good place to observe migrant redwings (Figure 4.10), who may be seen feeding on the berries.

You will soon reach the end of the path and Greenside Parish Church on Blenheim Place, where you will need to cross the cobbles to enter Calton Hill.

Figure 4.10: In winter we receive migrant thrushes from Scandinavia, and it can be a real pleasure to see them feasting on the berries. Their markings are distinctive; the red underwing clearly sets them out from our resident thrushes.

2 Blenheim Place to Calton Hill

After crossing Blenheim Place, you will find yourself at the foot of Calton Hill, with Greenside Parish Church to your right. Follow the path ahead of you that climbs steadily, with a set of railings on your right.

The vegetations to left and right is worth scanning for tits and other feeding birds. The hawthorn buds when they first emerge are in demand – a little bit like the very first crop of spring greens our ancestors might have enjoyed as they emerged from winter. Pay attention to who has spotted them and is enjoying them; it can be quite amusing to watch a plump wood pigeon manoeuvring his or her way to the ends of branches to reach those tempting buds. The smaller, terminal branches may sag under the strain, and you may be able to watch a pigeon seeking to negotiate the delicate path that lies between gravity and temptation.

Wood pigeons appear to have a greedy streak. Their appetite is impressive (Figure 4.11a) and at this time of year it can be interesting to watch them peruse nature's menu and tell you what's in season. The more obvious wood pigeon's dining preferences at this time are also shared by, amongst others, the bullfinch. These most colourful of birds are sur-

Figure 4.11a: This wood pigeon is delighting in the fresh green surge of hawthorn leaves as they burst from their buds. Here the pigeon's weight is supported by some larger branches. It can be amusing to watch how they seek to gain access to the tastiest buds on the outermost, pliable branches. Note the yellowy green iris and the white splash of colour on either side of the wood pigeon's neck.

Figure 4.11b: The male bullfinch has a fine beak that is well suited to nibbling buds and exploiting this excellent source of nutrition. This propensity has in the past earnt them the ire of gardeners and farmers, who do not welcome the bullfinches laying claim to such food sources. Of course, this begs the question of who is really greedy, for nature's bounty was always meant to be shared. When seeing a male bullfinch, recognised here by that beautiful belly, it is always worth looking out for his partner, for she will not be far away, such is the pair-bond they enjoy. Her colouring, however, is understated, so spotting her will test your powers of observation.

prisingly discreet, and their presence is often only given away by their gentle '*pew pew*', the flash of their white rump and, in the right light, the male's magnificent robes (Figure 4.11b).

3 Exploring Calton Hill

At the top of the rise, a path bears left. Pursue this to a viewpoint out across the city as the ground falls to the Firth of Forth. Above you, you will see the monuments that dominate the hill, namely the Nelson and National monuments as well as the observatory. This latter building was designed in 1818 by William Henry Playfair. In 1834 Professor Thomas Henderson was appointed Scotland's first Astronomer Royal. He was based in this building, and it was here that he discovered how to measure parallax and the distance of the stars.

Take your time taking in the views this site offers. You may want to consult the 'Sense of Place' document provided by Edinburgh World Heritage: https://tinyurl.com/4292h5tb.

The area can be pretty busy, however, and may not be the best place to observe wildlife unless visiting early in the morning or when the weather is such that most people are dissuaded from venturing out.

To exit the hill, follow one of the paths from the Nelson Monument that drop to the monument to the Scottish Parliament. Continue down a set of steps to the top of the road that passes immediately behind the former Royal High School (1829–1968).

Of an evening it is possible to see tawny owls in the area, and such an encounter can be most memorable. Pay attention to the silhouette they present (Figure 4.12a); this is a useful skill to develop, as it can help you observe the shape and profile of birds (Figure 4.12b).

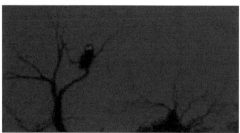

Figures 4.12a–12b: Working with silhouettes can be challenging, especially when it is unclear how to gauge size. In Figure 4.12a, note the well-rounded head; this is that of a tawny owl – a crepuscular visitor to Edinburgh's parks. In Figure 14.12b, this flock of birds demonstrate a clear crest over their heads: they are waxwings – a common winter visitor to Edinburgh parks.

4 Royal High School to Regent Road Park

At the roundabout, cross over the road and turn left to follow the pavement to the Burns Monument (Figure 4.13a). A little beyond the monument, you will see the entrance to New Calton Burial Ground. This can be surprisingly quiet even during tourist season, especially if the exit onto Calton Road is closed, as is often the case. Take your time to explore the cemetery, looking out for signs of life among the stones.

Leave the burial ground by the way you came in, and continue along Regent Road to reach a gate into Regent Road Park. This park is worth exploring, and can be a good place to spot both rabbits and grey squirrels.

In the centre of the park, you will find a beautiful Scots pine tree amid a fascinating collection of stones (Figures 4.14a–14b). These stones are part of an exhibit entitled 'The Stones of Scotland', and are drawn from the 32 regional councils of Scotland. These

Figure 4.13a: The Burns Monument, looking out over Holyrood Park, commemorates the life of Scotland's bard, Robert Burns. Among other great works, he wrote 'To a Mouse: On turning her up in her nest with the plough'. He was clearly someone who appreciated the need for us to consider more deeply the impact of our actions on the animal kingdom.

*Figure 4.14a: A fine Scots pine (*Pinus sylvestris*) stands among the paving stones in the centre of the exhibit and in spring adds her own flowers to the display.*

Figure 4.14b: The Stones of Scotland monument was first created by human artistry but now swells and falls by the artistry of a Scots Pine. In the distance can be seen the Scottish Parliament building and, beyond, Salisbury Crags.

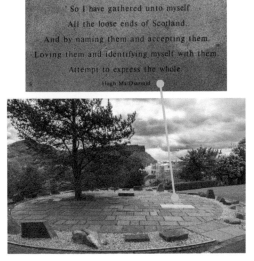

stones, in many respects, reflect Scotland's rich geological history, and during the conceptualisation of this exhibit, local communities were actively engaged in the selection of the stones chosen to represent them.

The exhibit, officially opened in 2002, was commissioned to celebrate the creative spirit of Scotland at the start of the new millennium. You can read more about this important geological exhibit in the following leaflet: https://tinyurl.com/4z4w6v4d.

The last five lines of Hugh MacDiarmid's wonderful poetic tribute to Scotland, the country of his birth, are engraved in a slab of Corennie pink granite accompanying the exhibit. The full poem is reproduced here and you are invited to read each line slowly and repeatedly, weighing the words and sentiment as it helps weave a sense of place deep within.

You can walk through the park and emerge at the entrance beside the Regent Community Bowling Club. You have now returned to the start.

Scotland

It requires great love of it deeply to read
The configuration of a land,
Gradually grow conscious of fine shadings,
Of great meanings in slight symbols,
Hear at last the great voice that speaks softly,
See the swell and fall upon the flank
Of a statue carved out in a whole country's marble,
Be like spring, like a hand in a window
Moving New and Old things carefully to and fro,
Moving a fraction of flower here,
Placing an inch of air there,
And without breaking anything.
So I have gathered unto myself
All the loose ends of Scotland,
And by naming them and accepting them,
Loving them and identifying myself with them,
Attempt to express the whole.

Hugh MacDiarmid (1892–1978),
with permission of Carcanet Press,
publisher of MacDiarmid's *Complete Poems,
Volume 1* (MacDiarmid, 2017, pp.365–8)

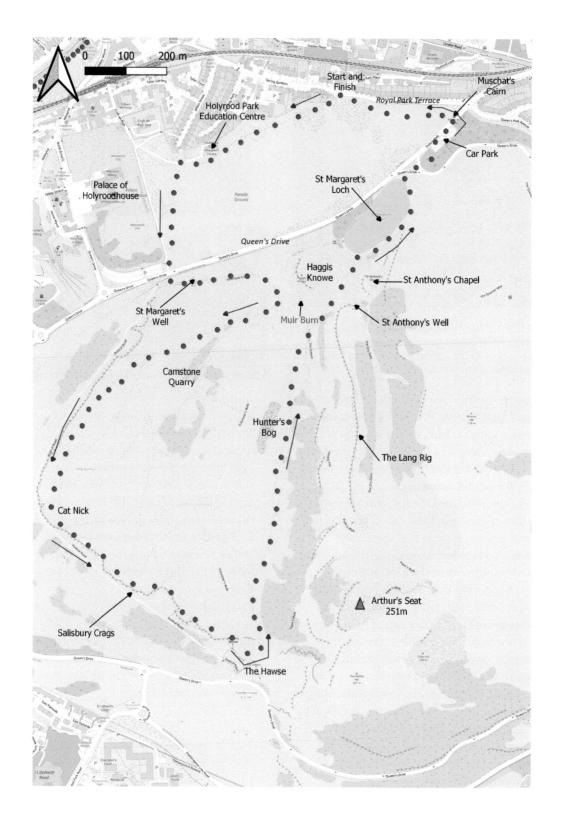

0 100 200 m

Start and Finish

Muschat's Cairn

Royal Park Terrace

Holyrood Park Education Centre

Car Park

St Margaret's Loch

Palace of Holyroodhouse

Parade Ground

Queen's Drive

Haggis Knowe

St Anthony's Chapel

St Margaret's Well

Muir Burn

St Anthony's Well

Camstone Quarry

Hunter's Bog

The Lang Rig

Cat Nick

Arthur's Seat 251m

Salisbury Crags

The Hawse

Walk 5

Salisbury Crags, Hunter's Bog and St Margaret's Loch

This walk is remarkable in the way it can allow you to completely forget that you are within a large city. There are times when the skyline is wild. At other times there are no signs of human habitation, with the vista extending uninterrupted out to the far-off Pentlands. At certain times of year, the park can be empty, and it is almost always quietest first thing in the morning. I also like to explore the park as a rain shower passes through, partly because things are likely to be quieter then, but also because the light can be magical immediately after the rain (Figure 5.1a). It can be wonderful to smell the wet earth and see the park reinvigorated by the watering.

This walk's highlights include:

- A fine example of unimproved lowland grassland – a habitat type rare across the UK, and which bears testimony to the life such habitats can support.

- The beautiful geological structures that give the park its unusual skyline.
- A rich variety of breeding birds, many of whom are clinging on despite the threats they have faced in recent times, and continue to face. These birds include skylark, fulmar, whitethroat, kestrel, mute swan, peregrine, sparrowhawk and grey heron.
- The views out across the city from Salisbury Crags, which are spellbinding; the vantage point provided by the crags is a great place to watch a number of birds, most notably jackdaws and fulmars, playing in the updraft.
- Hunter's Bog, a valley that can feel remarkably wild given that it lies at the heart of a large city.
- St Margaret's Loch, which hosts a variety of birdlife and can be a great place to sit, rest, watch and try to make sense of bird life.

Figure 5.1a: Arthur's Seat and Salisbury Crags combine to form an instantly recognisable silhouette that can look particularly dramatic as rain showers pass through.

Figure 5.1b: As you walk towards the Education Centre, look to your left to see the tilted dolerite sills that make up Long Row and Salisbury Crags. The lava that forms the Long Row flows runs for some 400 metres in a northerly direction until it is cut by the St Anthony's Well fault line, resulting in the creation of an outlying section of sill known as Haggis Knowe. This can be seen here, immediately behind the tree, with the Long Row behind, in the shade.

Figures 5.1c–1d: The profile of the tilted basalt sill that forms Salisbury Crags is an unmistakable part of the Edinburgh skyline – more instantly recognisable, perhaps, than the moon (which you may spot in Figure 5.1d). Salisbury Crags are the product of a tilting of the basalt dyke laid down during a period of volcanic activity. The hummocky nature of the ground falling down to the road is all that remains of the various attempts to extract valuable rock from this area. The steep cliff faces of the crags on the right have also been produced by quarrying, and it is these faces that now offer a safe home to a number of exciting breeding birds, including the fulmar.

ꜱ Summary

This walk starts from the entrance to the park on Royal Park Terrace (NT 274 741). It can equally be started from the car park beside St Margaret's Loch.

Follow the path along the north edge of the park to reach the Holyrood Park Education Centre. Then cross the grass to reach the car park beside the wall of Holyrood Palace, providing fine views of the palace and the abbey as well as of Arthur's Seat and Salisbury Crags. Next, climb Salisbury Crags and follow the edge before dropping down to the head of Hunter's Bog. The path descending northwards through Hunter's Bog emerges beside St Margaret's Loch, which you contour round to reach the car park.

🏛 History

Any understanding of the history of Holyrood Park must integrate both geological time and the human chronological time that we are perhaps more familiar with. This is not easy, however, for doing so will challenge us to consider our place in the history of the cosmos. This chapter gently introduces you to elements of this history as they arise over the course of the walk and you explore this sanctuary at the heart of Scotland's capital city.

The park is described on the 1853 map[37] of Edinburgh as the 'Sanctuary of Holyrood House'; this is because from the 1500s Holyrood Abbey offered sanctuary to those who could not pay their debts. These debtors, known as 'Abbey lairds', were granted shelter from their creditors within the abbey boundaries, which included Holyrood Park. Since its enclosure by James V in 1541, the park has continued to offer sanctuary in various ways. With the exception of some quarrying, land drainage and military activity, it has remained largely undeveloped with agricultural activity continuing until the 1970s. Centuries of sustained grazing have created a network of grassland habitats, in particular acid and calcareous lowland unimproved grasslands. These habitats were a key reason, along with the remarkable geology, for the park's designation as a Site of Special Scientific Interest (SSSI) in 1953, 1972, 1986 and 2011. Today, the park offers sanctuary to an unusual mix of wildlife, locals and tourists.

🍂 Habitats

Mature woodland, unimproved grasslands, scrub, wetlands, shallow lakes.

🚌 Transport links

The start of the walk is a 5–7-minute walk from the Meadowbank Stadium bus stop on London Road. This is served by buses 4, 5, 26 and 44. The park itself is accessible via National Cycle Route 1, from where the quiet route running through the park along Queen's Drive can be picked up. Cycle stands are available in the parking beside St Margaret's Loch.

☕ Refreshments

A detour into Abbey Hill or Meadowbank will lead you to a number of excellent cafés and eateries, including the Red Kite Café and Century General Store. The Café at the Palace is perhaps, however, the closest, and has a secluded and surprisingly quiet garden with a view into the park.

🪧 Directions

---

1 Royal Park Terrace to the Education Centre

On passing through the swing gate, follow the tarmac path ahead of you as it heads towards the back of the palace. A range of

---

37 https://maps.nls.uk/view/74426700

Figure 5.2a: A male bullfinch perches on the dried and browning branch of a seed-bearing plant. The fact that these are not mown but left to mature into the autumn is a godsend for finches and other seed-eating birds, especially when other food sources dry up.

Figures 5.2b–2c: The bullfinch's short beak is well suited to chewing up the tiny seeds that form the seed heads of cow parsley and other umbellifera flowers. The early morning sun is playing on the magical colours of this male and warming him up for the acrobatics required to reach the ends of these thin branches and the rewards they hold. One plant can hold some 800–1,000 seeds, so this represents a valuable food source – it is easy to understand the impact of mowing on autumn and winter feed supplies.

native trees, including oak, bird cherry, wych elm and rowan, provide excellent cover here for birds. The grass is also allowed to grow and go to seed, which means that in winter many seed-eating birds are drawn to the seedheads (Figures 5.2a–2c). The sound of goldfinches singing is often to be heard in this area throughout the year. You are also likely to hear and see blackbird, song thrush, wren, chaffinch and great spotted woodpecker.

As you walk along the path, look out for surprises like overwintering garden snails sheltering together (Figure 5.3a). The wych elm that stands at the back of the Education Centre can look particularly splendid in spring when lit by the morning sun (Figure 5.3b).

The views from this path can take the breath away at times. The profile of the tilted basalt sill that forms Salisbury Crags is an unmistakable part of the Edinburgh skyline – more instantly recognisable, perhaps, than the moon, which can often be seen floating over the crags. These are the product of a tilting of the basalt dyke laid down during a period of volcanic activity, while the hummocky nature of the ground falling down to the road is all that remains of the various attempts to extract valuable rock from this area. The steep cliff faces of the crags on the right have also been produced by quarrying, and it is these faces

Figure 5.3a: This remarkable collection of garden snails have decided, somehow and quite remarkably, to seek shelter together in this tight gap between two cherry tree trunks.

Figure 5.3b: The design of Holyrood Park's Education Centre is unusual, allowing the park and the Park Ranger Service to watch over each other. Rising above the centre stands an old wych elm whose leaves and seeds are brought to light in the morning as the sun rises in the east. Both the tree and the centre are watchers and reflectors, each benefiting from a rigorous, and yet markedly different, design process.

that now offer a safe home to a number of exciting breeding birds, including the fulmar.

2 Education Centre to St Margaret's Well

From the Education Centre head over to the car park at the back of the palace and cross over the road (Queen's Drive), turning left to reach the path that climbs diagonally to pass above St Margaret's Well.

You will not see any red deer here today, however, and there is scant evidence of an extensive forest. But there will be other treats, for the park's status is that of a Royal Park, an SSSI and a Scheduled Ancient Monument. Part of the park's designation as an SSSI is because of the grassland, a rich habitat that has in the past hosted as many as 10 to 13 skylark territories. The near-complete loss of the skylark as a breeding bird in the park is part of the story of the path you are about to tread.

3 St Margaret's Well to Salisbury Crags

The path above the wellhouse arrives at a junction. The main path bears round to the right and continues up Hunter's Bog. On this bend turn right, leaving the 'main path'

St Margaret's Well and the Legend of Holyrood

The wellhouse you see there today was originally sited at the earlier St Margaret's Well, in Meadowbank. It was a site of pilgrimage, for its waters were considered holy, but all that is left at the site of the original well is a memorial stone bearing the following inscription:

This stone marks the site of St. Margaret's Well. The dressed stone work of the fifteenth century wellhouse built over this ancient medicinal well and centre of pilgrimage was removed in 1859 and used to build a replica of it over St David's Well in the Queen's Park and the remains of the medieval building were filled in in 1969.

So this well was originally called St David's Well; it is around here that King David I of Scotland was attacked by a stag. The legend tells that on 14 September 1128, after taking mass, he and his court went out hunting in the forests to the east of the palace. At some point during the hunt he halted on the northern slopes of the crags, close to a well. A stag resting beside the well charged him, and he was thrown from his horse and gored by the stag. It is said that, on seizing the antlers and wrestling with the stag, he saw a cross appear on its antlers, whereupon the stag is said to have vanished. It is this tale that gave rise to the nearby well being named after the king, and the park being called Holyrood.

to head uphill onto Salisbury Crags. During the bird breeding season, you will usually see discreet signs, erected by the Ranger Service, reminding dog walkers that between April and August they are required to keep dogs both on the paths and on the lead. The reasons for this are made clear; the skylark population has crashed in recent years, for the nests of these ground-breeding birds are vulnerable to disturbance. Disturbed nests are likely to result in a catastrophic breeding season for the skylarks, and if these rules are not respected the skylark will become extinct locally. The delightful sound of skylarks is uplifting, and I sincerely hope you have the opportunity to hear the male's singing over their breeding territories. If you do hear them, try spotting them high up against the heavens, and allow yourself to admire how they project their voices from this fluttering vantage point.

The path uphill is obvious, and will take you between the remains of Camstone Quarry on your left and the edge of the crags on your right. Camstone Quarry, now rewilded, is home to gorse bushes, a resurgence of young trees and a geological richness that amounts to so much more than quarried stone. As you pass above the quarries that dot the length of Salisbury Crags, it is worth considering what it takes to move from extractive processes that take hand over fist to a sustainable way of acting in the world, one that recognises we cannot take without giving back.

Today, the vestiges of Camstone Quarry are hard to detect, and the area is a great place to listen and look out for whitethroat, dunnock and other birds who clearly value the cover and food provided by the scrubby vegetation hereabouts.

One item of food that appears on the menu through April and into May is the St Mark's fly (*Bibio marci*). This long-legged creature emerges on or about 25 April: St Mark's Day.

Figure 5.4a: The long trailing legs of the St Mark's fly, together with those backward-curving antennae, make it instantly recognisable. Hordes of such flies gather around blossoming hawthorn and gorse in late April and May.

Figures 5.4b–4c: The female chaffinch, pictured here, can't get enough of these flies, diving repeatedly to pluck them from the air. How many flies do you think she has managed to arrange across her bill, and at what point will she decide she has collected enough to justify returning to feed her chicks?

Figure 5.5: After rain, the gorse, even out of season, can be seen to be home to a host of invertebrates who we might otherwise be oblivious to. Attending to the magic of spider's webs and watching closely to observe their creators can be rewarding. It may also be worth seeing who is being caught.

Whilst the precise time of emergence is not set in stone, it is enough to have earnt these flies their name. They are also known as the hawthorn fly, and can be seen hanging around hawthorn, gorse and other bushes throughout the month of May (Figure 5.4a), providing a reliable food source for many birds working hard to feed their chicks (Figures 5.4b–4c).

It can be hard sometimes to realise just how much in the way of invertebrates are to be found in such scrubland. A rain shower can help you see and better appreciate some of the many creatures living here (Figure 5.5).

As you continue uphill, you might like to consider following a less well-defined path running closer to the edge, in order to get the best of the views down onto the palace and parliament buildings (Figures 5.6a–6d) from this incredible vantage point.

Figure 5.6a: Looking down on the Scottish Parliament and across to Calton Hill.

Figure 5.6c: Looking down on the Palace of Holyrood from Salisbury Crags.

Figure 5.6b: The path climbing up Salisbury Crags passes a few trees, sculpted by the wind, through and past which the Balmoral Clock Tower and the National Monument can be glimpsed.

Figure 5.6d: Looking down on the tented roof of the Dynamic Earth Planetarium and the Scottish Parliament.

*Figure 5.7a: In May the hollows along Salisbury Crags are aflame with the beautiful flowers of red campion (*Silene dioica*). Close attention will allow you to recognise that these flowers have five petals, each split in two in such a way that the flower appears to have ten petals.*

*Figure 5.7b: Rosebay willowherb (*Chamerion angustifolium*) in June, when the seedheads are developing. Here, only the uppermost flowers are blooming, but a remarkable succession line of flowers await their turn, and it is not hard to see how this plant is able to colonise far and wide.*

In spring on the ascent, it is worth looking out for flowers such as red campion (Figure 5.7a). Later in the summer, the pink of rosebay willowherb (Figure 5.7b) seems to take over and dominate the area. Its flower spikes are impressive, and the brown, dried remains will remain long after the pink flowers have fallen and the lanceolate (lance-shaped) leaves have disappeared. At one point this plant was uncommon. In the first half of the 20th century it benefited, however, from the deforestation and burning of the countryside. Such disruptions create space for colonising plants that have the ability to take seed quickly, giving them an advantage. The seedheads that succeed the rosebay willowherb's flowers are largely responsible for this ability; the seeds are equipped with fluffy, cottony parachutes that allow them to disperse far and wide when lifted by the slightest breath of wind. Each plant can produce up to 80,000 seeds, and it can be quite astounding to sit on a breezy day among the rosebay willowherb as the seeds take flight en masse.

As you continue along the steady climb, look out for signs of many of the birds nesting hereabouts. The cliffs below are the favourite haunt of carrion crow (Figure 5.8a) and

jackdaw. If you are lucky, you may spot a peregrine flashing by (Figure 5.8b).

The latter's presence in the landscape could not be more different from that of corvids. To understand this better, it helps to consider the intelligence of each bird. We have a tendency to think of intelligence in terms of IQ; in doing so we pay a disservice to the exquisite intelligence that arises in every life form. To truly understand intelligence we need to go back to the original meaning of 'genius', an ancient meaning lost in time that we desperately need to resurrect in our impoverished and overly competitive society. Genius can be understood as a locus: literally, what comes together in any one place at any given time. The spirit of a place, according to David Whyte (2014, p.17), 'describes a form of meeting of air, land and trees, perhaps a hillside, a cliff edge, a flowing stream or a bridge across a river. It is the conversation of elements that makes a place incarnate, fully itself'.

So, as you walk the cliff edge and feel alive, contemplate how the crow, the jackdaw and the peregrine each come to life in the moment – a moment that arises at the intersection of the wind, the cloud, the weather, the rock, the grass and the generations preparing for

Figure 5.8a: A carrion crow contemplates the city from the edge of Salisbury Crags. What will you contemplate, and how will you make sense of your own genius?

coursing through them, from wingtip to wingtip. Jackdaws are performers who are happy for their genius and their joyful performances to be made freely available to the world. So you can enjoy such moments with them.

Moments shared with the peregrine are of quite a different texture. They can pass in a blink of an eye, with no encore. The peregrine's genius is a meeting of very different elements. Peregrines have to live with the fear that their presence sows when their image etches itself on the retinas of other birds. The intelligence you develop when others are afraid of you is different. If you can conjure up the silhouette of an ominous cloud and the primordial chill that its shadow can cast, you will have some idea of the panic most birds feel when they perceive the peregrine's presence. So peregrines are great habit breakers, and know that the birds below must be allowed to settle. They can cover vast distances and appear or reappear in an instant. Their presence stays hidden: part of the peregrine's genius is to appear from nowhere. They can stoop from a great height at close to 200 mph and use one of their claws to cut open their

this moment. The genius of the jackdaw lies in their jackdawing, the way they throw themselves into the wind and embrace the elements. Nature's embrace of the jackdaw also feeds into this locus, for it informs who they are and the potential of each moment. Jackdaws and other corvids are social birds, and surf the weather world together. The feeling they enjoy when surfing the wind as it enters into conversation with the cliff face is one of absolute mastery. They were born to this. They were born for this. This is genius, and it can be felt joyfully

Figure 5.8b: The peregrine banks and turns just off the crags, and in an instant disappears off across the city towards distant hunting grounds. This is part of the falcon's genius.

Figure 5.9: A view down over Hunter's Bog from Salisbury Crags. Here a path can be seen descending through the grass, passing a young rowan tree in blossom. It is mid-May and the few remaining skylark here are likely to be on their nests. The sign shown here emphasises to walkers that skylark populations have crashed and that dogs must be kept on the lead and stick to paths.

prey, like the most skilled of swordsmen. Their genius fuses a fuselage of exquisite design with purpose and artistry. They can come out of the sun and, like the sun, can light up the sky. Moments shared with the peregrine are thus gifted to us, rare and precious. One second they are there, rending the air like a scythe or a sunbeam – the next, they are at vanishing point, out beyond Edinburgh's castle. In their wake, pigeons, gulls and other birds are alarmed, their calls and behaviour often the only indication of the peregrine's passage.

As you pass along the cliff edge, then, look out for whosoever' flight crosses your path. The fulmars (see the special feature) may fly out from the cliff to your right, whilst to your left over the grassland you may hear the uplifting voice of skylarks.

Skylark Tweet of the Day: https://www.bbc.co.uk/programmes/b03tht7c.

The grassland here is left unmown, so provides good cover for the last remaining pairs of these ground-nesting birds. You will see the signs (Figure 5.9), mentioned earlier, emphasising to walkers the impact that dogs can have on these vulnerable birds, and instructing that between the months of April and August dogs must be kept to paths and on leads. This uneasy balance arises because the park is heavily frequented by city dwellers and their canine companions. The right of access is incontestable but is not absolute. Rights only exist because they carry responsibilities, and the challenge is thus to promote awareness of this reciprocal relationship – one of the challenges of nature conservation.

★ Special Feature – the fulmar

The fulmar (*Fulmarus glacialis*) is perhaps the most ocean-going of British common breeding birds, for they visit land only during the breeding season. This is entirely consistent with their status as a close relative of the albatross; their flying abilities are legendary, and there is something profoundly magical about watching them dancing effortlessly over the waves, immune to the sea's best efforts to envelop them. That we can see them in the heart of Edinburgh (Figure 5.10a) is a treat, and is something we owe to their seeking out cliff ledges on which to nest.

There was a time when their range in the UK was limited to St Kilda. But then throughout the 19th century, they expanded across much of Scotland, and by 1930 had reached Pembrokeshire in south-west Wales. Remarkably, however, this extended range probably originated from the southern expansion of the Iceland and Faroe Island populations rather than from the population on St Kilda. Today they can be found breeding on cliffs along much of the coast of the island nation we share. More recently, this colonisation has seen them take to breeding on suitable ledges on crags and quarries inland. These sites can be up to 12 miles inland, for such distances pose little obstacle to such excellent fliers.

Figure 5.10a: The fulmar's stiff, elongated, grey wings, a pale splash of white over the inner primaries, together with their white head and neck, rounded heads and those tube-nosed beaks, are features that clearly mark this bird out from other seabirds. It is the effortless grace of their flying that usually alerts me to their presence, even when they appear out of place, as here over woodland.

Figure 5.10b: Seeing them flying out from the cliffs of Salisbury Crags over the heads of visitors to the park and the palace walls always brings a smile to my face. Few would realise that this bird is no 'seagull'. Note how straight those long wings are, and how the white patches on the fanned inner primaries stand out against the grey. Watch the fine adjustments, the fanning of the tail, and the tilted body that allows it to bank and turn – this is genius in action.

According to Scottish Wildlife Trust records, the first record of fulmar breeding on Salisbury Crags is from 1981. In 2012 the population rose into double figures, with a further three pairs nesting on Raven Rock. The ledges they nest on allow them to drop off and take to the air instantly. Their legs are not designed for life on land, and on the rare occasions they land on deck or are seen walking, this becomes very clear. Walking just isn't their thing. And that's fine, because flying most definitely is.

Their preference for feeding on plankton and krill (a form of plankton), meant that they would often be found near whale species whose diet similarly relies on these crustacea". This association led to whalers coming to recognise the bird and exploit the relationship as a way of seeking out their quarry.

Today our impact on sea life is evident in a different way, for many fulmar ingest the plastic that now blights our seas; everything from bubbles of expanded polystyrene to plastic bags. It is the vast quantity of plastic beads, however, entering the marine environment that is perhaps most concerning. These beads or pellets, termed 'nurdles', typically enter the marine environment when container ships clean out their tanks at sea after transporting loads of these processed pellets for manufacture. Spillages occur in other ways too – none of them excusable.

You can learn more about nurdles and the catastrophic impact they are having on our birdlife and the ecosystem that we depend on at: https://www.fidra.org.uk/nurdles/

The good news is that organisations such as FIDRA, based in East Lothian, are doing incredible work to raise awareness of the issue and address it. We can all do our part by reducing and ultimately eliminating the plastic whose production we are responsible for. The widely publicised but risible attempts at plastic recycling are not the answer, certainly as things stand, due to the huge variety of plastics leading to the expense and the near-impossibility of sorting them into those that can be reused or recycled and those that can't.

So, if you see fulmars on your walk, think about what they are finding out at sea and bringing back to their nests. It could be our plastic waste. If we want our water and our food to be free of plastic and associated toxins, we need to work collaboratively to address plastic production at source.

The story of the peregrine and the fulmar are tied up with ours. It was our use of DDT that devastated the peregrine, until we woke to that menace. Our use of plastics is having a similarly disastrous effect on seabirds such as the fulmar. We are waking up to that too. It is a shame that awareness dawns so slowly, though.

Figure 5.11a: From the highest point of Salisbury Crags a fine view stretches out across the city. Several key landmarks, including Edinburgh Castle and St Giles Cathedral, stand out.

Figure 5.11b: Hunter's Bog is the flat area of ground between Salisbury Crags and the slopes of Arthur's Seat. Your return route passes along the right-hand edge, seen here as a grassy path hugging a series of copses of young trees.

One of the highlights for me along this stretch of the walk is the appearance during the latter half of the year – typically from July through to November – of the Scottish harebell. This magical flower casts an azure spell over the crags, and I have devoted a special feature to celebrating their form and beauty.

The highest point of Salisbury Crags is reached near Cat Nick, and provides another fine vantage point across the city (Figure 5.11a). From here you descend, following the line of the cliffs, to reach the Hawse. Care may be needed over some of the rockier ground on this descent. As you walk down towards the flatter ground at the head of the Hunter's Bog, you will see this broad valley dropping more gently away, and will be able to spy out your return route (Figure 5.11b).

From the Hawse (where the path comes through from the road below you to your right), turn left to descend Hunter's Bog. Ignore the main path that drops down the left-hand side of the valley. Instead follow the path that follows the right-hand side, passing a copse of Scots pine. Look out for whitethroat singing in the gorse (Figure 5.12) and keep listening out for

Figure 5.12: Whitethroat return to the UK from their African wintering grounds south of the Sahara. The park is an excellent place to hear and watch these handsome warblers, as they favour the cover provided by the gorse and shrubby vegetation.

*Figure 5.13a: Water mint (*Mentha aquatica*) gives off an incredible fragrance if crushed, and used to be strewn on the floors at medieval banquets so that guests would smell this on entering and crossing the room. You can appreciate the smell equally well, however, and more respectfully, by gently caressing the leaves. The plant to the right is a horsetail.*

corvids. Carrion crows often visit the marshy area at the heart of the bog to enjoy a spot of sociable and profitable foraging, but should you hear a deeper corvid voice it is worth looking upwards, as the park is home to raven.

One of the rewards awaiting those exploring the wetter ground is the delightful fragrance of water mint (Figure 5.13a). You can best appreciate this by running your fingers gently over the leaves; they will pick up the exquisite minty aroma without inflicting any damage to the plants.

Soon you will reach the main path running from left to right before the rocky outcrop of Haggis Knowe. The view here stretches out to Calton Hill, and it is worth pausing to take it in (Figure 5.13b). Pass to the right of the outcrop and descend to St Margaret's Loch. As you approach the loch, look out for a large well-established patch of butterbur (Figure 5.13c).

St Margaret's Loch is worth pausing at, to see who is about. This can vary considerably according to the time of year, for the birds' relationship to this loch changes with the seasons. A large number of non-breeding swans can usually be found there, and it can be a real treat to see a group of them coming in to land on the water. At other times these birds can be

Figure 5.13b: Looking past Haggis Knowe to the Scottish Parliament and Calton Hill. In the foreground the white flower heads of cow parsley are in full bloom.

Figure 5.13c: The large leaves of butterbur soon grow to such a size that they obscure the flowers that precede their appearance.

Figure 5.14a: Non-breeding mute swans (Cygnus olor) gather in numbers on St Margaret's Loch.

seen grazing on the fresh lush grass growing beside the road. There is something different about seeing swans, rather than sheep or cattle, grazing at the roadside. Grass, it should be remembered, is swans' natural diet, and is what their digestive system is geared to deal with. Processed bread is distinctly lacking in nutrition, and whilst it may attract the swans,

I would strongly encourage you not to feed bread to the birds. If small amounts of food are to be fed, this should be wholegrain bread or, much better, grain. When food is scarce, especially in winter, such supplementary feeding may be welcome to swans, gulls, ducks and other birds gathering on the loch (Figures 5.14a–14b).

Figure 5.14b: Other visiting birds, including greylag geese and black-headed gulls, seek refuge on the loch in winter.

Figures 5.15a–15b: Tufted ducks (Aythya fuligula) are easily recognised by the tuft of feathers cascading down the back of their heads. In good light, these diving ducks can be seen to be far more colourful than initial appearances would suggest. Feast your eyes on those head colours on the male as they catch the light. The bill is the palest of blues – and that eye! ... a glimmering piece of gold on a bed of velvet.

Other birds to look out for include the tufted duck (Figures 5.15a–15b) and heron (Figure 5.15c). During the early summer it can also be a real pleasure watching swallows flying low over the water to catch insects. On one occasion I have seen a sparrowhawk appear from the undergrowth and take a swallow in mid-flight above the water. So remain alert to such surprises, especially if you are there at quieter times of the day.

Walk round the loch to reach the car park at the far end, and your finish.

Figure 5.15c: The juvenile grey heron on the right is learning to fish. It's all about the focus, that mesmerising stare, that fascination – and then a superswift, coordinated extension of the neck. What must it feel like to do that for the first time? What must it be like for the parent looking on to see their offspring pulling fish from the water? Yes, even in St Margaret's Loch there are plenty of fish to keep these herons busy.

Figure 5.16a (left): Harebells flower from July through to November, and can be seen springing up from the thin dry soil along the top of Salisbury Crags.

★ Special Feature – Scottish harebells

The Scottish harebell (*Campanula rotundifolia*) is often known as the Scottish bluebell in recognition of the exquisite way the flower's five pale- to mid-violet-blue petals fuse to form a bell. Another old Scottish name for this flower is witch's thimble. This association with witches may also lie behind the name 'harebell', for it was believed that witches had the ability to transform themselves into hares. I prefer, however, to see this association as hinting at the respect that wise women had for these delicate flowers.

This campanula occurs across Europe, from the Mediterranean to the Arctic. It tends to favour nutrient-poor grassland and heathland, and the established, mature plants seem able to compete with tall grass (Figure 5.16a).

These flowers are also able to colonise cliff faces (Figure 5.16b), and it can be a delight to watch their bells chiming away as they are blown about by the wind pummelling the crags. For such an apparently delicate flower, they are remarkably robust.

It was perhaps this trembling resilience that inspired the 19th-century English poet, Christina Georgina Rossetti, best known for writing the Christmas carol 'In the Bleak Midwinter', to write a poem entitled 'Hope is like a Harebell'. The first two lines run:

Hope is like a harebell, trembling from its birth
Love is like a rose, the joy of all the earth.

Hope is always worth seeking out, and the harebell can thus serve as a reminder for us to reconnect with what we are grateful for and what we remain hopeful for.

Figure 5.16b: Their ability to colonise the cliffs overlooking the palace and resist the blustering of the wind seems nothing short of miraculous.

Walk 6

St Mark's Park and Warriston Cemetery

This walk takes in a section of the Water of Leith Walkway and some of the hidden paths that fortunately attract only the more curious wanderers amongst us. The walk also explores one of Edinburgh's hidden treasures – a largely forgotten cemetery whose deepest recesses see little footfall, and whose wildlife clearly values this tranquillity.

This walk's highlights include:

- An opportunity to explore a community woodland initiative.
- A historic section of the Water of Leith Walkway.
- A delightful section of cycle path, lined with some particularly attractive birch trees.
- A detour into the hidden depths and delights of Warriston Cemetery.

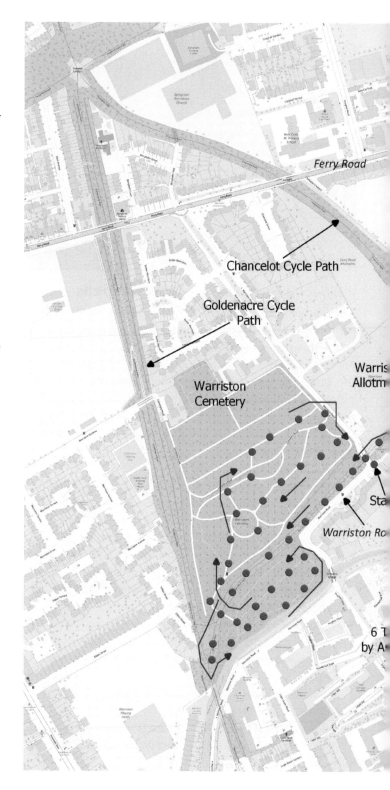

Ferry Road

Chancelot Cycle Path

Goldenacre Cycle Path

Warris
Allotm

Warriston Cemetery

Sta

Warriston Ro

6 T
by A

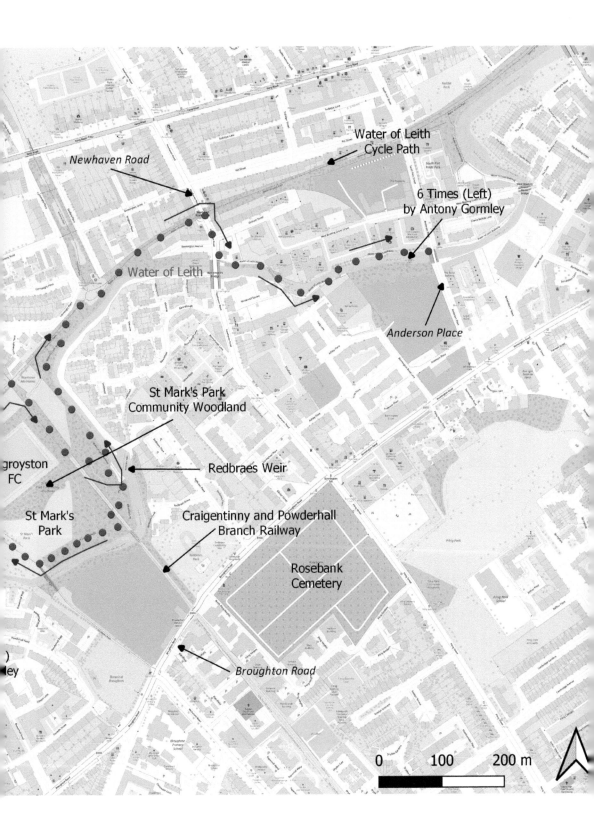

Water of Leith
Cycle Path

Newhaven Road

6 Times (Left)
by Antony Gormley

Water of Leith

Anderson Place

St Mark's Park
Community Woodland

groyston
FC

Redbraes Weir

St Mark's
Park

Craigentinny and Powderhall
Branch Railway

Rosebank
Cemetery

Broughton Road

0   100   200 m

:ə Summary

This walk starts from the entrance to St Mark's Park on Warriston Road (NT 255 757). Follow the cycle path to where it joins the Goldenacre Path. From here, you can gain access to the lower half of Warriston Cemetery, close to the river. After exploring this area, find a tunnel that leads under the cycle path and allows you to explore the upper half of the cemetery. Rejoin the cycle path and follow it all the way to South Fort Street, where it rejoins the Water of Leith. Follow the river upstream, past West Bowling Green, Anderson Place and Newhaven Road. After passing Redbraes Weir, pick up a path that provides access to St Mark's Park again, with the opportunity to explore the delightful community woodland that now stands beside the football pitch.

🏛 History

For the purposes of this walk, you may be interested in learning a little more about Warriston Cemetery and the Water of Leith. Recent human history has left its imprint on both of these, and this is relevant to any understanding of the biodiversity you may encounter on the walk, for we are part of the ecosystem that gives rise to life. The way we commemorate our dead and the ways in which we use and abuse the rivers running through our communities is thus of great historical relevance.

The following map, from 1852, can help transport us back over a century and a half, and see the extent to which the Water of Leith has been industrialised. It is also possible to see the layout of the oldest part of Warriston Cemetery, which would then have been nine

Figure 6.1a: A quiet morning on the cycle path linking St Mark's Park and Warriston Cemetery can be a real treat, for the birch trees lining the path are unusually shaped and patterned.

years old, having opened on 3 June 1843 as Edinburgh's first garden cemetery: https://maps.nls.uk/view/74426700

The Garden Cemetery Movement is a Victorian phenomenon that arose in response to the overcrowded nature of the town's burial grounds. The movement sought to promote the creation of grounds in which family members could be interred and monuments erected, and that the public could enjoy visiting to learn about their ancestors and respectfully pay homage to them. In 1840 the Edinburgh Cemetery Company was founded. Its first cemetery was designed by David Cousin, who went on to design those at Dalry, Dean, Newington and Rosebank. These are all worth visiting, for they have each become havens of peace and for wildlife. We have much to thank the garden cemetery movement for; in such places we can find peace and restful respite in life as well as in death.

Perhaps Warriston's most renowned occupant is the obstetrician and pioneer of anaesthesia for childbirth, James Simpson (1811–1870). At the age of 28 he became Professor of Medicine and Midwifery at the University of Edinburgh. In 1847 he discovered for himself the effects of chloroform, which previously had only been used on large animals; his experience led him to explore the drug's potential as an anaesthetic agent.

Such was his fame that on his death his family were offered a site in Westminster Abbey – which they declined, in favour of Warriston Cemetery. On the day of his interment, a public holiday was declared, with some 100,000 citizens lining the route taken by the cortege to his final resting place.

A very different historical character whose roots are firmly embedded in this part of Edinburgh is an ancient common pear tree (*Pyrus communis*) in Rosebank Cemetery, with a girth of 2.36 metres, measured at

1.5 metres from the ground. The tree can be found in the cemetery that sits quietly on the south side of Broughton Road (NT 260 756). It can be accessed from Pilrig Street.

Habitats

River, woodland, urban park and cemetery.

Transport links

The start of the walk on Warriston Road is well served by two Lothian Bus services. The bus stop on Broughton Road (at the foot of McDonald Road) is a 5-minute walk from the start, and is served by bus services 13 and 36. If you are cycling to the start, a quiet cycling road along McDonald Road allows you to reach the start via St Mark's Path. Alternatively, the start can be accessed via National Cycle Route 7r (and the Chancelot and Warriston paths).

Refreshments

You could make a detour to access a selection of excellent cafés in Canonmills, including the Orchard, the Coffee Angel and the Blue Bear.

Directions

1 Craigroyston Football Club to Warriston Cemetery

If you enter St Mark's Park from Warriston Road, walk past the Craigroyston Football Club to access the cycle path immediately beyond the clubhouse and changing rooms. Turn left onto the path and head south-west, passing under Warriston Road. This section of the path is lined with a delightful series of silver birch trees (Figures 6.1a–1b). As you walk along these paths, it is worth appreciating the ribbons of nature they have now become; where once there were noisy smoke-belching trains, we have been able to establish a fantastic network of tranquil tree-lined cycle routes.

A little further on, you pass over a bridge with impressive views down into Warriston Cemetery. At this point look out for a fine mosaic of a carrion crow on the left-hand wall (Figure 6.1c).

The ivy-clad walls hereabouts are often a good place to look out for dunnock, robins, blackbirds and carrion crows. You will then pass a turning onto the Goldenacre path,

coming in from your right. A little beyond this, look out for a path dropping through the trees to your left. Follow this to arrive at a gap in the wall (Figure 6.2a). Take care on stepping over the wall. On arriving in the cemetery you may want to consciously slow down, for you are in many respects about to travel back in time.

I suggest that you take a loop through the lower half of the cemetery between the old railway line (now cycle path) and the river, before passing beneath the stone bridge (Figure 6.2b) built in 1845, to keep the two parts of the cemetery connected when the Edinburgh Leith and Newhaven Line was put in.

Figure 6.1b: Each birch tree is unique, and it is worth pausing to run both your eyes and your hands over their bark, pondering perhaps the story such inscriptions might tell. The horizontal lines are porous structures, known as lenticels, that provide openings for gas exchange. The white pigment in birch bark is due to a compound, botulin, that protects the tree from intense sunlight, and may explain why birches are one of the most northerly found deciduous trees. Botulin is also increasingly used for its anticancer and anti-inflammatory properties.

Figure 6.2a: An obvious path cuts through the trees from the cycle path, providing access to the lower part of Warriston Cemetery via a dip in the wall.

Figure 6.1c: A delightful mosaic of a corvid adorns the lichen-covered stone of the bridge. Next time you see a crow walking purposefully forwards, it might be worth wondering whether the artist was right to suggest they walk as if in high heels.

Figure 6.2b: The gothic stone archway provides a dramatic way of transitioning between the lower and upper parts of the cemetery, passing under the old railway line in the process.

Figures 6.3a–3b: One day in May the overnight rains had left multiple pools of water on the floor of the lower part of the cemetery. These caught and reflected the fresh green of the leaves. They also attracted a number of birds grateful for the opportunity to take a bath. Bathing is an essential activity that birds eagerly seek out and appear to enjoy. It helps them to eliminate parasites and attend to their feathering, ensuring it is kept in tip-top condition and looking good. It can be a real delight to observe a bird such as this female bullfinch demonstrating her preferred bathing technique. This frantic movement seems to recruit all manner of muscles; it really is a head-to-toe affair. Water flies everywhere. Feathers are ruffled and brought into conversation with the cleansing qualities of water. And then, as if by magic, those feathers are all reordered.

Many of the gravestones have been left to do their own thing, and the cemetery pays its deepest respects to the cycle of life by welcoming nature back in. Every visit seems to yield new surprises, and it is your own curiosity that will help you discover these. The images that follow are but a few suggestions of what you might care to look out for (Figures 6.3a–3f).

Figure 6.3c: As the days start to lengthen again there is something magical about the emergence of snowdrops.

Figure 6.3e: Warriston Cemetery contains a significant number of war graves, and this magnificent Cross of Sacrifice. This is an example of the Commonwealth War Memorial designed in 1918 by Sir Reginald Blomfield for the Imperial War Graves Commission; it is generally present in Commonwealth war cemeteries with more than 40 war graves. The cross stands on an octagonal base and is typically made of limestone, and a bronze longsword is affixed, blade down, to the cross. The whole serves as a reminder to us all, perhaps, of the fragility of life and the folly of humanity.

Figure 6.3d: Snails too seek out a safe passage through the winter, even introducing themselves between these two kissing doves. How peaceful. Elsewhere, the stones that you could argue commemorate the fallen and all our losses offer hope for a lightening of the darkness and a lifting of the spirit.

Figure 6.3f: A jumble of stones is certainly not forgotten by nature, whose loving embrace reclaims everything. Splashes of blue and green say as much to the immortal memory, perhaps, as the words on the stone. What does it mean to be reborn again?

Figures 6.4a–4b: Who is this little character? Can you tell? Focus your attention on the silhouette and that puffed chest ... are you reminded of a familiar garden bird? If you are patient, their persistent calling may allow you to deduce that this is a fledgling. And if your patience leads you to establish a safe distance, you may encourage the adult to appear and feed the youngster.

The cemetery is a quiet place whose silence and tranquillity are much appreciated by wildlife. Bird song travels further on the clear air here, and it can be an excellent place to come and listen to a dawn chorus in spring. The chorus typically starts well before dawn and reaches its peak in the 30 minutes either side of sunrise, so if you are an early riser you may want to visit at least one hour before sunrise to be in position to watch and listen to the singers gradually taking the stage and singing their hearts out. By doing so, you are more likely to hear the soloists – but then as the singers start to sing en masse that becomes harder, and you may just want to let this glorious sound wash over you without straining your ears to pick out particular voices.

Spring is also, of course, together with early summer, synonymous with new life, so you can expect to encounter many young birds as they fledge and venture forth from their nests. These can present some interesting identification challenges. When you see a bird you do not immediately recognise, particularly if they are behaving a little naïvely, pay attention;

they are quite likely to be fledglings, and their first coat of feathers may only be dimly suggestive and/or reminiscent of those they will sport as adults (Figures 6.4a–4c).

Figure 6.4c: In this case, the adult that came to feed the youngster was a robin. Who'd have guessed? But if you look carefully at the fledgling, you will recognise the silhouette and the wing shape. Your sense of the essence of a bird is developing ... what a reward for paying attention!

2 Warriston Cemetery to Chancelot Path

Retrace your steps back out of the cemetery and onto the cycle path. Head back the way you came (direction Leith) to pass the entrance to Craigroyston Football Club. Continue beyond this, to reach the junction with Chancelot Path (NT 256 758).

You now have a choice. If you want to follow the cycle path all the way to South Fort Street and then join the Water of Leith, you are invited to continue straight ahead. If, on the other hand, you would like to follow the Water of Leith down to South Fort Street (heading downstream) and then retrace your steps upstream again, you are invited to turn right here and follow the path of the old railway line until you reach the river. These two options are described as options 3a and 3b respectively.

3a Chancelot Path to South Fort Street (via cycle path)

The hard surface of the cycle path heads straight ahead in a north-easterly direction. It passes under Newhaven Road and continues on, to pass under South Fort Street. Stay on the cycle path, which will emerge on the bank of the Water of Leith (NT 263 762).

The merit of this option is, perhaps, that it allows you to walk a circuit rather than an out-and-back route. It also allows you to experience the green corridors that the old railways of the city have bequeathed us and that allow us to enjoy traffic-free circulation through the city.

Figure 6.5b: One of the surprises I have enjoyed feasting my eyes on, growing from among the gravel and sleepers of the railway line, is this white variety of Herb Robert (Geranium robertianum). The stems are a typical red, and the leaves too have a red tinge, as seen here. The flowers are usually a light pink, so this white variety is quite unusual. The crushed leaves of this plant have a mousey smell, in part due to the essential oils they contain (including geranium). This may account for its reputation as an insect repellent.

Figure 6.5a: The old Powderhall to Craigentinny railway line on the north side of the river.

Figure 6.5c: A group of four mallard drakes drifting down river towards Redbraes Weir. The seeds on the water were those of the elm tree and proved irresistible to the passing ducks who happily dabbled for them. It is always worth getting curious as to what foods are in season, whether you be mallard or human …

3b Chancelot Path to South Fort Street (via Water of Leith)

Should you decide to turn right and follow the earthen path towards the river, you will find yourself on the old line that used to run from Craigentinny to Powderhall. Until 2016 a two-mile section of this line was kept open to service the local waste management site, now also closed; waste was transported by train from this plant to a landfill site in an old limestone workings near Dunbar. It is hoped that in time this railway line, which links Abbeyhill and Meadowbank, will be developed as a cycle path. At the time of writing, it stands empty and desolate.

As you walk along the path you will see the railings enclosing the remaining tracks that cross the bridge over the Water of Leith. The line has been reclaimed by nature and is full of surprises (Figures 6.5a–5d). Whilst you are discouraged from venturing onto the line and the bridge for safety reasons, it is certainly worth taking a closer look through the railings to see how this space is rewilding itself. Nature's ability to reclaim and rewild reminds us that biodiversity is not so much a thing as a process; so perhaps we should be more willing to speak of biodiversification rather than biodiversity.

Keep the railway line to your right and follow the earthen path. You will find this leads you down to the Water of Leith close to Redbraes Weir. You can then follow the river pretty much all the way to South Fort Street, by following the signs for the Water of Leith Walkway.

Figure 6.5d: Two mallards are dabbling for elm seeds on the surface of the water. Below them a shopping trolley lurks as a reminder of the misuse and abuse we inflict on waterways. Fortunately, the Water of Leith Conservation Trust organises clean-up days, which can be very rewarding to contribute to, knowing that you are helping restore the ecosystem and repair some of the damage arising from mindless human behaviour.

4 South Fort Street to Redbraes Weir

The cycle path rejoins the Water of Leith Walkway a little under 100 metres downstream of South Fort Street (NT 263 763). At this point I would invite you to turn and follow the river back upstream.

Immediately after South Fort Street, you will come across an Antony Gormley statue (Figure 6.6) standing beside a majestic old willow tree. This location can also be a good place to spot kingfishers zipping up and down the river and perching in the branches of the willow (see the special feature).

Continue following the Water of Leith Walkway, crossing two bridges that take you from one bank to another, until you reach Redbraes Weir.

Figure 6.6: The statue you can admire from the walkway upstream of South Fort Street is part of an outdoor exhibit called 6 Times. The work is by Antony Gormley, the Turner prize-winning artist perhaps best known as the creator of the Angel of the North. The 6 Times project was initiated in 2010 and undertaken in collaboration with the Scottish National Gallery of Modern Art. For the project, Gormley produced six statues positioned between the Gallery of Modern Art and the sea. Four of these stand in the Water of Leith itself, and help us gauge the height of the river. This way, they interact with the elements and draw our attention to the elemental force that is water, which can both sustain and overwhelm us. Originally they had been designed to move with the water, but have since been redesigned so that they are permanently secured to the riverbed.

★ Special Feature – the kingfisher

Figure 6.7a: What do you see? Do you notice those lichens on the branch, the out-of-focus lanceolate leaves of the willow tree, or perhaps the fish? I suspect not, for the kingfisher is king. How can we fail to be dazzled by that bejewelled crown and the regal robes and that stare? There is so much to take in: all those brilliant and not-so-brilliant blues, the white cravat, the oranges and browns of the chest. And then there is the rapier-like bill that only kings can carry. It is sobering to realise that of the kingfisher's 16.5-centimetre body length, four of those centimetres are the bill! Without such a weapon this bird would be little bigger than a sparrow. When bearing arms, however, this predator is 'all tooled up', as they say. And that fish sitting in the beak bears testimony to the king's proficiency as a fisher.

As a child I grew up learning all the twists and turns of the river that ran through my home city of Bristol. The highlight of every such visit was the flashing brilliance of a kingfisher streaking upriver or down, cleaving nature's palate asunder with a set of colours whose capturing has challenged the best nature writers. Jim Crumley, in his beautiful book *Kingfisher*, perhaps captured this best when he wrote 'Colour is to kingfishers what slipperiness is to eels'.

And so I will let these two images (Figures 6.7a–7b) speak for themselves, whilst drawing your attention to particular features that appear worthy of comment. I say 'worthy'. But I know that my words will fail to do justice to the wizardry of this wonderful creature. Maybe, though, just maybe, they will help the kingfisher to cast a spell on you, as it has on me.

So …. slow down. Pay attention as you walk. You may be the one to see the lightning strike – and to marvel at those who walk on by, oblivious to all but their mobile phones, messages, chatter and the intoxication of consumerism. There is a gulf between mindlessness and mindfulness, and in that gulf a kingfisher can appear and disappear: a loss to the mindless, a gift of inestimable grace to the mindful. Which would you rather be?

Figure 6.7b: The bird pictured here is a male: if you look carefully you will see that the lower mandible is all black. (In females the base of the lower mandible is reddy-orange for about half the length of the bill.) You will also note that the fish is held with the head pointing forwards. This has been arranged so that the bird can be swallowed head first by the young, who will be eagerly waiting in a nesting chamber somewhere deep in the riverbank.

If we are mindful of kingfishers, what might reveal itself? That's a very good question – one that may require us to revisit what it might mean to be mindful …

We may need to be patient, very patient. But appreciating the kingfisher extends beyond glimpsing it flash by. Life itself can, lest we forget, flash by in an instant if we fail to pay attention and seize each and every moment. The kingfisher is thus our invitation to stay in the present.

We may need to slow down and create the time and space to see beyond the magnificent colours. We might need to let go of our tendency to admire all that glitters, and to see the emperor rather than the emperor's clothes. We might need to wrinkle our noses and embrace these creatures in all their fishiness. When feeding their young, these expert fishers can bring back over 100 fish per day to the nest. This makes for a lot of fish bones, and as those young develop, the metre-long tunnel becomes increasingly smelly and messy. On emerging from the tunnel, the kingfisher can thus typically be seen making a series of dips to clean off the debris from their feathers before heading off for more fish. During the breeding season, work is unrelenting.

We may also need to close our eyes and listen for the kingfisher's flight call. This I would suggest you do before visiting the riverbank, however, so that you have a chance of recognising that zipping call that might be described as *'zii'*. A good place to start is Radio 4's Tweet of the Day: https://www.bbc.co.uk/programmes/b02twpwl.

And then when out in the wilds you hear that call, be sure to study the river.

As well as being mindful, I would also invite you to be curious. Can you imagine how young kingfishers who are born naked make sense of the eruption of all these bright colours from their skin? Can you imagine what it might be like for them to emerge for the first time into the light of day and head out to befriend the willow tree and start learning the essence of their craft?

The kingfisher's essence is the kingfisher's essence. There is neither good nor bad, as Mary Oliver has so exquisitely captured in her poem:

The Kingfisher

The kingfisher rises out of the black wave
like a blue flower, in his beak
he carries a silver leaf. I think this is
the prettiest world — so long as you don't mind
a little dying, how could there be a day in your whole life
that doesn't have its splash of happiness?
There are more fish than there are leaves
on a thousand trees, and anyway the kingfisher
wasn't born to think about it, or anything else.
When the wave snaps shut over his blue head, the water
remains water — hunger is the only story
he has ever heard in his life that he could believe.
I don't say he's right. Neither
do I say he's wrong. Religiously he swallows the silver leaf
with its broken red river, and with a rough and easy cry
I couldn't rouse out of my thoughtful body
if my life depended on it, he swings back
over the bright sea to do the same thing, to do it
(As I long to do something, anything) perfectly.[1]

To be mindful of kingfishers is thus to accept them wholeheartedly, and perhaps to appreciate that such acceptance can also be extended to ourselves. As David Whyte once said, we are the only species who seem to wish we were someone other than ourselves. The kingfisher, he reminds us, never wakes up in the morning thinking it would like to be a crow for the day, and eat carrion.

Kingfishers grace the river with their presence because they are meant to be there – providing, of course, that the river sustains them. A sustaining river implicates us, however, and requires us to collectively respect the river and ensure it sustains the loach and minnows and stickleback that the kingfishers feed on. The grace of kingfishers is thus so much more than a set of magnificent robes and a rapier-like beak.

Figure 6.8: Redbraes Weir used to divert water into a lade that fed the mills at Bonnington. The level of water in the lade was controlled by a sluice gate. Studies conducted back in 2009 to explore the possibility of installing micro-hydro turbines at the weir have so far come to nothing.

5 Redbraes Weir

The impressive weir you see ahead of you (Figure 6.8) once fed a number of local mills. Water was diverted from the river and fed via a lade to the mills at Bonnington, where the water power generated was used to mill grain. There were other mills, too, where cloth was woven, leather tanned and paper manufactured.

Mallard ducks and heron can often be seen around the weir, and it can be fascinating to pause and study what they are up to.

Figures 6.9a–9b: Moorhen can be fascinating to watch as they construct their nests and then set about raising their young. In 6.9a, one of the adults is covering the eggs, one of which has recently hatched. The parents take it in turns to share this duty, and the changeover is remarkably affectionate, with a little gift of food being passed between them. After the exchange, the brooding parent rises from the nest and heads off in search of food, leaving their mate to settle back onto the nest.

Figure 6.9c: When the nest has been vacated, the returning parent inspects the remaining egg and recently hatched chick before very carefully stepping into the nest and assuming the correct position.

Figure 6.9d: The parent moorhen settles back into the nest and finds herself well hidden among the surrounding ivy leaves. Should you identify the location of a nest, please maintain a respectful distance and take care not to disturb the owners. If you do keep your distance, your presence may become acceptable and your return may not be unwelcome, allowing you to observe the comings and goings and the development of the chicks. Paying appreciative attention to the daily changes can be an enriching experience, particularly if you get to see the young moorhens leaving the nest and taking their first tentative steps into the big wide world.

6 Redbraes Weir to St Mark's Park and Craigroyston Football Club

From the weir, continue following the river-bank upstream. This can be a good place to look out for moorhen (Figures 6.9a–9d) who in spring and early summer may be actively rearing their young.

Look out too for flushes of some of our most beautiful woodland plants, including cow parsley and wood aven.

★ Special Feature – wood avens

Between the months of May and August our woodlands can sparkle with the delicate five-petalled yellow flowers of wood avens (*Geum urbanum*). This effect is sometimes particularly pronounced when the light filters back through the woodland canopy after a rain shower. On such occasions,

Figure 6.10a: This image illustrates the three-lobed structure of the leaves of wood aven and the extent to which this pattern, whilst normally followed, can vary.

with the light picking up and setting off water droplets on the heavily veined and oh-so-green leaves and those delicate yellow petals, you cannot help but stop and pay attention (Figure 6.10a). The expanses of flaming delicate flowers are visited by all manner of pollinating insects, and it can be intriguing to watch them as they move from flower to flower.

A member of the rose family, this species has leaves whose initial form is often heart-shaped before becoming trilobed. It has also been known as St Benedict's herb, and it is likely that its association with Christianity is due to the leaf and petal structure (the three lobes a reminder of the holy trinity, the five petals of the five wounds of Christ (Figure 6.10b).

Figure 6.10b: The five-petalled flower heads are an exquisite yellow, and it can be very rewarding to examine their shape and structure under a magnifying glass. In this case, paying attention to the way rain has pooled on each petal further contributes to the awareness we can develop of shape and structure. Easily overlooked perhaps, the reward is there for those who pause to look. You might wish to go further and consider how flowers respond to and cope with rain when they meet, as they inevitably do.

Figure 6.10c: As the petals are lost the seedheads are left exposed, and gradually mature to form little balls whose red prickles are easily picked up by passing animals. This process thus aids seed dispersal.

Wood avens are also known as herb bennet and cloveroot. The latter name has as its 'root' (pun intended) the flavour and smell of the plants' roots. If you have permission from the landowner, you can forage for and dry these, and use them as a flavouring similar to cloves. If you do collect any, respect for the plant and for your own health is essential. When harvesting roots, never take more than a third of the root, and take care to replant the plant such that it can continue thriving. When preparing wild food ensure your identification skills are excellent and you are not misidentifying the plants you consume. A good way to help ensure this is to undertake dedicated foraging courses.

For further information on foraging courses in Scotland and on how wood avens can be utilised, please consult a good provider of such courses, such as Galloway Wild Foods.

Figure 6.11: The tunnel under the railway line leads onto a curving path that climbs gently to give access to St Mark's Park.

Your way back to St Mark's Park takes you through an intriguing tunnel along a curving path (Figure 6.11). On emerging from this you can either continue following the river back into the park, or branch right onto a delightful path that runs through a section of the community woodland (Figures 6.12a–12b). Allow yourself to wander here and be surprised by whatever happens to be 'in season'. There is something magical that happens when you visit a familiar plant and catch up on its 'news' (Figures 6.13a–13b).

Figure 6.13a: Many of us will have no trouble recognising the holly leaf. Perhaps because, as evergreens, hollies are ever-present through the year and therefore ever-present. We can probably also call to mind the red holly berries. But how many of us can call to mind holly flowers? This fine example was photographed on a holly tree in the community woodland a short distance from the football pitch.

Figures 6.12a–12b: The curving path leads you onto a delightful tree-lined path that will see you emerge beside a bridge across the Water of Leith. If you pay attention as this tree-lined path opens up before you, you may see a discreet path leading off to the right. In May, however, this path is well hidden by the flush of cow parsley that grows, flowers and attracts pollinators, then goes to seed.

Whichever path you follow, you will soon emerge onto the grassy area of St Mark's Park and see ahead of you the concrete path that runs from the bridge over the Water of Leith (to your left) to the football clubhouse (to your right). As you approach the clubhouse, you will see the exit out of the park onto Warriston Road. You have now made it back to the start of the walk.

Figure 6.13b: The flower of the garlic mustard pictured here has received a visitor. This little beauty is a hoverfly (Eupeodes luniger), who is migratory in nature. The males hover at height, and when we are walking through woodland we can see them hovering in sunlight, providing yet another reason for us to appreciate the way light filters through the canopy and contributes to life.

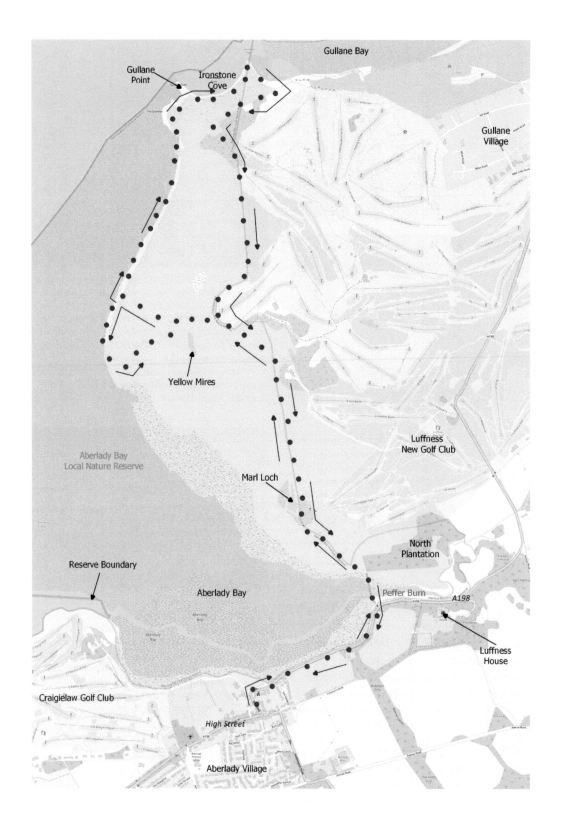

Gullane Point

Ironstone Cove

Gullane Bay

Gullane Village

Yellow Mires

Aberlady Bay
Local Nature Reserve

Luffness
New Golf Club

Marl Loch

North
Plantation

Reserve Boundary

Aberlady Bay

Peffer Burn

A198

Luffness
House

Craigielaw Golf Club

High Street

Aberlady Village

Walk 7

Aberlady Bay
Local Nature Reserve

This walk takes you out of Edinburgh to the East Lothian village of Aberlady and a veritable jewel of Scotland's natural history: the Aberlady Bay Local Nature Reserve. This reserve, established in 1952, was the UK's first such reserve.

It is a magical place to visit at any time of year, for it welcomes a rich variety of both breeding and overwintering birds as well as a host of life evolved for and appreciative of the habitats that the reserve protects and nurtures.

This walk's highlights include:

- An opportunity to cross Aberlady Bay (Figure 7.1a) and explore one of the best nature reserves in southern Scotland.
- In the autumn, the sight of as many as 30,000 pink-footed geese visiting from Iceland to roost and feed before moving on again.
- The many birds, including curlew, redshank, oystercatcher and shelduck, attracted to the intertidal zone to feed.

- A wonderfully rich variety of breeding birds, including whinchat, stonechat, wheatear, whitethroat and reed bunting.
- The uplifting song of a healthy population of skylark, who are protected from disturbance by dogs and are thus able to flourish on the reserve.
- An opportunity to explore sand dunes and the biodiversity supported there.
- A delightful stretch of beach with views back to Edinburgh and across the Firth of Forth (Figure 7.1b).

⏱ Summary

This walk starts in the village of Aberlady and follows the A198 out of the village in the direction of Gullane. This section along the road follows a wide pavement and provides an opportunity to scan the estuary and salt marshes between the village and the reserve car park. At the car park, cross the estuary to gain access to the reserve; the walk then follows the main path past the Marl Loch, to reach the sand dunes above the beach. At this point, your walk loops round to the left, exploring a stretch of Gullane Sands before

Figure 7.1a: The footbridge across Aberlady Bay provides you with an opportunity to cross over the estuary and observe the birdlife drawn in to feed on the mudflats exposed as the tide ebbs.

picking up a path that loops back into the sand dunes. You could then take a further loop by following the beach towards Gullane before cutting inland to explore the dunes. This leads you to the main path skirting the edge of Gullane Golf Course. Follow this path back to the Marl Loch, picking up your outbound route to return to the start.

🏛 History

Today, both breeding and overwintering birds know Aberlady as a place of sanctuary. So it is perhaps hard to imagine that it was only in 1952 that this, Britain's first Local National Reserve (LNR), was declared, in response to the indiscriminate shooting of wildfowl. An account of the tensions that arose between waterfowlers and conservationists, marking the creation of this reserve, is provided at the end of this chapter.

An LNR is designated by a local authority as a way of protecting a specific area of land because of its special natural and educational value. In Aberlady's case, the reserve is managed by East Lothian Council, whose reserve managers do a fantastic job of caring for this special place. One such manager was Russell

Nisbet who, writing in *Scottish Birds* in 1979, provides a delightful account of what it was like to birdwatch at Aberlady.

In October I have experienced the best migration movements of all. One windy morning I was walking past the Marl Loch when a flock of Redwings flew low overhead, shortly followed by another flock. I noted the numbers, and was about to put my notebook away when a third and fourth large flock of between 80 and 100 each flew past. I noted flock after flock coming in at buckthorn height, and within about an hour 4,675 Redwings had flown over my head. Over 200 Song Thrushes came in with them, as well as small flocks of Bramblings. In calm weather I have watched flocks of Redwings passing over almost out of sight. The Fieldfares tend to come later and not quite in the same numbers. Over 60 Siskins, over 50 Snow Buntings and occasional Crossbills and Waxwings have been seen on a single day. This is the time too for small parties of Barnacles to be seen passing Gullane Point. October is Great Grey Shrike time, and the small hawthorn bushes spread

Figure 7.1b: Looking across Aberlady Bay from the east. The water glints, and in the distance the silhouettes of the Pentland Hills and Arthur's Seat can clearly be made out. In the foreground, two skylarks can be seen hovering; a little further back, a roe deer stands on the tideline, looking out across the bay.

out over the wet grassland make ideal perches. In November the finch and thrush movements continue, and the geese have by then reached their peak of around 6,000.

Nisbett, 1979, pp.230–231

Russell's account provides a real flavour of why this place is so very special, not just to those who have been privileged to work as the warden here but also all those who visit and make the effort to appreciate this reserve.

Today, this reserve is part of a much larger SSSI, and continues to host a remarkable variety of birds.

🍃 Habitats

Aberlady offers a remarkable range of habitats, most notably sand dunes, saltmarsh, the mudflats of the tidal zone of the estuary, a freshwater loch and burn, buckthorn spinneys, scrub, small areas of woodland, grassland, a sewage works – and of course the neighbouring golf course.

🚆 Transport links

This walk is well served by the 124/X24 bus route running from Edinburgh to North Berwick. This bus stops on the coastal road as it leaves Aberlady for Gullane, providing remarkably good access to the reserve: https://www.lothianbuses.com/timetable/?service_name=124

☕ Refreshments

Aberlady offers a number of excellent locations for refreshments, including Ducks, and the Old Bakehouse Tea Room.

▌ References and further reading

Jones L., Garbutt A., Angus S. and others. (2011) 'Coastal margins' (Chapter 11). In: *UK National Ecosystem Assessment.*
Understanding nature's value to society. Technical Report. Cambridge, UNEP-WCMC, 411–457.

Nisbett, R. G. (1979.). 'Birdwatching at Aberlady Bay Nature Reserve'. *Scottish Birds 10 (6)*, pp.229–233.

Tranter, N. (1981). *Nigen Tranter's Scotland.* Harmondsworth, England: Penguin Books.

🚏 Directions

1 Aberlady village to Aberlady Local Nature Reserve entrance

The road out of Aberlady makes a right-angle bend as it leaves the village, providing you with your first view of the bay. The grassy area has a well-situated bench that can be worth stopping at in order to scan the estuary and get a sense for who is around (Figure 7.2a).

You may want to sit a while with your eyes closed; allowing yourself to direct your attention ahead of you to the estuary, then out to your left, before directing your attention to the sounds behind you and finally off to your right, can help you settle and attune yourself.

Figure 7.2a: The shoreline can easily be scanned with binoculars, and will often turn up curlew and redshank. Seeing them side by side like this provides a valuable opportunity to compare size, silhouette, beak shape and other useful features that can be hard to pick up otherwise. You can then integrate this awareness into how you pay attention to waders.

Figure 7.2b: At low tide it is possible to see the bed of the Peffer Burn as it snakes out into the Firth of Forth. Many are the times when I see cruise ships out in the estuary, and feel perfectly happy to be sharing a little peace and quiet instead, with the birds of Aberlady.

Figure 7.2c: In autumn as many as 30,000 pink-footed geese arrive from Iceland to roost and feed in the bay. Their calls, whether out in the bay or as they fly overhead in wave after wave of V-formations, are a quite magical phenomenon to savour here.

Figure 7.3a: Male teal; teal, our smallest duck, are a delight to observe. Their plumage is an endless series of surprises, from the yellow patch on the side of the lower abdomen to the bright green panel on the wing, which itself is exquisite when it is revealed and catches the light. Here a breeding pair are dabbling together in the shallow waters, using their bills to sift small seeds and other food items from the water.

Figure 7.3b: This carrion crow is turning and tossing strands of bladder wrack in anticipation that food will sooner or later be uncovered. The crow's strong, prehensile bill is well suited to this activity.

The estuary in front of you is likely to host curlew, redshank and oystercatcher, whose calls are very distinctive and worth learning. Behind you on the grass you may hear starlings flocking to feed, although they too may venture onto the intertidal zone.

With practice, you will become aware of the distance over which sounds travel and how sounds orchestrate themselves and who might be conducting. The soundscape will vary depending on where the tide is sitting (Figure 7.2b) and by the seasons (Figure 7.2c).

Follow the pavement to the bridge that crosses the burn and provides access to the reserve. As you approach the car park beside the bridge it can be worth scanning the pools of brackish water; if you are lucky, you may be treated to the sight of a kingfisher hovering above one of the pools before diving for fish.

A more dependable sight will be the birds gathering on the water and/or mud below the bridge. These can include shelduck, curlew (see Special Feature), teal (Figure 7.3a) and carrion crow (Figure 7.3b). The bridge provides you with an opportunity to study

how different species exploit the food sources available to them, and how they call on their intelligence and sensory powers to do so. A greater contrast between the dabbling bill of the teal and the long, curved probing beak of the curlew is hard to imagine.

If you are lucky enough to see and hear teal in flight, you may pick out the musical bell-like tinkle that rings out and, together with their rapid wing beat, helps identify them in flight.

Teal are much sought by waterfowlers, and it is sobering to realise that according to the British Trust for Ornithology 97 per cent of the ringing returns are from birds that have been shot. Waterfowlers refer to this diminutive duck as the 'half bird'. In reality, they are closer to a third to a quarter of the weight of a mallard. Try to let your eyes learn to pick out this size difference, for it will help you recognise teal at a distance. Were it not for the heavy toll of waterfowlers on this bird, they might hope to live for over 18 years; indeed, the longevity record stands for a bird ringed in Essex in 1970 and recovered in 1988 – that is 18 years, 20 days later.

★ Special Feature – the curlew

Figure 7.4a: Whether captured as a reflection in the water or seen against the sun that sets the bay a-sparkle, the superior size, long neck and slender downward-curving bill of the curlew marks them out from other waders.

Even at a distance the silhouette of the curlew, whether stalking the shallows or in flight, is almost always instantly recognisable. Look at the gentle sweep of the throat that levels as it meets the beak, which then plunges in a delicate curve (Figure 7.4a).

The name 'curlew', or 'courlis' in French, is onomato-poeic, capturing something of the bird's call in the same way that the calls of the cuckoo and chiffchaff are reflected in their names.

Where the curlew is concerned, however, the name only hints at the magical haunting call of these birds and the manner by which they can evoke other-world-ly feelings. Scotland's national bard, Robbie Burns, wrote that he had never heard the call 'without feeling an elevation of the soul'. More recently, Ted Hughes has

Figure 7.4b: This curlew's bill is feeling for invertebrates deep under the mud. The bundle of sensory receptors at the bulbous tip of the bill allows the curlew to recognise worms and other food items, which can then be artfully seized and dextrously drawn from their tunnels to be eaten.

Figure 7.4c: This curlew has a small worm clasped in their bill. In pondering how this catch was achieved, it is worth noting the slight bulge at the terminal end of the bill. This is often termed a 'bill tip organ', and it is rich in sensory receptors that pick up vibrations and pressure cues, allowing its owner to detect invertebrates deep in the mud, then catch them.

captured something of their essence, declaiming them as 'wet-footed gods of the horizons', who 'in April hang their harps over the misty valleys'.

Where once the curlew provided an essential contribution to the orchestral performances that hold up the heavens over estuaries in winter and their upland breeding grounds in summer, there is now no guarantee that our descendants will hear this magic. The curlew, sadly, is now in peril here in the UK; between 1995 and 2012 the breeding populations declined by 55 per cent in Scotland, and 30 per cent in England. In Wales between 1993 and 2006 a decline of 81 per cent was seen, whilst in Northern Ireland between 1985–87 and 2013 a decline of 82 per cent was recorded. This is tragic, given the international importance of the UK breeding population, which makes up between 19 and 27 per cent of the global population.

So I invite you, on visiting Aberlady, to pay attention to the curlew and to contemplate the spectre of a Silent Spring devoid of their and other birds' calls. In addition to listening attentively to their calls, I invite you to watch them feeding and to marvel at the pure genius of these birds as they use their bills to probe deep into the mud in search of food (Figure 7.4b).

*Figure 7.4d: The low-angled autumn sun dances off the curlew's beak, eye and plumage, and causes the red of marsh samphire (*Salicornia europaea*) to blaze. Also known as common glasswort, samphire is, like the curlew, to be sought out and appreciated when exploring the salt marshes with your binoculars.*

2 Aberlady LNR entrance to the Marl Loch

After crossing the bridge, follow the obvious path all the way to the Marl Loch. The path will be flanked at one point by a dense spinney of sea buckthorn. As you emerge from this, you will see the Marl Loch appear on your left-hand side.

The loch can be a great place to settle down and spend some slow time. There is always something to see, and you might be treated to the sight of a heron stalking the shallows or flying low over the reeds. Flapping languorously to gain height above the reed beds, the heron's black primaries and secondaries become evident as, with wings unfolded, they are no longer tucked away, hidden under the grey coverts.

In summer, the water surface is kissed by swallows and house martins sipping water on the wind. Your eyes may pick out moorhen and little grebe (Figures 7.5a–5b) among the reeds. There are other delights too, including flag irises, damselfly and dragonflies. You may want to pay attention to their behaviour as

Figure 7.5b: Partially submerged, this individual has periscoped up to look around before diving again. The still, vegetated waters of the loch are well suited as a habitat for this, the smallest British grebe.

Figure 7.5a: The little grebe is a secretive bird, well adapted to diving and fishing among the reeds. A certain amount of patience is required to observe them, for they are quick to dive and are constantly moving, rarely breaking out of cover and onto open water. It can be particularly rewarding to watch a pair of little grebes with their young, helping them explore the reedbeds and teaching them to fish.

they hunt for small insects around the loch, and to their breeding displays and mating habits. After mating (Figure 7.6), the female will devote her time to finding a suitable site to lay her eggs in, hovering over the water as she does so. Some eggs are laid inside the tissues of plants, others in the water. During this period, the male is likely to hang around, guarding the female from rival males.

Figure 7.6: These mating blue-tailed damselflies are fascinating to try to make sense of. Can you work out whose tail is where, and who the male might be? The formation thus achieved during mating is called the 'wheel' or 'heart', for when viewed from the right angle it is heart-shaped. The male initiates the shape by grasping the female at the back of her head, using a set of claspers at the end of his abdomen; thus secured the pair can fly around together in tandem. If the female is sexually receptive, she lifts up her own abdomen to make contact with the male's secondary genitalia, allowing sperm to be transferred.

3 The Marl Loch to the dunes

From the loch, follow the main path as it wends its way across the Yellow Mires towards the dunes that rise up, blocking any view of the beach beyond. This whole area lies on an old cockle bed, which serves as a rich source of calcium, so you will see evidence of plenty of crustacea (snails) on the vegetation.

As you pass the sea buckthorn in winter and early spring, it is worth looking out for birds feeding on the nutritious orange berries, which represent a veritable pantry of delights during this sparser time of year (Figures 7.7a–7b). You may also see and hear herring gulls raucously calling from behind these bushes, and wonder what they are up to. The answer is to be found in what lies behind these mature bushes, for hidden from view is Aberlady's sewage plant – and it is the plant, not the buckthorn, that attracts the gulls!

Some 750 metres or so beyond the Marl Loch, the path meets a grassy track. Ignore the track heading straight ahead and turn left onto the track where a sign indicates 'footpath'. This will take you through to impressive network of sand dunes whose colonisation by plants follows a natural process termed 'dune plant succession', in which the youngest dunes are colonised by 'pioneer species'. With increasing distance from the sea, there is a corresponding increase both in the plant cover and in the number of species contributing to that cover. This reflects the increased availability of moisture, humus and other nutrients, and the development of soil. The shrubs and oak woodland that should normally be found on the oldest, stable dunes further inland are largely absent at Aberlady, as they have largely been removed to make way for the golf course. Further details about dune ecology can be found on the CEH website: https://www.ceh.ac.uk/our-science/projects/sand-dunes

Figures 7.7a–7b: In winter the berries of the sea buckthorn attract a steady stream of diners, including the resident carrion crow and a handsome visiting thrush from Scandinavia: the fieldfare. The blue-grey head of this large thrush is a reliable distinguishing feature. The same colour can also be seen on the bird's rump when flying away from you. These social birds typically travel in flocks of up to 200 individuals and may be seen with redwing, so do scan through the buckthorn to see who else has joined the feast.

Figures 7.8a–8b: Many a wonderful moment can be spent watching and being watched by the rabbits who have colonised the dunes. Take up a discreet position near a rabbit run, away from the main path. If you are lucky you will see them appear, making good use of the cover provided by the marram grass that helps stabilise the sand dunes.

The highest dune ahead of you forms an impressive ridge that reaches between 4 and 5 metres in height. The hollows between the ridges of sand dunes, termed 'slacks', are a great place to watch rabbits (Figures 7.8a–8b) and other wildlife including, in summer, two particularly delightful migrant visitors: the wheatear and skylark (see the special feature).

You may want to wander off the path, lie down, close your eyes and sink into this space. Allow yourself to smell the sand, the marram grass and the salt in the air. Allow yourself to listen to the birdsong, and marvel at the speck in the sky whose song falls like a golden shower.

★ Special Feature – the skylark

Figure 7.9a: The skylark, a ground-nesting bird, requires open ground to avoid predators. They prefer vegetation 20–50 centimetres high and sufficiently open to allow them easy access to the ground. The dunes at Aberlady provide this in abundance.

So much inspiration can be found in nature and, for George Meredith (1828-1909), author of one of the English language's great poems, 'The Lark Ascending', such inspiration owes much to the exquisite aerial display and musical prowess of the skylark. Before heading out, or perhaps on returning, you might want to read the 120 lines of the poem and see which resonate most exquisitely. Here is a taster, one of my own favourite passages:

As up he wings the spiral stair,
A song light, and pierces air
With fountain ardour, fountain play,
To reach the shining tops of day,
And drink in everything discern'd
An ecstasy to music turn'd
Impell'd by what his happy bill

Disperses; drinking, showering still,
Unthinking save that he may give
His voice the outlet there to live
Renew'd in endless notes of glee,
So thirsty of his voice is he,
For all to hear and all to know
That he is joy, awake, aglow.

The whole poem is available at: https://www.poemhunter.com/poem/the-lark-ascending/

And if that tribute to the skylark seems to capture something of the essence of the skylark, you may find the musical work by Vaughan Williams of the same name equally uplifting. The links should take you to a performance of this great work by the violinist Janine Jahnsen (https://www.youtube.com/watch?v=2XT9KLu86EE), and to one by Nigel Kennedy (https://www.youtube.com/watch?v=yU-1zqUo80U).

In short, skylarks gift us one of THE sounds of summer, and we should be deeply concerned at their plight. Why so? Well, because their decline, since it was first identified in the 1970s, has continued at an alarming rate as is clearly shown in the graph, from the BTO/JNCC BirdTrends Report, reproduced here.

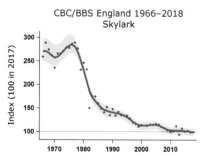

CBC/BBS England 1966–2018
Skylark

Between 1970 and 2001 the UK population of skylarks fell by some 54 per cent. A similar trend has been seen across the range of the Eurasian skylark (*Alauda arvensis*) and both internationally and here in the UK the skylark has consistently made the Red List. This fall has been attributed to the intensification of grassland management and to the widespread switch from spring to winter cereals.

You can read more about this by following the links below: https://tinyurl.com/2p95434e, https://tinyurl.com/bdfmsmp2.

The tragic crash in skylark numbers across British farmland has made the bird emblematic of the cause that is the recovery of the farmland environment. The silencing of this wonderful voice is telling us something of crucial importance about the way farmland in this country has been managed to the detriment of biodiversity. The good news here at Aberlady, however, is that the dunes and the roughs around the golf course offer excellent habitat for skylarks, meeting many of their essential needs.

Figures 7.9b–9c: The skylarks appreciate the sand dunes of Aberlady in many ways. The wide-open spaces provide them with an ideal habitat over which to sing and to establish their breeding territories. At Aberlady they are also free from the menace of dogs, who pose a significant threat to ground-nesting birds. The sand also provides them with opportunities to meet another essential need – the need to bathe: not in water but in sand. Should you see a skylark hunkering down in the sand, stop a while and watch them as they undertake their ablutions, making use of the sand to remove lice and other irritants.

Figure 7.9d: Often the skylark's form can barely be picked out against the heavens as they attain heights of 50 metres or more – sometimes as much as 200 metres – above the ground. There they hang and sing for an average of about two minutes, although song flights have been recorded to extend to 30 minutes. One of the delights here in the dunes is to see them ascend from the ground and gain height, wings and tail all a-tremor.

Figures 7.10a–10b: The sand martins keep up a busy schedule of visits to their nest sites as they keep their young supplied with insects.

4 The dunes to the beach

To reach the beach, follow any one of a number of paths that allow you to pass over the large sand dunes colonised with the marram grass that can be a pleasure to watch as it dances in the wind. In summer, as you pass over this area look out for sand martins, who can often be seen flying low over the dunes and surrounding beach. Where the roots of the marram grass have sufficiently stabilised the dunes, the martins are able to excavate their nesting tunnels. Every year they return to nest along this bit of coastline, but the shifting nature of the dunes means that these sites change. Once you have located one, though,

it can be very rewarding to sit at a respectful distance and watch the birds as they fly to and from their nest sites (Figures 7.10a–10d).

On the beach, you may wish to explore the tideline and marvel at the number of razor shells that are to be found on this piece of coastline. At low tide, the remains of two miniature submarines can be seen and inspected (Figure 7.11). These lie approximately three quarters of a mile out across the sands and it will take you 15 minutes to reach them. So, if planning to walk out to them, you are advised to check the tide times:

https://www.bbc.co.uk/weather/ coast-and-sea/tide-tables/7/223

Figures 7.10c–10d: Sand martins in flight can be a joy to watch, such is their playfulness and acrobatic prowess.

Figure 7.11: The wreck of one of the two midget submarines littering the mouth of Aberlady Bay can be visited at low tide. These tiny submarines were only about 16 metres long and, amazingly, had a crew of four. In September 1943 they were employed in a daring raid on the German battleship Tirpitz in a Norwegian fjord. The two submarines you see here were used as part of a bombing exercise in May 1946 to determine whether their armour could be pierced by shells dropped from Spitfires and Mosquitoes. Their wreckage has clearly never been cleared up, for the circular economy championed by the likes of Ellen MacArthur (https://www.ellenmacarthurfoundation.org) has not yet emerged. As such this wreckage will continue to sit there, partly sunk into the sands.

You may want to walk a small loop heading up the coast looking for a path that heads back inland and swings back to regain the foot of the dunes. As you walk the tideline, it can be fascinating to see what the receding sea has deposited and who else has passed by (Figure 7.12).

In summer the stretch back through the slacks here can be a great place to look out for wheatear. Unlike the skylark and meadow pipit, who may not migrate away from our shores but move instead to lower altitudes and southwards, the wheatear is a true migratory species. They overwinter in a broad belt across Africa, from Senegal in the west to Kenya in the east. This stretch also boasts several beautiful willow trees (Figure 7.13) that can be appreciated in every season.

Figure 7.12: The tideline is a remarkable place, a veritable treasure trove of flotsam and jetsam and, of course food. The tracks in the sand here are those of a carrion crow. This species can often be seen foraging for food among the seaweed that usually populates the tideline. Here though, a large quantity of beechmast and twigs have been washed down from some distant woodland upstream.

Figure 7.13: Watching buds bursting open is one of the joys of spring.

5 Along the beach

If you want to prolong your walk, you can delay the return back through the reserve, and walk northwards along the beach to reach the headland known as Gullane Point. As you walk along the beach, look out for sanderling foraging and running along the tideline (Figures 7.14a–14c). Looking beyond the tideline and out to sea, it is always worth keeping a weather eye out for gannets and terns diving. Try to spot them as they locate fish, hover and prepare to dive. If you manage to get them in your binoculars before they initiate the dive, you can watch the whole spectacle. It beats watching platform diving any time.

6 Returning to Aberlady

Whether you walk the beach or not, your return path will see you retrace your path back to the Marl Loch and onwards back to the footbridge over the Peffer Burn.

If not walking the beach, pick up the path at the back of the dunes that you came in on and retrace your steps.

If walking the beach: on reaching Gullane Point, pick up one of the multiple paths that bear gently uphill to reach the main track (NT 463 829) that heads south-east initially and then south, to rejoin the track you came in

Figures 7.14a–14b: The sanderling is a bird whose short stature means it exploits the habitats and food sources that are revealed as the tide descends. Here the exposed shellfish are investigated as a potential tasty snack.

Figure 7.14c: One of the joys of walking along the pristine beaches of the East Lothian coast is watching sanderlings sprint along the tideline as they follow the waves in and out, taking care to stay out of the surf whilst ensuring they can lay claim to the food served up or uncovered by the sea. Their feeding ground is distinct from that of waders with longer legs – watch them carefully and you will start to get a feel for the ecological niche they have evolved to occupy.

Figure 7.15: From the path, a view opens up across the Aberlady LNR. In the foreground the anti-tank defences are clearly visible, and if you are good at picking out silhouettes you may just make out a roe deer to the right of the tree in the centre of the image.

on. Follow this track to regain the footbridge over the river and your starting point.

As you do so, you will see below an impressive arrangement of anti-tank defences. This can be a great place to look out for deer (Figure 7.15). The tank defences can be worth wandering through and can be a great place to observe skylark and other Aberlady specialties (Figures 7.16a–16b). Keep your ear out for other surprises, for this area can be a good place to see sedge warbler (Figure 7.17a), stonechat (Figure 7.17b), linnet, reed buntings and some wonderful butterflies (Figures 7.18a–18b). Further opportunities to observe deer abound, so do keep your eyes peeled (Figure 7.19).

Figures 7.16a–16b: Wandering down and through the anti-tank defences can yield some nice surprises, including this view of a skylark on top of a clump of succulents and, in 7.16b, sunbathing on the warm concrete. Note the distinct crest on the top of the head in the image above.

Figures 7.16c–16d: Among the dunes and anti-tank defences, viper's bugloss (Echium vulgare) appears to thrive, and can be seen in flower between May and September. The spotted stems may account for the reference to a snake in this flower's name. The flowers themselves are popular with a variety of insects, including buff-tailed and red-tailed bumblebees, and large skipper and painted lady butterflies.

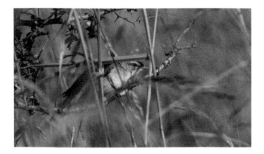

Figure 7.17a: As you walk back along the track with the anti-tank defences below you and the golf course to your left, listen out for sedge warblers singing from deep within the vegetation. If you are lucky enough to see them, the prominent white supercilium is quite distinctive.

Figures 7.17b–17c: Some birds are just challenging to identify. This is particularly so when the young have fledged and left the nest. These juveniles can really confuse things, and so it is worth picking up clues, including behavioural traits. If the young appear to be calling for food, it can also be worth hanging around to see if the parents return to feed these young. In the above image a young stonechat is showing a flash of the characteristic white wing panel. There is, however, no sign of a collar yet.

Figures 7.18a–18b: The small pearl-bordered fritillary (Boloria selene) is an exquisitely coloured and patterned butterfly who likes to take nectar from brambles and thistles. Close examination of the patterning on this individual's wings reveal two heart shapes, can you find them. It can be a real challenge to identify butterflies in the field and it is worth photographing both the under and upper wing as this can help with identification.

Figure 7.19: This walk can be a great opportunity to spot roe deer and, with practice, your eyes will get better at picking out their white rumps and their rounded ears. When they turn to look at you, you will also get a hint of a white moustache. Quite what they make of cruise ships coming up the Forth is anyone's guess!

★ Special Feature – a look back at the historical conflict between wildfowlers and ornithologists

To better appreciate the tension that surrounded wildfowling at Aberlady, it is helpful to cite the author and Aberlady resident Nigel Tranter, who founded the East Lothian Wildfowler's Association and coordinated the opposition to the creation of the reserve. In his book, *Nigel Tranter's Scotland*, (1981) he tells of how he came to settle in Aberlady:

> *Oddly enough it was the ducks which brought me to East Lothian – wild ducks. ... In those days I was a keen shooting man, and Aberlady Bay is a great place for wild ducks and wild geese, its fifteen-hundred acres of mudflats, sandbars, saltmarsh and dune country the haunt of wildfowl and waders innumerable. (1981, p.19).*

To his mind, most wildfowlers are naturalists too, although he does not define the term – and certainly not in terms of appreciating the extent to which humans have decimated the natural world and left nature with few refuges. Tranter's primary argument centred around the status of the foreshore, which in Scotland is public property held in trust by the Crown, whereas in most of England it is Crown property. Tranter and two other wildfowlers were charged with breaking the new byelaw that prohibited the shooting of ducks and geese. They initially won their case, only for this decision to be overturned by the High Court. The byelaws were thus established, although 'the Secretary of State for Scotland ... added a clause to the effect that duck could continue to be shot but only by permit granted by the Nature Reserve Committee'. This led Tranter to join the committee and contribute to the issuing of some 25 permits annually.

All this provides some indication of the significance of affording Aberlady Bay its protected status. The significance of this sanctuary, when so much of our native wildlife is under immense pressure, should not be underestimated. And if you find yourself relaxing and enjoying the peace of the reserve, it is worth asking yourself whether the wildlife might feel something similar.

Walk 8

Hewan Bank, Roslin Glen and Roslin Castle

This walk takes you out of Edinburgh to explore the River North Esk between Springfield Mill and Roslin Castle, returning via the old railway line and Bilston Wood.

This walk's highlights include:

- An opportunity to explore the ancient, semi-natural, undisturbed and tranquil deciduous woodland that thrives on the banks of the North Esk where it runs through Roslin Glen.
- An opportunity to encounter and marvel at woodland fungi as they work to break down dead wood and complete the cycle of life.
- The rich birdlife of the wooded valley, including green and great spotted woodpeckers, jays, buzzards and goldcrests among some 60 recorded breeding bird species.
- An opportunity to plumb the depths of the impressive gorge that cradles the North Esk and marvel at the fluency and patience of water; the river's persistence and artistry have, over a few thousand years, sculpted out this geological masterpiece.
- Views of the historic Roslin Castle and Rosslyn Chapel.

Summary

This walk starts from Polton Road, near Springfield Mill, where the road crosses the River North Esk in the village of Polton. It then follows the footpath along the west bank of the North Esk all the way to Roslin Castle, skirting the castle to pick up the Penicuik to Dalkeith railway line walk. Follow the line

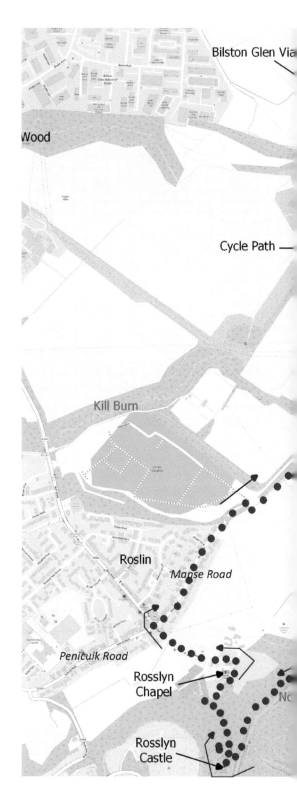

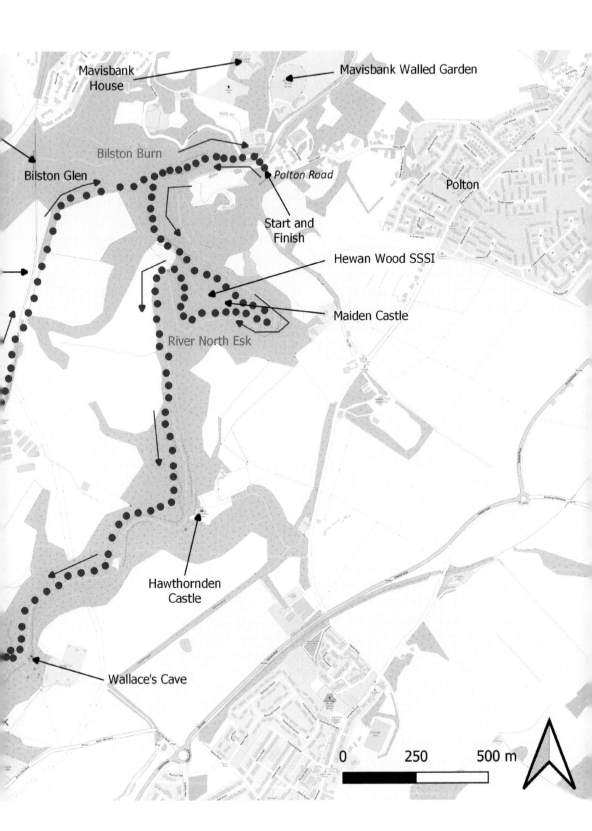

Mavisbank
House

Mavisbank Walled Garden

Bilston Burn

Polton Road

Polton

Bilston Glen

Start and
Finish

Hewan Wood SSSI

Maiden Castle

River North Esk

Hawthornden
Castle

Wallace's Cave

0   250   500 m

of the old railway for a short distance before picking up a path that runs along the edge of the Hewan Bank and back to Polton.

🏛 History

It is said that the name 'Roslin, often spelt Rosslyn,' derives from the Celtic *ross*, meaning 'stone', and *lynn*, meaning 'waterfall'. Together these elemental features sum up much of the character of this remarkable steep-sided glen. Roslin is also the sight of the Battle of Roslin, fought in February 1303, some 11 years before Bannockburn; it saw a Scottish army of some 8,000 soldiers win a series of three decisive victories against English forces number-ing close to 30,000. The English forces had been raised by Sir John Segrave, the English governor of Edinburgh Castle, who had been expecting to marry Lady Margaret Ramsay of Dalhousie, only to find that she had promised herself to Henry St Clair, Baron of Pentland and Roslin. Many of the English soldiers captured after each encounter were ruthlessly slain, and it is said that less than a tenth of the English force survived. This slaughter is im-mortalised in local names, including the Kill Burn and the Hewan (meaning 'hewing''). There is even a Shinbane field, so named because of the number of human shinbones encountered by the plough. Henry St Clair's ancestors subsequently built Rosslyn Chapel on the site of the old castle, and a new castle on the promontory above the river.

🍃 Habitats

This walk visits two Sites of Special Scientific Interest (SSSIs): the Hewan Bank and Roslin Glen itself. The Hewan Bank runs through the Hewan Wood, which offers a delightful mix of deciduous woodland. Roslin Glen is similarly wooded, and the valley floor cradles

a relatively fast-flowing river. Two urban areas are included and some of the latter half of the walk touches on farmland.

🚏 Transport links

This walk is well served by the number 31 bus running from Edinburgh to Poltonhall, with a journey time of some 30–35 minutes. This then leaves a short walk down Polton Bank to reach Springfield Mill. This service is operated by Lothian Buses: https://www.lothianbuses. com/timetable/?service_name=31

If cycling from Edinburgh, Quiet Route 61, which runs from Portobello to Roslin,[1] passes through Loanhead. There you can leave the cycle path and pick up Polton Road and Polton Bank, which drops you down into the Esk Valley.

Parking is available at Springfield Mill on the east bank of the river, just before the bridge.

☕ Refreshments

The village of Roslin offers a number of locations for refreshments, including the café at Rosslyn Chapel, although this does require you to pay the entrance fee. Other options include the Original Rosslyn Inn and Dolly's.

🪧 Directions

1 Springfield Mill to the Hewan Bank

This walk starts on the east bank of the North Esk, at Springfield Mill, before crossing Polton Bridge. This can be a great place to take in the views both up and down stream (Figures 8.1a–1b) and to marvel at the rehabilitation of the large industrial site that until very recently would greet those crossing the bridge (see the special feature).

On the far side of the bridge, keep left and follow the road, taking care to listen for

---

1   https://www.edinburgh.gov.uk/cycling-walking/places-can-go/7

Figure 8.1a: The North Esk flowing downstream towards the Forth, viewed from Polton Bridge. Take your time to imagine what stories the waters flowing beneath you might have to tell of their journey from the heights of the Pentlands above Carlops.

Figure 8.1b: Looking upstream from the bridge; the patchwork of autumn colours above the river is a balm to the eyes.

traffic. After crossing the North Esk, the road climbs via a series of bends to reach the village of Loanhead. A short distance beyond the bridge (NT 287 648), the walking route leaves the road, allowing you to pick up a delightful woodland trail that climbs high above the river.

Let your senses soak in the smells; in autumn and winter the musty smell of damp leaf litter can be quite captivating, whilst in spring the scent of wild garlic and few-flowered leek (Figures 8.2a–2c) will accompany you on your climb up the Hewan Bank.

★ Special Feature – Springfield Mill

Figure 8.2a: A carpet of few-flowered leek and wild garlic greets you on the Hewan Bank in spring. The presence of wild garlic, also known as ramsons, is a good indicator of undisturbed ancient woodland.

For those with a little time to spare, either at the start or the end of the walk, the site of the old paper mill, which used to stand on the flood plain that the river contours round in a graceful arc, is well worth visiting. The site has been rehabilitated as a wildlife sanctuary and as a place for people to enjoy.

The story of this project is itself worthy of a special feature.

The old papermill that once stood here is said to date back to 1742 and was one of two paper-mills at Polton and of a series of industrial mills locally that drew on the river for power. In return, these mills repaid the river with a legacy of pollution that we are only now setting to rights.

Springfield Mill closed in 1960 and was inherited by Midlothian District Council in 1975. Over the next quarter of a century the site became derelict, and in this state of abandonment nature started to reclaim the site. In 1999 the Springfield Mill Action Group formed to raise awareness of the site's value for wildlife, setting the scene for a collaborative project that allowed the site to be gradually restored. This work was completed in 2009, and today the site boasts a wildflower meadow, ponds and an area of woodland. The viewing platform overlooking the river provides a great view of the Hewan Bank with its mature woodland and colony of sand martins. In summer this can be a great place to watch the sand martins and other insectivores, including Daubenton's bats, out hunting for insects.

Figures 8.2b–2c: The flower heads of wild garlic (Allium ursinum) *are like a constellation of twinkling stars. When you move up close, you will be further rewarded with a powerful smell. Close your eyes and breathe it in to savour this seasonal treat, and take a few leaves home to flavour your supper (but be careful not to disturb the roots). During World War II onions were hard to come by, and your grandparents may have stories of how their generation foraged during that time of scarcity.*

🜛 Weblinks

A collection of images of the mill before it was demolished is available from: https://tinyurl.com/3r837sc2.

A timeline documenting the history of the site is included in the following excellent historical leaflet: https://tinyurl.com/2sv6as82.

Figure 8.3a: The path running along the top of the Hewan Bank is flanked by some fine old beech trees, and provides a breathtaking view down onto Bilston Burn and the North Esk.

2 The Hewan Bank

The path along the Hewan Bank provides a fantastic vantage point. The ground to either side falls away steeply. To your right the slopes plunge down to Bilston Burn, whilst to your left the slopes plunge down to the Esk (Figures 8.3a–3c).

The ground under your feet is composed of glacial deposits left behind during the last ice age. Immediately under your feet are the sediments of sand and gravel left behind by the meltwater flowing under the ice. Beneath these lie the older angular rocks that were broken up and left behind as the ice itself moved over the ground before the

Figure 8.3b: The Hewan Bank falls steeply on the left to the North Esk and is prone to landslips. The walkway constructed here provides walkers with a fantastic elevation that allows the grandeur of this site to be appreciated in all seasons.

Figure 8.3c: After the rain the bare branches of the trees that clothe the Hewan Bank as it plunges towards the Esk glisten where the sun catches the rain droplets as they hang beading, waiting to be shaken free. Such are the delights of walking immediately after a shower has passed through.

ice sheets receded; this deeper bed is known as till.

The rivers that shaped the landscape after the glaciers receded have cut through these sediments to produce the deep gorge you see today. The deposits that make up the Hewan Bank are vulnerable to landslides, the most significant of which may have been that of 9 December 1979. At 3.30 pm that day something like 100,000 tonnes of debris plunged down the bank in the direction of Springfield Mill. Such was the volume of the slide that the river was dammed and diverted into the mill, threatening the small housing estate beside the bridge.

How did this happen? It is helpful to consider the nature of the local geology and the weather. The glacial deposits were already known to be unstable, and the summer of 1979 had been marked by significant rainfall. At the time there was still a ruined cottage on the bank, and it is said that a visitor to the cottage reported that the floor of the cottage nearest the river had dropped by over a foot. The accumulation of glacial deposits on top of the bank were clearly moving. All that was needed was a further trigger, and this was

provided by the heavy rain that fell between 7 and 9 December.

The landslide was immense. The sand, mud, gravel, trees and associated debris, measuring up to 25 metres in depth, effectively dammed the river. The timely actions of the property manager at the mill, David Tuddenham, alerted people onsite and the council, and together they were able to break down a wall and temporarily return the river to its bed. The North Esk then cut a channel through the dam, further reducing the threat posed to the housing estate. Today you have to use your imagination to recreate where the cottage stood and the scene of that devastation.

3 The Hewan Bank to Maiden Castle

Follow the path until it meets a wide track that drops to your right, towards Bilston Burn. Bear left along the track. Listen out for mountain bikers and horse riders along this stretch. A short distance further on, a gate on your left takes you to the top of the landslip where a display panel provides information about the landslip that destroyed Hewan Cottage. The main path curves round to the right. A smaller path heads straight ahead to reach the promontory known as Maiden Castle, which is thought to have been the site of the Battle of Roslin.

4 Maiden Castle to view of Hawthornden Castle

The main path drops down towards the river, leaving behind the spur that leads to Maiden Castle. To your right an area of grassland, the Hewan Bog, opens up. This can be a good place to see buzzard. Listen out for their mewing call, and then try to spot them as they circle above the trees.

The path soon joins the river, and there is a delightful section off to your left beside a dead-end channel of water. In spring the

Figure 8.4a: The path along the Esk passes under a series of mature trees, including oak, Scots pine, beech, sycamore and larch. Further upstream, the Esk flows peacefully in a northerly direction, with many mature trees overshadowing the river and providing both shade and food, in the way of leaf litter, to sustain the river and river life.

ground here is carpeted with bluebells (see the special feature) and is well worth exploring.

The path continues along the west bank of the river, heading upstream. Pass through a swinging metal gate and continue along the riverbank, following a delightful path which passes under a series of ancient trees (Figure 8.4a). The North Esk flows straight and steadily almost south to north for some 800 metres. The waters creep peacefully under the branches, and it can be rewarding to pause a while and contemplate the waters as they flow by (Figure 8.4b) before continuing to explore a charming path through the woodland.

The path soon starts to climb, gaining height above the glen. Soon Hawthornden Castle, on the far side of the river, comes into view (Figure 8.5). It comprises a 15th-century ruin with an L-shaped 17th-century house attached. The poet Sir William Drummond of Hawthornden was born here, and it was he

Figure 8.4b (left): Looking back along the woodland path in spring sees the understorey carpeted with green growth as plants, including the great wood-rush (Luzula sylvatica) seen here, take advantage of the light that will be blocked by the canopy of leaves later in the year.

Figure 8.5: Viewed through the trees, from the west bank of the North Esk, Hawthornden Castle's stone catches the light on a sunny day.

who was responsible for the L-shaped extension, built in 1638. Hawthornden is famous, among other things, for the Hawthornden apple: a primrose yellow and lightly flushed pinky-red dual cooking and eating apple. First recorded in 1780, it was popular during Victorian times, but its popularity waned because although the tree is hardy the apples bruise easily. As a culinary apple, it is said to cook to a creamy, well-flavoured, brisk purée.

The rock beneath the castle is sandstone, and is riddled with caves, which are thought to date back to the Bronze Age and in the 18th and 19th centuries were much noted by visitors to the area. One such visitor was the Welsh naturalist, traveller and writer Thomas Pennant (1726–1798). He made two visits to Scotland, in 1769 and 1772, and his accounts of these tours made him arguably the best-known writer on Scotland, inspiring Dr Samuel Johnson and his companion, James Boswell, to undertake their tour of Scotland and the Western Isles. In Pennant's second tour of Scotland, he visited Hawthornden and found that: 'The vast mural fence, formed by the red precipices, the mixture of trees, the grotesque figure of many of the rocks, and the smooth sides of the Pentland Hills, appearing above the wild scenery, are more striking objects to the contemplative mind' than the caves. So your attention is indeed best prevented from straying across the river, and is better directed to the trees and cliffs, for there is much there to enthral the eye.

★ Special Feature – bluebells

Of all the many woodland delights that burst forth from the ground in spring, the common bluebell (*Hyacinthoides non-scripta*) is perhaps the most magical. It has long been associated with ancient woodland where its dominance of the understorey has made it an indicator species for such woodland. Its well-earnt reputation as one our best loved and most unmistakeable woodland flowers is highly deserved, for it possesses an incredible ability to transform woodland floors into a carpet of blue and green (Figure 8.6a), the nodding blue bells that festoon each flower stem contrasting with the vivid green of the long, narrow drooping leaf fronds.

How does this transformation arise? The soil of bluebell woods can contain literally millions of bulbs, which mean that these perennial flowers can overwinter safely underground. They spring forth before the trees overhead have developed a canopy of leaves, and this allows the deep green leaves of the bluebell to capture the energy of the sun. In order to do so, the bulbs must send forth shoots capable of pushing through a thick layer of leaf litter. The bulbs produce contractile roots that are able to draw the bulbs deeper into the earth where they can secure the water they need.

The bluebell's range extends from north-western Spain and Portugal, northwards through France, to Ireland, Britain and Holland. It is in the British Isles, however, where it appears to thrive, and it is estimated that between 25 and 50 per cent of all common bluebells occur here. British archers used to extract glue from the bulbs of bluebells, which contain muselage and inulin, using this to stick feathers to their arrows. Book binders similarly used bluebell glue to bind their books. Over the years, the number of threats to bluebells has increased; the loss of large swathes of woodland, coupled with heavy visitation and footfall to the few remaining bluebell woods, has been compounded by the threat of hybridisation.

Figure 8.6a: In April and May the floors of ancient woodland are transformed by the appearance of a carpet of common bluebells.

The threat of hybridisation

Hyacinthoides non-scripta is related to several other species of bluebell, including the paler-coloured Spanish bluebell (*Hyacinthoides hispanica*). These two species are thought to have separated some 8,000 years ago. They differ markedly, and are easy to tell apart; the common bluebell's flowers are darker and more heavily scented, and are distributed along a single side of the stem; it is this distribution that gives rise to the graceful arc of our bluebell's inflorescence (flower head). The bells of the Spanish bluebell, in contrast, hang on all sides of the upright flower stem.

In the UK, the Spanish bluebell's introduction threatens the common bluebell with hybridisation. The offspring are viable, and were this hybridisation to continue the remarkable sight of thousands of nodding, heavily scented bluebells, loaded with pollen, would be threatened. This is in turn a threat to humans, to pollinators and to many other woodland visitors, and a threat that should arguably alert us to the impact of plant introductions on ecosystems.

Protection

In the UK, under the Wildlife and Countryside Act (1981), landowners are prohibited from collecting for sale common bluebells on their land. It is also a criminal offence to remove the bulbs of wild common bluebells. In 1998 this legislation was reinforced, making any trade in wild common bluebell bulbs or seeds an offence punishable by fines of up to £5,000 per bulb! A reminder that the preservation of ancient woodland requires us to develop our awareness of the damage that exploitation causes. A reminder too, perhaps, that the value of bluebells lies in them enhancing their own surroundings rather than profits potentially generated by them.

Figure 8.6b: What would our ancestors feel and think if our senseless and thoughtless trampling destroyed the last remaining carpets of bluebells that still stretch from tree to tree. Our footprint on our woodland needs to be lightened and even eliminated ...

Why do bluebells need protection?

Bluebells are fragile flowers in many respects. If the soft green leaves, which capture the sun's energy, are trampled and damaged, the plant's ability to stock its energy reserves in the bulb is seriously compromised. The compaction of soil above their bulbs is another serious threat to bluebells, impacting on their viability. These impacts lead to wide carpeting sweeps becoming fragmented into patchy islands. For these reasons, it is essential that visitors to ancient woodland stick to the paths and do not wander onto and walk over the lush green carpet. By visitors sticking to the paths and respecting the green shoots, the sight of bluebell carpets can be preserved for the benefit of all (Figure 8.6b).

Figure 8.6c: Sometimes the bluebells spring up en masse; elsewhere they may be found growing with other plants, including bracken and greater stitchwort.

Figure 8.6d: The common bluebell's bells are distributed along a single side of the stem, which encourages the stem to arc and the bells to nod.

An appreciative exercise:

In seeking to develop your awareness and appreciation of the bluebell, I invite you to undertake the following sensory exercises:

- Observe the inflorescence carefully; a pair of binoculars or a magnifying glass can help with this. How many bells do you see on each head? Does this number vary? What is the largest number of bells you can see on any one head?
- Taking care not to damage the bluebells, sit down – lie back, even – and close your eyes. A tree trunk might be a suitable place to do this. Allow your breathing to draw the scent of the bluebells into your nose, and savour the aroma. What do you feel about this experience? What would it be like to lose this?

Figures 8.7a–7b: The cliff edge appears quite suddenly and is unguarded. Care is therefore needed when approaching it to take in the view. A clear path then climbs away from the cliff edge, passing through the trees.

Figure 8.8a: Look out for the splendid white flowers of the wood anemone (Anemone nemorosa). The number of perianth (petals and sepals) segments varies between five and nine. In this image, most of the flowers appear to have seven such segments.

Figure 8.8b: Wood sorrel is springing up among the moss on this fallen tree.

5 Hawthornden Castle to Roslin Castle

The path continues through rich woodland, and offers impressive views across the river gorge from the top of a rocky outcrop (Figures 8.7a–7b). Take care here, as there is a significant drop and the cliff edge is unguarded.

Further on there is the possibility of dropping down towards the river, but this path has been officially closed following a landslide, and you are not encouraged to take this as there is at least one fallen tree trunk to navigate, and a short, exposed drop.

The upper path leads to General Monck's Battery (NT 278 630), the site from which the general, in his role as Oliver Cromwell's commander-in-chief in Scotland, besieged Roslin Castle in 1650. The woodland path leading to the battery rewards you with a rich flora in spring, including wood anemone (Figure 8.8a), wood sorrel (Figure 8.8b), ramsons, bluebells and bilberry (Figures 8.8c–8d). Look out for shaggy ink cap too (Figure 8.8e). A little beyond the battery, the path is lined on its west side by a row of yews set atop a low stone terrace (Figure 8.9). This marks the path's passage through the remains of the gardens of a 19th-century villa, Rosebank House. This whole section of woodland is particularly

Figures 8.8c–8d: Perhaps more often thought of as a plant of heath and moorland, the bilberry (Vaccinium myrtillus) is also often found in woodland, as here in Roslin Glen. In late spring and early summer (April to May), the pink bell-shaped flowers appear, as seen here. Later in the year, the plant will bear the blue-black fruits that are known in Scotland as blaeberries.

Figure 8.8e: The shaggy ink cap mushroom (Coprinus comatus) is very edible when young. The hidden gills are white initially, turning pink and then black, as shown here. Within the space of a few hours the blackening ink caps disintegrate and the spores can be disseminated by the wind.

Figure 8.9: Old yews whose roots are engulfing the remains of the stone terrace marking the edge of the gardens of Rosebank House. According to the Ancient Yew Group, the average girth of the yews in an avenue of yews can be used to determine whether they should be considered 'ancient', 'veteran', or 'notable'.

Figure 8.10a: The archway at Roslin Castle, surrounded by a carpet of snowdrops in spring.

Figure 8.10b: The ruined towers and the bridge of Roslin Castle, with the renovated east range of the castle visible beyond the hedge.

rich and undisturbed; see the special feature on the Life and Death of Trees.

Follow the path as it drops back down towards the river and approaches the remains of Roslin Castle, curving round to pass under an impressive archway (Figure 8.10a). This impressive structure, dating back to the 14th century, stands precipitously above a loop of the river. As such it was well sited, for it was protected on three sides; on the fourth the promontory was breached, to further

protect the site. This gap was spanned by a drawbridge which, when the castle was rebuilt during the 16th century, was replaced with a stone bridge (Figure 8.10b).

Pass under the bridge, then turn right to climb steeply up to gain the wide pathway that crosses the bridge to Roslin Castle. The bridge offers a fine view of the glen and the ruins of the castle itself. The east range of the castle was renovated in the 1980s, and is now a holiday home.

★ Special Feature – the life and death of trees

Figure 8.11a: The path running along the North Esk bears ample evidence of the havoc wreaked by high winds. This image shows at least three broken trees; that to the bottom right has toppled down the slope towards the river, whilst others can be seen in various stages of decomposition beside the path.

One of the more interesting aspects of the woodland lining the edges of Roslin Glen is arguably the way that the natural cycle of tree growth, death and decomposition can be observed. The woodland consists of a rich thriving mix of sessile oak, wych elm, ash, Scot's pine, holly, sycamore, beech and larch, of all ages. Many of the trees, including the yews pictured in Figure 8.9, are centuries old, and will have fathered many generations of younger trees.

Whilst trees may be longer lived than humans, they are still subject to the cycle of life, for it is in dying and undergoing decomposition that nutrients are recycled and can give rise to new life.

In human culture, decomposition and decay have come to be viewed negatively. This represents a distortion for, as our Celtic ancestors would have realised, life is circular, not linear. Decomposition and growth form two halves of the whole; this is how natural ecosystems are constituted and sustained. All life must come to an end, and when it does the building blocks of life locked up in the plant and animal remains must be liberated. Failure to do so can only give rise to a shortage of nutrients and a reduction in new growth.

In order for the loop to be closed, trees must die and be broken down. And it is this that is in evidence within the glen. In addition to the shedding of leaves and the breaking of branches, the passage of storms coupled with the steep sides of the glen mean that there are many fallen trees (Figure 8.11a). Look out for them. Pay attention to how they have been laid low, and whether they are still alive or are slowly being broken down. Other trees may have succumbed to disease without falling. Standing dead wood helps sustain forest life, providing rich feeding ground for invertebrates and nest sites for woodpeckers, owls and other species favouring cavities. And yet humans have historically had a tendency to tidy up and remove this dead wood rather than leaving it to make its contribution. In nature, all contributions are important; it is our warped thinking that fails to recognise this. The contribution made by 'detritivores' is no different.

The decomposition of plant cellulose, and indeed all forms of organic matter, falls to a group of organisms known as detritivores. The detritivore community feed on dead and decaying matter, and collectively ensure its breakdown. This happens slowly, inexorably and largely out of sight, for most members of this community are small. Insects such as beetles and flies (and their larvae) collaborate with fungi, slime moulds, bacteria, woodlice, millipedes, earthworms, slugs and snails to transform the organic matter on the forest floor.

The fibres of woody plants are much tougher than those of herbaceous plants, so they take much longer to break down. Many species of fungi contribute to this, establishing themselves and growing in the dead wood (Figure 8.11b), feeding on the cellulose and lignin, and converting this into a softer tissue. They send out fungal hyphae that penetrate deep into the tree's tissues, facilitating this digestive breakdown and allowing bacteria and beetle larvae to join the party and do their bit. It is deeply humbling to recognise that even great oaks are recycled by grubs and mushrooms!

Figure 8.11b: Many species of fungi have evolved to break down the tough lignin and the more flexible cellulose fibres in dead wood. They do this by releasing enzymes that degrade and mineralise these fibres. Recent scientific work has revealed that there are far more species of fungi involved in this process than had previously been suspected. It has now become apparent that the fungi responsible for breaking down different tree species are specific to that species. This reflects the specialist nature of the trees and their fungi after co-existing together for millennia.

Figure 8.12a: Rosslyn Chapel viewed from the path to the south of the chapel. The path, passing to the right, allows you to walk round the chapel.

Figure 8.12b: Looking back along the hedge-lined lane towards Rosslyn Chapel.

6 Roslin Castle to Rosslyn Chapel and the village of Roslin

With your back to the castle and the bridge, head along the path towards the cemetery either side of the path. Look out for a small path on the right before the path meets the T-junction ahead of you. This path will allow you to walk round the side of the chapel and view its impressive architectural layout (Figure 8.12a). As you round the chapel, turn left and head along the road past the car park (Figure 8.12b). The hedge row to your right is a rich mix of four different species of trees: beech, hawthorn, holly and ivy. Continue, to reach the main road opposite the Original Roslin Inn, and the village of Roslin itself.

Figure 8.13: One of the surprises that can be encountered along the cycle path is the tree sparrow (Passer montanus). These are easily overlooked, and it is worth noticing the rich chestnut brown headcap, black cheek spot and white collar that distinguish them from the more familiar house sparrow. Tree sparrows are birds of farm and woodland, and have experienced a significant decline in recent years. They were listed as an IUCN Red Species of Conservation Concern after their breeding population crashed by 93 per cent between 1970 and 2008.

7 Roslin village to Polton

From the main road, turn right and follow Manse Road to the end and onto the cycle path. Look out for a gate on the right and a path (NT 276 636) that leads through to a quiet track that runs parallel to the cycle path. A section of the old railway line lies between these two paths, and is rewilding itself. The vegetation and the hedgerows along the track can play host to a range of woodland birds, including goldfinches and tree sparrows (Figure 8.13).

As you reach the farm buildings, turn left onto a bridge (NT 278 638) to cross the railway line and regain the cycle path. Turn right and follow the cycle track as it heads north. Look out for a track dropping down to the left. Follow this path as it bends right and passes under the cycle path (NT 280 643). If you miss the track, an opportunity comes up further on, to your right, to rejoin the track from the cycle path – but if you reach the viaduct over Bilston Glen you have gone too far and will need to retrace your steps.

The track you are now on diverges slightly from the cycle track as it plunges into Bilston Wood. This track can be followed all the way to the gate (NT 283 647) above the Hewan Bank, which you passed earlier. A rich stretch of mixed woodland, replete with birdlife, stretches down on your left to the burn below. It is worth marvelling at how the precipitous nature of these river glens has saved them from human exploitation. When mapped out across the country, these green arteries can be seen to provide wildlife corridors for all manner of species, even in urban areas.

Leaving the gate you passed earlier on your right, continue along a short section of sunken path until it bends to your left and starts dropping steeply towards Bilston Burn. At this bend, do not descend. Instead, turn right onto the path running along the top of the Hewan Bank, which you followed earlier. You can follow this all the way back to Polton and your starting point on the other side of Polton Bridge.

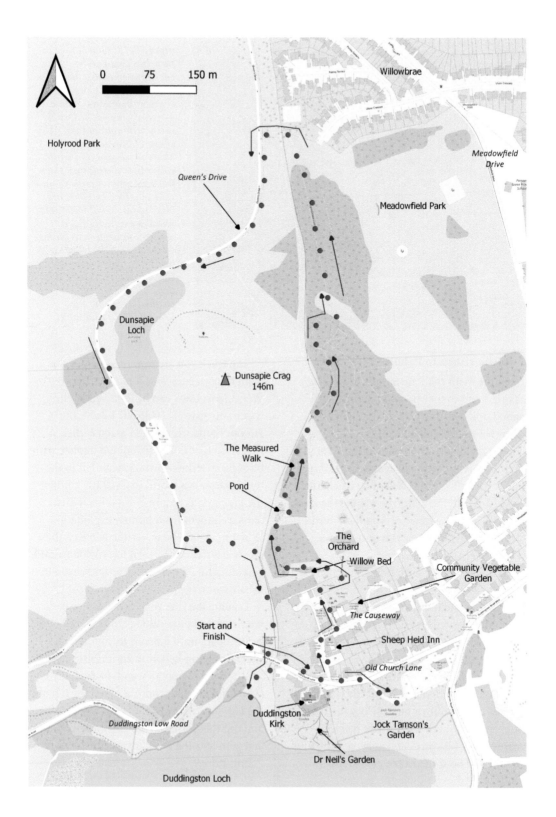

Holyrood Park

Queen's Drive

Willowbrae

Meadowfield Drive

Meadowfield Park

Dunsapie Loch

▲ Dunsapie Crag 146m

The Measured Walk

Pond

The Orchard

Willow Bed

Community Vegetable Garden

The Causeway

Start and Finish

Sheep Heid Inn

Old Church Lane

Duddingston Kirk

Jock Tamson's Garden

Duddingston Low Road

Dr Neil's Garden

Duddingston Loch

0   75   150 m

Walk 9

Duddingston Orchard, Meadowfield Park, Dunsapie and Duddingston Loch

This relatively short walk explores Duddingston village, the south-eastern corner of Holyrood Park, and neighbouring Meadowfield Park.

This walk's highlights include:

- An opportunity to explore the historic village of Duddingston and visit Dr Neil's Garden.
- A visit to Duddingston's community orchard with its collection of Scottish apple and pear trees.
- An opportunity to discover the willow bed and the remnants of old woodland linking the orchard with Meadowfield Park.
- The breeding mute swans of Dunsapie Loch, and the annual migration of toads who descend upon the loch to breed.
- The waterfowl of Duddingston Loch (Figure 9.1).

👣 Summary

The walk starts from the car park at the park gates a little beyond Duddingston Church. The route takes you back towards the church to visit Dr Neil's Garden before heading up to the Sheep Heid Inn and on to Duddingston's community garden and orchard, the Field, and then Meadowfield Park. After pass-

Figure 9.1: The shoreline beside the Boat House on Duddingston Loch is a great place from which to contemplate and watch the resident and visiting birdlife, including these two mute swans.

ing through the woodland running parallel with the edge of Holyrood Park, the route enters the park and heads over to Dunsappie Loch, and you regain your starting point by descending a long series of steps. I would suggest, however, that before completing the walk you spend some time exploring the northern shore of Duddingston Loch.

🏛 History

Duddingston is something of a hidden secret in many respects, for hints of its long history contribute to the unique character and quaint 'village feel' of this place. Malcolm IV of Scotland bequeathed the land hereabouts to the monks of Kelso Abbey in 1128, when Holyrood Abbey was founded. They subsequently feued[2] the estate to a Norman knight by the name of Dodin de Berwic. It has been suggested that the area then became known as Dodinestun, and that this may be one of the possible origins of the name Duddingston. At the same time, Duddingston is not an uncommon name, composed of the Old English words *dodda*, meaning 'enclosure' or 'farm', and *tun*, meaning 'town'. Another explanation offered is that the name has Gaelic origins and indicates a house on the sunny side of the hill. Certainly, the loch and village are a great place to enjoy the winter sun when its absence from the northern aspects of Edinburgh is felt quite strongly. Further aspects of Duddingston's history will be touched on in the walk directions.

🍃 Habitats

This walk explores a community garden, orchard and woodland, with several venerable trees of character along the margin. There then follows a stretch through an area of relatively young deciduous woodland, known as Meadowfield Park,

before entering Holyrood Park to pass by a small freshwater loch before descending back to the much larger freshwater loch of Duddingston.

🚍 Transport links

Duddingston village can be accessed on foot or bicycle via the Innocent Railway Line; on emerging from the railway tunnel, take the turning on the right and follow the path up to the Queen's Drive, which can then be followed into Duddingston. If travelling by bus, take the Lothian Buses route 42, which stops on Duddingston Road West opposite Holyrood High School.

☕ Refreshments

The Sheep Heid Inn is perfectly located at the start and end of the walk, and can be a great place to call in for coffee, a drink or even a meal. https://www.thesheepheidedinburgh.co.uk/

🪧 Directions

1 Duddingston Church to the Sheep Heid Inn

From the car park at the park gates, walk back towards Duddingston's 12th-century church. Built in or around 1124 on land in the hands of the abbot and monks of Kelso Abbey, the church can claim to be one of the oldest still in use in the east of Scotland.

The gatehouse you pass is much more recent, however – constructed in the early 19th century to allow elders of the church and relatives of the deceased to guard against body snatchers. The demand for bodies for anatomical dissection was such that for three weeks following a funeral, watch would be kept over the grave! The iron collar and chain beside the gatehouse was used during the 16th to 18th centuries and, it is said, shamed

---

2   Sold off, usually to be split into separate properties.

people into repentance for their wrongdoings. The adjacent block of stone, known as the 'loupin-on stane', was used by churchgoers as a mounting block.

You may wish to explore the churchyard or carry further along Old Church Lane to visit Dr Neil's Garden. Alternatively, visit them at the end of your walk. On exploring the churchyard, you may find yourself contemplating the oak doors of the church itself, on the north wall. The oak for these doors is local, sourced on the Duddingston Estate; this is noteworthy, given that you will encounter several old oak trees on this walk. The doorway was unveiled in 1922 and is dedicated to the fallen of World War I. The door itself was crafted by Mr John Hay, a local joiner, Justice of the Peace and elder of the kirk, who had lost three sons in the war.

From the church gate continue a short distance up the lane, before turning left into the Causeway (Figure 9.2). This is followed up to the Sheep Heid Inn, where the road bears round to the right. It is said that there has been an inn on this site since 1360, which would make the Sheep Heid the oldest pub in Edinburgh. The name may reflect the fact that Duddingston was where the sheep raised in Holyrood Park

Figure 9.2: The Causeway makes a left turn off Old Church Lane, immediately after the church, and heads down towards the inn.

were historically slaughtered before their meat was sent to Edinburgh's Flesh Market, in the old town; there being little demand for the heads, these were used by enterprising locals, who produced both a sheep's head broth and a singed sheep's head dish. An alternative explanation suggests that the name can be traced back to the gift of an ornate ram's head snuffbox from Scotland's King James VI.

2 The Sheep Heid Inn to Duddingston Community Garden and Orchard

From the inn, continue a short distance along the causeway, looking out for a gate on your left, between numbers 56 and 58, which provides access to the Community Garden and Orchard. This stone-flagged lane is known as the Pend.

As you move up the lane, note the old stone beds for cartwheels. Look out, too, for a small path on your right that leads to the community garden, which is tended by volunteer gardeners and contains a most exquisite collection of herbs, vegetables and other produce. A little further along the Pend is a large open grassy space that once housed a tennis court. At the top of the Pend, pass by the yew tree and gatepost, into a cobbled and bricked yard. This, stretching off to your right, leads up to the Field, with its orchard, herb-rich meadow and other habitats.

The area of land you are heading into is managed by the local community, who have established a charitable structure (a Scottish Charitable Incorporated Organisation) for the purpose. This represents a wonderful example of a community-building initiative that nurtures the interests of the whole. You can find out more about the ethos informing this collaborative project at: https://thefielddud-dingston.wordpress.com/

★ Special Feature – exploring Duddingston's Community Orchard

Figures 9.3a–3b: In spring, the apple and pear trees in the orchard are decked in white and yellow blossom. The local bees will move from one tree to the next, ensuring the pollination of the flowers and therefore the crop of apples that follows. The genes present in the apple pips will be a mix of both the mother apple and pollen parent. The offspring is thus a unique individual, albeit with characteristics from both parents.

A large area of the meadow above Duddingston village has become the site of a remarkable project to grow all of Scotland's native apple and pear trees and many others. You will find an unparalleled variety of apples here, and may be able to taste some in the autumn, when the community leave apples out for visitors to sample. These even include the Hawthornden apple, mentioned in Walk 8. At the time of writing the trees are still young, having been planted in 2012 or more recently.

Given the limited number of apples we are used to seeing on supermarket shelves, a visit to the orchard serves as a welcome reminder of the variety and rich heritage we have where apples are concerned, and of the need to preserve this diversity. They have after all, evolved to cope with, and thrive in, the local climate and environment. Table 9.1 lists the names and numbers of the apple and pear trees in the orchard.

I suggest that you wander through the orchard in whatever way feels right for you. Allow the trees to surprise you. You may want to pay attention to the blossoms (Figures 9.3a–3b), the scents, the insect life visiting the trees, the names themselves and the stories they hint at (Figure 9.3c–3f); there is such rich diversity for the savouring.

Some of these varieties are well known, others less so. Some were first recorded over two centuries ago, others much more recently. The Orleans Reinette (Figure 9.3d), for example, was first described by a Dutchman, Knoop, in 1776. It is an old French variety that became popular in the UK during the 20th century. It is a sweet apple that ripens late, typically in December. The Jupiter (Figure 9.3c) is much more recent, having been raised in 1966 by Dr Alston as a cross between Cox's Orange Pippin and Starking Delicious. The apples here are recognised either as eaters or

90 Bess Pool	91 Beauty of Bath	92 Kidd's Orange Red	93 Bountiful	94 Jupiter	95 Sunset	96 Scotch Dumpling	97 Bramley's Seedling	98 Laxton's	99 James Grieve
80 Lady of the Wemyss	81 Pine Golden Pippin	82 Bloody Ploughman	83 James Grieve	84 Sunset	85 Orleans Reinette	86 Discovery	87 Greensleeves	88 Clydeside	89 Red Windsor
70 Beauty of Moray	71 Thomas Jeffrey	72 Oslin	73 Ashmead's Kernel	74 Ellison's Orange	75 White Melrose	76 Katy	77 Worcester Pearmain	78 Lothian Red	79 Rajka
60 Hood's Supreme	61 Maggie Sinclair	62 Elstar	63 Adam's Pearmain	64 Lane's Prince Albert	65 Tydeman's Late Orange	66 Fiesta	67 Scotch Bridget	68 Saturn	69
50 Tom Putt	51 Lemon Queen	52 Red Falstaff	53 Hood's Supreme	54 Ribston Pippin	55 White Paradise	56 Coul Blush	57 Ryan's Seedling	58 Lord Derby	59 Katy
40 Cambusnethan Pippin	41 Thorle Pippin	42 Love Beauty	43 Pine Golden Pippin	44 Court Pendu Plat	45 Discovery	46 East Lothian Pippin	47 Port Allan Russet	48 East Lothian Pippin	49 St Edmund's Russet
30 Lemon Queen	31 Galloway Pippin	32 Egremont Russet	33 Elstar	34 Lady of the Lake	35	36	37 Rock (Lanarkshire)	38 Suntan	39 Cutler Grieve
20 Ashmead's Kernel	21 Hawthornden	22 Stark's Late Delicious	23 Stirling Castle	24 Suntan	25 Cambusnethan Pippin	26 Nexton Wonder	27 Golden Monday	28 James Grieve	29 Eve
10 Worcester Pearmain	11 Belle de Boskoop	12 Lord Rosebery	13 Cutler Grieve	14 Pine Gold Pippin	15 William Crump	16 Yorkshire Aromatic	17 Sunset	18 Lady Sudeley	19 Early Julyan
	1 Bramley's Seedling	2 Rosemary Russet	3 Hawthornden	4 Lemon Queen	5 George Cave	6 Seaton House	7 Megginch Favourite	8 Scrog	9 Rev W. Wilks

Table 9.1: The apple varieties planted in the orchard: the names alone are intriguing, the blossom and fruit of the trees themselves an even greater treat.

Figures 9.3c–3f: Each of the apple and pear trees in the orchard is numbered and identified, and it can be very rewarding to discover the many varieties planted here. Those of us who visit regularly can appreciate the opportunity to visit a particular (perhaps favourite) tree through the seasons and watch it as it flowers, and then, later, prepare to bear fruit and yield what is theirs to give.

cookers, although a number of them, including the Kingston Black, have a reputation as cider apples. The Scotch Dumpling is a cooking apple introduced into Scotland in the mid-20th century; the Stirling Castle had a reputation in the 19th century as one of the very best cooking apples.

The White Melrose is, however, both a cooker and an eater. It was recorded as far back as 1831; it is thought to have been introduced by the monks of Melrose Abbey, and it was widely grown in the Borders and Tweeddale during the 19th century. It is an apple that is both sweet and sharp.

At the bottom of the orchard there is a row of ten pear trees. Of these, you may be forgiven for knowing only the Conference. The others include Craig's pear, which was first recorded in 1875 and originated from near Perth.

The Orchard Project is the national charity dedicated to the creation, restoration and celebration of community orchards. To find out more about how they are working closely with community groups to design and create new orchards in hubs across Scotland and England, please visit their website: https://www.theorchardproject.org.uk/

3 Duddingston Community Orchard to Meadowfield Park

After visiting the orchard, pick up the path, known as the Measured Walk, that heads off past the willow bed, gaining height as it approaches the old stone wall on the western edge of the Field, before following this boundary line as it climbs to the northernmost tip of the Field.

The willows are a collection of delightful thriving young trees (Figure 9.4a). Further up you will see crab apple trees and a collection of young trees that include a large number of oak, ash, birch and alder (Figures 9.4b–4c).

As you move along the path listen out for signs of the many birds visiting the Field. You may hear bullfinch, chaffinch, goldfinch, blackcap, willow warbler, wood pigeon and stock dove. You may also pick out the calls of geese and other waterfowl coming up from Duddingston Loch below you. Look out for a small path heading off on your left about two thirds of the way up the ascent. This takes you round to a quiet bench that can provide a great 'sit spot': somewhere to sit down and listen to the birdsong, the trees or even the sunset at the end of a summer's evening.

Figure 9.4a: The path climbs up with the willow bed on the left, before curving round to the right.

Figures 9.4b–4c: Allow yourself to slow down as you appreciate the unique character of the different tree species found in the orchard. This can shift with the light and the weather, giving rise to different visual and auditory effects. The willow trees (in 9.4b) look and sound different from the birch (9.4c) when the wind moves through them and the rain beads on the branches.

The trees along the boundary wall have witnessed many changes. Many of them show the scars from when the Field was used to graze horses – their bark stripped away in places, laying bare the wood underneath. They include a number of fine old oaks, an ancient chestnut tree and several fine ash trees. I would encourage you to pay attention to the oaks, and appreciate some of their many attributes and the life they sustain (see the special feature).

Figures 9.4d–4e: The willow trees in the bed can be appreciated in many ways: for their beauty as well as their various other qualities. Their supple young branches have long been valued by weavers; the shoots are harvested and made available to basket weavers and other craftspeople.

★ Special Feature – ancient oaks, and oak apples

Figure 9.5a: On the younger oak trees planted in the Field, the old coppery leaves are retained throughout the winter. Beside them you can see the russet-brown buds that protect next year's leaves. Take your time to observe the shape and colour of these buds, as well as the way they cluster together at the end of the branch. These observations will help you recognise oak buds and therefore the oak trees who have lost their leaves to the ravages of the storms that mark the tail end of the year. The oak seen here is a pedunculate oak (Quercus robur), *otherwise known as the English oak. Its leaves are almost stalkless, and are bilobed at the base with between four and five earlobes along the edges of the rest of the leaf. The acorns hang on long stalks, hence the name 'pedunculate'. By contrast, the acorns of the sessile oak have no stalks, and the leaves are much less lobed, with a more obvious stalk.*

Both the Field and Meadowfield Park are home to several impressive old oak trees and a large number of much younger oaks. This special feature plays tribute to our encounters with the oak.

In the early months of the year many of the younger oak trees will have retained their bronzed leaves, for the winds of autumn and winter do not strip these shorter trees of their leaves. Overhead, the canopy of the older oaks is bare, so you may find yourself challenged to identify these trees. Telling them apart from other tree species, even in winter, is possible, however. For a start, the buds that burst open in spring, liberating as they will either leaves or flowers, will have been prepared in advance. Look for them; pay attention to their colour, shape and configurations (Figure 9.5a).

One of the nice things about having young and old trees beside each other is that you can see the buds together with the leaves in these younger trees, and then visit the older, leafless, trees to observe their buds. Of the old trees lining the back wall of the Field, there are only a few species to distinguish from the oak: the chestnut and the ash. The buds of each are very different – so pay attention, and enjoy the magical experience of watching spring unfold.

By visiting a particular tree regularly, you will become more familiar with how it weathers the seasons and sees the year through. Watching spring bursting forth from the buds of the oak tree will have you yearning to return, to see what happens next (Figures 9.5b–5c). You will not be the only one to be watching the oak trees, for there are also parasitic wasps watching for these buds to form. In Britain there are some 70 different species of gall wasp, so called because their

Figures 9.5b–5c: As the buds burst open, spare a little time to observe what springs forth. The fresh green leaves of the oak are an exquisite pale lime green. The catkins follow soon after, and release pollen to the wind. This is borne to the female flowers that appear on the same tree, as oaks are monoecious, meaning that they bear both female and male flowers on the same plant.

larvae, when laid in the tissues of the oak tree, induce a reaction that ultimately leads to the formation of a protective structure known as a gall. The female wasp targets different parts of the tree, including the leaf buds, flower buds and acorns, even the roots. On hatching, the grubs secrete chemicals that repro-gramme the tree's normal growth processes, so that instead of normal oak tree tissues a gall forms around the developing grub.

These galls come in a range of forms. The galls of the oak apple gall wasp (*Biorhiza pallida*) arise on twigs and have a delightful pinky hue that has earnt them the name of oak apple (Figures 9.5d–5e). Unlike most other galls, these contain not one but many larvae.

The presence of galls on an oak tree, whilst reflect-ing parasitism and having a potential impact on acorn crops, are not a concern for the oak tree. They are part of the diversity of life on oak trees, providing critical food for native wildlife. There are even some special-ised species of gall wasps that inject their eggs into the larvae of other species of gall wasp. There is so much life unfolding in oak trees! Allow yourself to be surprised – who knows what you might see?

Figure 9.5d (above): Among the oak catkins, an oak apple gall wasp has laid her eggs, and the larvae have wasted little time in hijacking the tree's growing tissues in order to build themselves a shelter.

Figure 9.5e (right): The gall, produced collaboratively by the oak apple gall wasp's larvae and the oak tree, bears a striking resemblance to an apple. Galls produced by the many other wasps who parasitise oak trees affect other parts of the oak tree, including the acorns, and can have very different structures.

*Figures 9.6a–6b: This venerable old oak
tree came down in a storm many years ago,
and now lies stretched out on the ground.
Amazingly, the tree's roots still maintain a life
support system, and every spring new growth
springs forth from the branches. Small suckers
rise from the trunk and seek the light. The
tree's ability to reinvent itself and flourish in
adversity is quite inspirational.*

4 Meadowfield Park to Holyrood Park

At the top corner of the Field, with the wall
on your left, pass up a set of steps and follow the path that leads into Meadowfield
Park. An area of relatively young woodland
planted by the council drops off to your right
and conceals an impressive old fallen oak
tree, whose existing root structure maintains
a life support system and allows the tree to
bear leaves and life every spring (Figures
9.6a–6b).

Follow the path gently uphill, taking care
here when the ground is muddy. You will
soon see a stone stile allowing you to pass
over the wall and into Holyrood Park. Stay
within Meadowfield Park, following the more
obvious path through the woodland and
keeping the wall in sight on your left-hand
side. You soon arrive in a clearing. Cross this
and pick up one of several trails that continues into the woodland. This can be a good
place to see two delightful pink flowers: herb
Robert and red campion (Figures 9.7a–7b).
In spring, look out, too, for bluebells and
ramsons. The ground and tree trunks in this
section of woodland are densely covered
with ivy (Figures 9.8a–8c).

*Figure 9.6c:
Amidst the
fractured
and broken
wreckage, the
broken wood
and splintered
limbs, the oak
tree sends forth
new life.*

Figure 9.8a:
In winter, the
young trees in
Meadowfield Park
are largely devoid
of leaves. Devoid,
that is, except for
ivy, whose evergreen
leaves clothe the
floor between the
trees and climb
up the tree trunks,
drawing on them
for support.

Figures 9.7a–7b (above): Two common pink woodland flowers are herb Robert (9.7a) and red campion (9.7b). Their leaf shapes and numbers of petals are quite different, so they are easily told apart.

Figure 9.8b: Even on a cold, wet and rainy winter's day, there can be things to appreciate on a walk. Here the rain adds a sheen to the ivy leaves and draws the eye to the delicate veins that course through each of the leaves. The veins provide structure and support to the leaves whilst also providing a transport system for essential nutrients, water and energy. While each leaf may perform the same function every one is different, yet we only notice this if we pay enough attention and greet each leaf as we would like to be greeted ourselves.

Figure 9.8c: The flower heads are green and easily overlooked. Whilst they may be little appreciated by most humans, they are much appreciated by insects, for they are one of the earliest flowering plants and provide nectar early in the season. So it can be worth stopping to observe who is visiting these flowers. The ivy bee (Colletes hederae) specialises on the ivy, and emerges early so as to profit from 'its flowers. As the bee is common in Europe and southern England, we can expect to see them appearing in Scotland as the climate warms.

Emerging into another grassy area, look out for an archway on your left, leading through the wall into Holyrood Park. Here, the ivy on the park wall to either side of the gateway can be seen demonstrating its ability to turn from the creeping plant we are familiar with into a dense shrub capable of supporting its own weight.

5 Holyrood Park to Dunsapie Loch

On emerging through the gateway into the park, head up the path ahead of you to join the road, whereupon a left turn will take you along the pavement to Dunsapie Loch. This artificial loch was created in 1844 at the initiative of Queen Victoria's consort, Prince Albert, who was also responsible for creating St Margaret's Loch and Queen's Drive.

Dunsapie Loch stands at 110 metres above sea level and can be a magical place to see the sun rise, with a warm palate of colours appearing behind the willow trees (Figure 9.9a) that now mark the loch's south and north-east ends. The loch is home to a number of natural wonders, including common toads (*Bufo bufo*) and mute swans (*Cygnus olor*).

Every spring many hundreds of toads set their sights on the loch and head down from their winter hibernacula on the wooded hillside above the road. This usually happens after a series of consecutive warm, wet nights, often after heavy rain. The road – and especially the kerbs – represent a serious obstacle to migrating toads, however, and it is fortunate that at this time the park wardens close the road to traffic. Volunteers often

Figure 9.9a: Dunsapie Loch sits between the road and the iron age fort of Dunsapie, and can be a magical place to see the sun rise behind the willow trees at the south end of the loch. The pair of breeding mute swans seen here are tolerant of Canada geese, tufted ducks and other waterfowl, but not of other swans. Once the pair's young have fledged and taken to the water you are likely to see the whole family on the loch.

Figures 9.9b–9c: The pen sits on her nest close to the edge of the loch amidst the young willows. Do not approach her, especially if you are walking with dogs; you should maintain a respectful distance. Failure to do so may cause her to become distressed, and you may also find yourself attacked by the male swan, who is capable of breaking an arm and of drowning a dog. Note how much flatter the female's cere is compared to the bulbous shape of the black cere above the male's bill.

turn up during the annual toad migration to help toads on their way to the deep waters of the loch. Across the UK, and indeed globally, it is estimated that many of our toads fall victim to road traffic, and this is having a devastating effect on the numbers of this charismatic amphibian.

The loch is home to the local breeding pair of swans and you are therefore highly unlikely to see more than two swans on the loch; the non-breeding adults and juveniles frequent St Margaret's Loch, and would not dare to run the gauntlet of the cob.[3] During the breeding season you will see the cob with his pen closely guarding their nest and the loch itself (Figure 9.9b). The cob can be identified by the large fleshy, bulbous cere over his bill, whereas the pen's cere is much flatter (Figure 9.9c).

The loch can also be a good place to see grey heron, tufted duck and Canada geese. But there is more! ... In 2020 the loch became famous for its resident otters, as not just one but three otters were regularly sighted in or around the loch. These lithe mustelids are now repopulating Edinburgh's waterways, and are exploring them and re-establishing their grip on a watershed from which they have been absent for far too long.

If you are lucky enough to spy an otter on the banks or in the water, please keep a respectful distance and keep any dogs on a lead. Undisturbed, the otters may treat you to some magical moments. Their bodies are made for moving in water, and it can be mesmerising to watch them dancing in their element. They dive under the surface, disappearing from sight but leaving a trail of air bubbles as the only sign of their underwater pursuits. When they do come up, you may see them chomping on whatever they have caught underwater. Their coats are incredibly dense and made up of two very different types of hair: long, glossy guard hairs, and soft, white underhairs. The guard hairs are waterproof and very efficient at shedding water; the underhairs, much shorter and close-packed, trap a layer of insulating air.

---

3   Male swans are called cobs, the females pens.

Figure 9.10a: The long guard hairs of the otter shed water by clumping together. When out of water and drying, a healthy otter's coat therefore dries in a collection of triangular tufts, creating a spiky appearance. The undercoat is incredibly dense and insulating. Otters, however, need to come out of the water regularly to dry and warm up. If prevented from doing so, they can become chilled and start shivering; it is therefore important to keep a respectful distance and not interfere with their natural behaviour.

Figure 9.10b: Emerging from the water, the otter's sleek and streamlined body is exquisitely made for this environment. The sensory whiskers that help the otter navigate and make sense of this environment (especially in poor light or murky conditions) and identify and catch prey are part of the otter's highly specialised equipment, and a veritable wonder of nature.

Figure 9.11: Sunset over Duddingston Loch with snow on the Pentlands, and the swans, geese and ducks clamouring for food.

6 Dunsapie Loch to Duddingston Loch

From Dunsapie Loch continue along the pavement. As you approach the metal railings on the left-hand side you will see a set of steps dropping down the hill to your left. Take these, paying attention if the ground is muddy. They descend gradually towards the stone wall that marks the boundary of the park. On the other side of the wall is the Field, which you explored earlier in the walk. Reaching the wall, turn right and descend a long flight of steps to reach the park entrance beside Duddingston Loch.

The car park where you started is off to your right. Before rejoining the car park or heading to the Sheep Heid Inn, you may wish to cross over the road and descend to the edge of Duddingston Loch. This can be a wonderful place to view the sunset (Figure 9.11) at the end of the day, and to note and observe a few species you may not have seen on your walk; great crested grebe, coot (Figure 9.12) and moorhen may be seen here.

Figures 9.12a–12b: Coot are incredible waterbirds, from the tip of their white beaks to the tips of their long green toes. Watching them feed and carry out their business on the loch can be quite cathartic, for they are strong characters.

Walk 10

A Pentland walk: Flotterstone, Turnhouse and Carnethy Hills, and Glencorse Reservoir

This somewhat longer walk follows the Pentland skyline and rewards you with fine views in all directions as well as with opportunities to explore hill and moorland habitats, and see a number of species that you are unlikely to find in Edinburgh.

This walk's highlights include:

- An opportunity to explore the Pentland Hills Regional Park and walk along the Pentland ridgeline that runs over Turnhouse Hill before reaching the walk's high point at Carnethy Hill (573 metres).
- An opportunity to see moorland birds including red grouse, stonechat, whinchat, wheatear and ring ouzel.
- An opportunity to follow the Logan Burn on its descent from the Loganlee Reservoir, and on to Glencorse Reservoir.

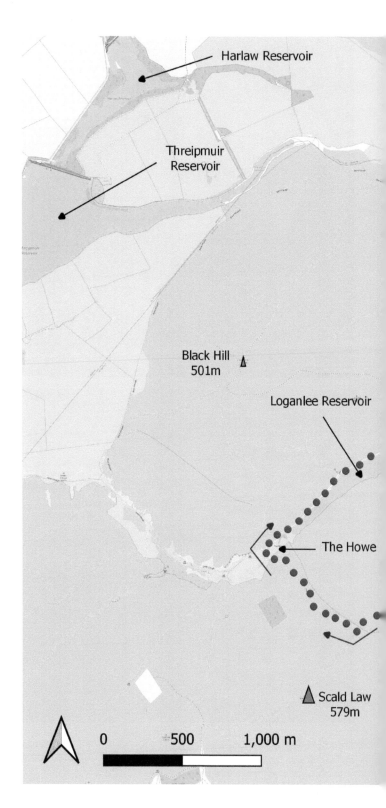

Harlaw Reservoir

Threipmuir Reservoir

Black Hill 501m

Loganlee Reservoir

The Howe

Scald Law 579m

0   500   1,000 m

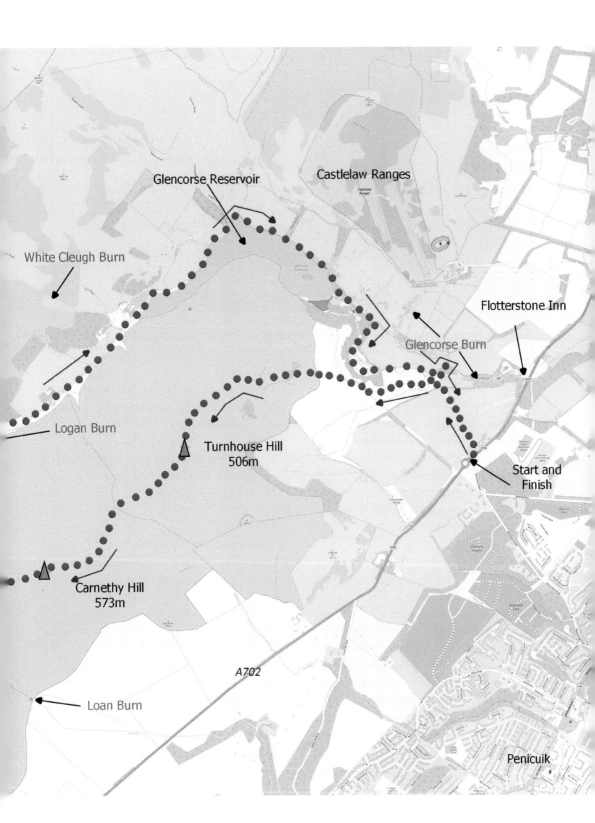

White Cleugh Burn

Glencorse Reservoir

Castlelaw Ranges

Flotterstone Inn

Glencorse Burn

Logan Burn

Turnhouse Hill
506m

Start and
Finish

Carnethy Hill
573m

A702

Loan Burn

Penicuik

Figure 10.1: The copse of trees on the ascent of Turnhouse Hill has a brooding quality about it that is in part due to the mix of species and silhouettes.

- The possibility of seeing some exciting birds of prey, including peregrine, merlin and long- and short-eared owls.
- Incredible, ever-changing views in all directions.
- Insights into the controversies surrounding land management practices in the uplands and the health of the upland river ecosystems.

🐾 Summary

The walk starts from the car park and information point a little beyond the Flotterstone Inn, which lies off the A702 south of Edinburgh.

After a short section through woodland, paralleling the road, pick up a path that crosses the Glencorse Burn and then climbs steadily towards a copse that clings to the hillside and dominates the skyline (Figure 10.1). This path gives access to the ridgeline that you can follow as it undulates over Turnhouse Hill (506 metres) and Carnethy Hill (573 metres) before descending to the col below Scald Law, the highest of the

Pentland Hills. The route then drops downhill to reach the Howe at the south-west tip of Loganlee Reservoir. Then it follows the valley floor all the way back to the start, allowing you to explore the heart of the regional park, and take in the peace and magic of Glencorse Reservoir.

🏛 History

The Pentland Hills might be thought to have been named because of the succession of summits that mark the ridgeline. Indeed, anyone walking the hills might be forgiven for wondering which five tops make up the 'pent' of Pentland. If this were true, the name would have Ancient Greek origins. The etymology can, however, be traced back to other languages: specifically to the Welsh or Cumbric. In these tongues, *pen* means 'head' and is often used to designate a hilltop, whilst *llan* means 'church', 'glade' or 'enclosure'. The hills are thus likely to have been named after the hamlet of Pentlant, which today is Old Pentland. Other hills in the range, including

Turnhouse, have been named after the farms below them.

The eastern flanks of Turnhouse Hill were the site of the only battle of the 1666 Covenanter Rebellion, also known as the Pentland Rising. A Covenanter army had formed following an uprising in south-west Scotland and, under the command of Colonel James Wallace, advanced as far as Colinton on its march towards Edinburgh, where it hoped to win support. The Covenanter forces stopped near Rullion Green as they made a retreat towards Biggar. It was here that a government army, under Sir Thomas Dalziel, finally caught up and engaged them in battle, defeating them after a stiff fight. The fields upon which the battle was fought are viewed from the heights of the ridge that this walk follows.

The Pentland Regional Park was designated in 1986 under the Countryside (Scotland) Act 1967, which defined regional parks as 'large areas of countryside, parts of which are available for informal countryside recreation'. The Scottish Outdoor Access Code now ensures that much of the park is available for recreation, providing the guidance of land managers is followed. The majority of the land falling within the boundaries of the park is in private ownership, which explains the kind of land management practices (including both sheep farming and shooting) evident in the area, that leave their mark on the local ecosystem.

According to the park's website, the City of Edinburgh Council is the managing authority of the regional park, although statutory duties are shared with two other local authorities: Midlothian Council and West Lothian Council. The Minute of Agreement between these three councils states that the park aims are as follows:

- To retain the essential character of the hills as a place for the peaceful enjoyment of the countryside;
- Caring for the hills so that the landscape and the habitat is protected and enhanced;
- Within this caring framework to encourage responsible public enjoyment of the hills;
- Co-ordination of these aims so that they co-exist with farming and other land uses within the Pentland Hills Regional Park.

Habitats

Deciduous woodland, heather moorland, freshwater reservoirs and hill burns.

Transport links

The Flotterstone car park can easily be reached by bus. Route 101 is operated by Stagecoach, running from St Andrew's Bus Station in the heart of Edinburgh. If cycling from Edinburgh, route 61 can be taken to reach Roslin. A series of minor roads and a short section on the A701 can then be taken to reach the A702 a little north of the Flotterstone Inn.

Refreshments

The Flotterstone Inn is perfectly located at the start and end of the walk, and can be a great place to call in for coffee, a drink or a meal. https://www.flotterstoneinn.com/

An alternative is the old visitor centre at Flotterstone, which has now been converted into a café and has been receiving great reviews. https://www.facebook.com/Pentland.Hills.Cafe.

References and further reading

Wright, S., Cairns, P. and Underdown, N. (2018). *Scotland: A rewilding journey*. Scotland: The Big Picture.

Figure 10.2: The sturdy wooden bridge crossing the Glencorse Burn lies among a cluster of gorse bushes that can be a great place to watch for a range of birds including chiffchaff, dunnock and stonechat.

⚐ Directions

1 Flotterstone car park to footbridge over Glencorse Burn

At the far end of the car park you can either follow the tarmac and enjoy the tinkle of the burn to your left, or pick up a path through the trees to the right of the road. The road remains level and provides easy going. Before it starts to rise and skirt the southern flank of Castlelaw, you need to turn off left and drop down to the Glencorse Burn. Look out for this obvious path and an obvious gate where the road leaves the burn and bends a little to the right (NT 229 631). The path keeps the burn on its left. At the fork, stay left to reach the bridge (NT 228 630), where it lies among the gorse bushes (Figure 10.2).

2 Footbridge to Turnhouse Hill

After crossing the footbridge, ignore the track coming down on your left. Instead, pick up a path that climbs through the gorse and follows a rising line that provides you with a fine view to left and right. To your right, the Scots pines massing like an ordered battalion on the southern slopes of Carnethy catch the eye. They are home to a large rookery, and you may see these black corvids floating above the trees, especially during nesting seasons, when these birds gather together to raise their young. The gorse bushes, meanwhile, provide good cover and feeding grounds for a number of breeding birds including chiffchaff, whose call is as the name suggests: an onomatopoeic *'chiff chiff chiff chaff chiff chaff'*.

As you climb through the gorse bushes and up onto the pastureland beyond, keep an

Figure 10.3: Dog violet is so named, in contrast to sweet violet, because it has no smell. It is typically a woodland flower but can also be found on pastureland, as here.

eye out – for what might lie both underfoot and close at hand as well as at a distance. Underfoot, you may see signs of dog violet (Figure 10.3), whilst overhead it would not be unusual to see raven or buzzards taking in the view from the tops of thermals (Figures 10.4a). In poor weather, there is little for them to see from such heights, however, and their hunting strategy will typically take them much lower (Figure 10.4b).

The path climbs relatively gently towards an impressive copse of trees that you pass through before reaching the crest of the hill. These mixed trees are worth admiring in all seasons, for their genius is born both of place and parentage. Every growth is the product of the trees' desire to fulfil their genetic potential as it engages in perpetual conversation with the elements of nature: the wind and the weather; the sun and the soil, when watching the weather come dancing in, the clouds and the branches swaying to the wind's pulsating rhythm – each

giving a little and yet never yielding fully, for clouds and trees are wedded to the cycle of life.

The invitation here is to admire these trees in your own way and to glimpse a little of their magic (Figures 10.5a–5b). Beyond them continue to climb the path until you reach the lower summit of Turnhouse (465 metres) and then a little beyond this the main summit (506 metres), where you will find a significant cairn and, on a good day, breath-taking views; to the south-east the land drops down to Penicuik, to the north it drops to Glencorse Reservoir before climbing to Harbour Hill and Capelaw Hill, whilst to the south-west it drops and climbs to Carnethy Hill (Figure 10.6), where this route takes you next.

Figures 10.4a–4b: On a warm day our common raptors, including the buzzard and the raven, can often be seen flying over at height or soaring on thermals. Their calls can alert us to their presence, and it is worth familiarising yourself with the coarse croaking call of the raven and the buzzard's mewing. In the upper image, a raven is passing high over Turnhouse. In poor weather, as in this Pentland snowstorm, birds of prey change their hunting and other behaviours, and will fly lower. Such encounters can be quite magical.

Figure 10.5a: The copse of trees on the spur that runs off in a north-easterly direction from Turnhouse's 465-metre top stands at an altitude of some 350 metres. Each of these trees is in itself a sculpture worthy of our admiration. Together these sculptures take the breath away, whether the day be sunny or snowy, brooding or breezy.

Figure 10.5b: The light, the branches, the clouds, the curves; all seem to bear testimony to nature's vitality.

Figure 10.6: A wintry Carnethy Hill viewed from Turnhouse.

★ Special Feature – of battles and forestry plantations

Figure 10.7a: Looking northwards, down onto Loganlee Reservoir and Logan Burn, a series of unnaturally straight lines can be seen. The edges of the conifer plantations are straight and angular, whilst on the hillside above some rectangular areas of muir burn are evident, where the heather has been burnt back as part of the land managers' work to encourage artificially high populations of red grouse for shooting.

From the top of Turnhouse Hill, you may want to take a brief look back in time: The map, whilst providing the location for the Battle of Rullion Green, fought on 28 November 1666, does not allow any impression to be gleaned as to the arrangement of the opposing forces. The opening skirmish of the battle was fought down near the Glencorse Burn, from whence you have just come. The Covenanters then took up positions in an arc stretching from Turnhouse Hill across towards Lawhead Hill. The battle itself marks an important event in the Kirk of Scotland's dissenting religious tradition, for the Pentland Rising, and the subsequent persecution of Covenanters that came to be known as the 'Killing Times', are deeply embedded in the psyche of Scottish Presbyterianism. The battle itself was the subject of 16-year-old Robert Louis Stevenson's first publication: *The Pentland Rising: A Page of History, 1666*. Whilst these events may have left their mark culturally, today there is little evidence of the battle on the ground other than the Martyr's Monument below and to the north of Lawhead (NT 222 623).

The same is not true of certain land management practices, by contrast. A look back to the 17th century provides us with an opportunity to consider how the landscape has changed in the intervening 350 years. At the time of the battle the land was not enclosed and would have been free of the walls and fences that you see before you. The late 18th- to early 19th-century plantation that stretches westwards from the Martyr's Monument probably stands on some of the positions occupied by the Covenanter forces. These plantations are a mix of deciduous trees and conifers. They were arguably part of the Plantation Movement, which saw species such as ash, beech, elm, oak and sweet chestnut planted for the purpose of producing wooden structures ranging from coffins to ships' keels. In Scotland, Scots pine was also favoured, and this kind of planting became something of a hobby.

Such plantings ceased by the end of the 19th century, as cheap imports outcompeted home-grown timber. The country's reliance on such imports, coupled with the increased demand for timber during World War I, led to severe timber shortages, and the response to this was the creation of the Forestry Commission in 1919 and a massive planting campaign that severely impacted the fragile ecology of heathland and moorland. In addition to the trees planted as part of the Plantation Movement, you will see examples of these more recent monocultures of single tree species, typically planted in straight rows and in blocks (Figure 10.7a) with little respect for soil and the ecology that the earth sustains in each and every part of the globe.

The situation is evolving, however, and there is hope that the Pentland Hills may see woodlands return, as a result of either land management policy change and official planting schemes or renegade and phantom initiatives. There is a precedent for the latter in the Pentlands; you may enjoy reading the Manifesto of the Phantom Tree Planters (Figure 10.7b). This thought-provoking document was written by Alastair McIntosh and published in Reforesting Scotland after being read out at the Spring Equinox, 1991, somewhere in the Pentland Hills.

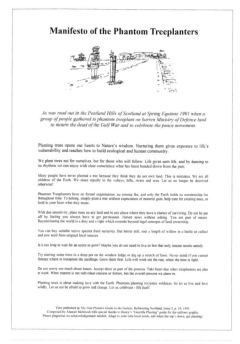

Figure 10.7b: Manifesto of the Phantom Treeplanters.

3 Turnhouse Hill to Carnethy Hill

The path descending from Turnhouse drops down some 80 metres to the south-west, to reach a narrow col (NT 207 622). Pass through the boundary wall and continue up the path ahead to gain the summit of Carnethy Hill, which at 573 metres is one of the highest summits in the Pentlands. The heather-clad flanks of Carnethy are home to red grouse, and you are likely to encounter these handsome birds skulking in the heather (see the special feature) – unless, of course, you approach too closely, and prompt them to fly off in alarm. By paying attention to more subtle signs of distress and keeping a respectful distance, you are likely to be granted some rewarding opportunities to take in the many features that make these birds so very handsome.

4 Carnethy Hill to the Howe

From the top of Carnethy, an obvious path continues in a westerly direction, dropping gradually down to reach a col at 440 metres, and a boundary wall. Turn right here and follow the path as it drops to the Howe, at the head of Loganlea Reservoir. As you do see look out for stonechat and whinchat as well as meadow pipit.

★ Special Feature – red grouse and grouse moors

The red grouse sports a delightful scientific name, *Lagopus*, that pays tribute to their feathered lower legs, which have been compared to a hare's foot. Such adaptations to the wintry conditions of the uplands of northern Europe characterise both the red grouse and ptarmigan. The latter is typically found at much higher altitudes than those of the Pentlands. The red grouse, by contrast, favours altitudes between 600 metres and 900 metres, where their preferred food is to be found. That food is of course heather, and as a species they rarely stray from heather moorland. This association with moorland has become very 'entangled', however, following the emergence of shooting estates during the Victorian era, when red grouse earnt themselves a reputation as the 'King of Game Birds'; 'entangled' in the sense that red grouse, whilst undoubtedly handsome and majestic (Figures 10.8a–8c), do not exist independently of humans. The assemblage of practices that produces grouse moors and therefore grouse means that we cannot think of grouse, in the purest sense, as independent creatures. Of course, if that is true of grouse then it is true of all of nature, except that in this case red grouse constitute an extreme example.

What is being emphasised here is that the red grouse you are likely to encounter in the Pentlands are in many ways a product of particular land ownership and management practices

Figures 10.8a–8b: Red grouse are likely to be lurking in the heather as you pass along the path that runs over the Carnethy Hill ridgeline. They are likely to keep to cover, and if you are to spot them you may need to pay careful attention. They will no doubt be watching you (and any accompanying dogs). In these images the red patch over the eyes is particularly noticeable and allows the bird to be identified as a male, for females lack this feature. It is not feathered but is, instead, made of a thick keratinised pad: a wattle. Unlike in domestic fowl, these wattles do not hang from the throat but sit over the eyes, where they bear testament to the male's testosterone levels, particularly during the breeding season.

coupled with the fact that these practices have largely passed unquestioned and unscrutinised. A singular truth was allowed to prevail; this truth is, like all truths, another fiction propounded by those best placed to impose their narrative. Truths, here, are understood to be a collection of data points and facts conveniently and persuasively stitched together so that they appear convincing. This is worth unpacking a little further, for it can help us to understand why much of our uplands have become ecological deserts, and why this has taken so long to enter the wider public consciousness. To understand how this sad state of affairs has come to pass, it is helpful to see how this narrative was established and then maintained, and why it is increasingly untenable.

In order to maximise the numbers of grouse available to shooting parties – a goal justified by the revenue it generates and the ways estates have historically been valued – the land is intensively managed. This is perhaps most evident as muir burning, but also involves several less evident practices, including predator extermination, carried out by gamekeepers. Since the latter half of the 19th century, shooting estates have come to dominate much of upland Britain, and the economic models and land management practices they tend to employ to ensure high densities of red grouse have become established as the norm to such an extent that those involved have come to believe that they are conservationists.

This is changing, however, for these practices are coming under increased scrutiny and have been heavily criticised on several levels. This is in part because the uplands of Britain are no longer the exclusive preserve of a tiny rich landed élite. Responsible access to the countryside has been secured and with the 'right to roam' has come greater awareness of how land is managed – or, indeed, mismanaged. Increased scrutiny of the work of gamekeepers has drawn attention to the extent to which they wage war on predators. A number of predators, including foxes, stoats and weasels, are not protected in law, and are targeted legally, although perhaps not legitimately. Other predators, specifically birds of prey such as golden eagles, peregrine and hen harriers, are also targeted, as is becoming increasingly clear through the monitoring and satellite tracking of these iconic birds and the post-mortem examination of birds found dead. According to a BBC report from 10 October 2018, a peregrine falcon was found dead in Green Cleuch, in the Pentlands Regional Park. A police investigation concluded that the bird had been poisoned illegally, but it appears that little or no action was taken to warn the public about the risk of poisoning in the park.

Alison Johnstone, then Scottish Green MSP for Lothian, is quoted as saying, in response to the bird's death, that she was shocked and saddened, and continued:

Scotland's birds of prey are supposedly protected, yet persecution is rife and rarely met with justice … That a protected species could be killed using a deadly poison in a regional park that is visited by over half a million people every year is shocking.

We appear to be witnessing a conflict between the traditional landowning classes and a public who are increasingly concerned about ecological matters. This, however, represents an oversimplification, for underneath we are witnessing a growing realisation that farming and land management practices founded on a factory model (a model whereby productivity can be improved through managing inputs and outputs, keeping costs down and maximising efficiencies) are simplistic and have hidden costs. These costs are passed on to future generations and to the environment. This is a classic example of 'shifting the burden', and is a sign that the core principles of sustainability are not being respected.

When viewed as a living system that draws on its own biodiversity to maintains itself in equilibrium, we can start appreciating that our uplands have been decimated: the Critical Zone of life that should exist there is largely missing. Overgrazing by deer and sheep means that the vegetation is no longer what it would be naturally. Heather moorland and high grouse numbers are forcibly maintained through a combination of muir burning, medication of grouse to address the diseases that arise in intensive situations, and intensive predator extermination, to name just three practices in the grouse moor assemblage.

The rewilding movement in Scotland is demonstrating that other assemblages are possible with different economic models and visions of the future, with deer excluded and/or culled (or keystone species reintroduced so that systems can rebalance themselves) and time allowed for the seeds in the soil to germinate and new forests emerge. You are invited to consider what might be possible here in the Pentlands, were similar approaches to be explored in this part of Scotland.

Scotland: The Big Picture is one of the leading organisations helping us to imagine what might be possible in Scotland. It defines rewilding as follows:[4]

Rewilding is an evolving process of nature recovery that leads to restored ecosystem health, function and completeness built around the following principles:

- Providing the space and conditions to re-establish dynamic natural processes, so that they shape and govern Scotland's land and seas.
- Recognising the critical role of all species – including missing native species – in sustaining functioning food webs and other ecological interactions.
- Nurturing nature recovery at different scales and accepting that approaches to rewilding can look and feel quite different and still offer valuable benefits.
- Improving connectivity across fragmented habitats to give species more freedom to roam, supporting biodiversity recovery and climate resilience.
- Helping communities to prosper in a diverse, nature-based economy that works in tandem with ecological recovery.

For more information on rewilding see Wright, Cairns and Underdown (2018).: https://www.scotlandbig-picture.com/our-take-on-rewilding.

Figure 10.8c: The mix of browns in the grouse's body feathering is exquisite, and allows both male and female to blend into the heather. If you are lucky, you may find feathers in the heather and can study the patterning more closely.

4   https://www.scotlandbigpicture.com/our-take-on-rewilding

Figure 10.9: A common sandpiper flies fast and low over the water, often sending out a haunting piping call that once learnt will help you spot these birds as they move about the shoreline.

5 The Howe to Glencorse Reservoir

Having descended to the valley floor and with the cottage to your right, cross over the stream by means of the bridge. You will then find yourself on a track that runs up to a gate. Pass through the gate and onto a road, and follow it along the edge of Loganlea Reservoir. This reservoir is heavily fished, and you may see lost fishing lines on the telegraph wires beside the road.

As you pass along the shore of the reservoir keep an eye out for common sandpiper flitting with wings flicking, low over the water (Figure 10.9). Their call is somewhat haunting, and their brown and white plumage, whilst unassuming from a distance, very smart. You may also see diving ducks such as goosander, as well as other birds drawn in by the fish. During the summer months, listen out for the cascading liquid call of willow warblers, who are likely to be perching in and hunting from the trees along the shoreline (Figures 10.10a–10b).

At the end of the reservoir, the road drops before passing beside Logan House. At this point, the Logan Burn will be to your right,

Figures 10.10a–10b: Willow warblers are one of the summer migrants who, after spending the winter in Africa, arrive to feast on the insects that emerge once our summer starts warming up. They are relatively nondescript, but have a clear pale eye stripe (or supercilium) running above the eye, and most helpfully a cascading song that makes it easy to identify them.

Figure 10.11: The quizzical look on this pied wagtail's face is born of the attention paid to flying insects that draw both pied and grey wagtails to the river.

6 Glencorse Reservoir and Glen Cottage to Flotterstone

and is a great place to watch out for dipper (see the special feature) as well as grey and pied wagtail (Figure 10.11). Upon reaching Glencorse Reservoir, it can be worth pausing to scan the area of wetland and open water to the left of the road. There can be some nice surprises in this habitat. The road sticks close to the shore of the reservoir until it reaches Glen Cottage, passing by an impressive line of Scots pine along the edge of the loch and casting shadows across the road when the afternoon light seeks to find ways past the trunks, branches and needles.

To familiarise yourselves with their call, visit Tweet of the Day: https://www.bbc.co.uk/programmes/b03zdbr0

After passing the end of the reservoir and Glen Cottage, you will find yourself with an area of mature mixed woodland on your right. After about 300 metres (NT 224 633) a path heads down through the woods to join the track running along the floor of the valley. This can make for a pleasant return route, as the enclosed valley with its woodland can provide a contrast to the open views out across the reservoir that you have just been exposed to.

Whether you take this path or follow the tarmac, either will lead you back to Flotterstone. The path follows the left bank of the burn (which should not be crossed) before rejoining the road at NT 229 631. Then follow the road back to the start where, hopefully, you will find the café or pub still open for refreshments.

★ Special Feature – dippers and mountain stream ecology

Our weather systems mean that water as a result of air rising and cooling, falls on high ground. A look at any map will show that this rain then flows downhill from the watershed (or the partitioning line, from *ligne de départition des eaux* in French), giving rise to the streams that feed our rivers. The Logan Burn is itself fed by water that rises at the Kitchen Moss, and descends to the Loganlee Reservoir, together with several streams whose waters rise from springs on the northern flanks of Carnethy.

Figure 10.12a: The dipper is a stocky, barrel-chested wren with a dark back and a characteristic white breast. The bird can dip not just their head under water in search of aquatic food, but can submerge themselves completely – and, remarkably, walk along the riverbed in search of food, defying the tug of the river and their own natural buoyancy.

Figure 10.12b: What is it you are hunting or searching for, Mr Dipper? Given what goes on underwater, it can be challenging for us to work out what is going on under the surface. With a little patience, however, all becomes clear. Patience, after all, is a virtue we all share, and it can be salutary to pay attention to the patience of other creatures. ... This dipper has collected five larvae from a single foraging outing lasting a matter of minutes. The water here is shallow, although the flow is still brisk. The bird's feet are exquisitely adapted to securing a purchase on the stream bed, and allow the bird to hunt out the larvae attached to the stones.

The Pentland reservoirs provide us with one of the essentials of life: water. And by 'us', we are to understand all life, not just human life. One creature that is intimately associated with mountain streams and rivers is the dipper (*Cinclus cinclus*), also known as the water blackbird (*merle d'eau* in French), water thrush or water ouzel. These names bear testament to the assumption that these birds are members of the thrush family, an understandable conclusion given their appearance. Perhaps surprisingly, they are in fact more closely related to the diminutive wren (Figure 10.12a).

Dippers are so named because of their innate bobbing movement, which has been described as curtseying. When I worked as a wildlife vet and contributed to the hand-rearing of a brood of dippers, I was amazed to see that this movement was present before they had even fledged, suggesting that it is innate rather than learnt. The young are also at home in water from an early age, as befits a bird who has evolved to feed on the insects and invertebrates that survive on the riverbed in even the harshest of winters. This is why you will still see dippers out and about on our mountain streams in winter, when the grey and pied wagtails (amongst many other less hardy birds) have flown to lower altitudes or further afield. The dipper is even known to plunge under ice to access the larder that nature has provided for them on the riverbed. But what are they finding down there (Figure 10.12b)?

The answer to this excellent question is a lot of caddis fly larvae (Figure 10.12c). These are the larvae of relatively inconspicuous and short-lived flies who lay vast numbers of eggs on vegetation surrounding freshwater streams. When these eggs hatch, the larvae that emerge fall into the stream, where they build protective cases. This is achieved through their ability to spin silk that can embrace a range of materials, including sand, gravel, twigs and vegetation. In fast-moving streams; the incorporation of heavier material prevents these larvae from being washed downstream. By contrast, in still water their cases tend to be lighter.

The larvae feed on the algae and periphyton that grow on submerged stones and other materials. It is suggested that they may be resistant to pollution, including low oxygen levels. At the same time, it is important to recognise that they can accumulate toxins such as lead, which can then bioaccumulate in predators who feed on the larvae, causing disease. Given that the reservoirs in this area have a long history of fishing, it is likely that there will be residues of lead in the water system. The extent of this is very unclear, however, as to my knowledge there have been no studies to evaluate this. Fortunately, lead shot for fishing was banned in January 1987, largely in response to growing awareness that waterfowl, including swans and ducks, were ingesting lost shot and succumbing to both acute and chronic lead poisoning. In areas where waterfowling was practised, much of the 'lost' shot is likely to have been fired from shotguns and spread across the environment. Nevertheless, what this highlights is our attitude towards invisible threats and the lack of a precautionary approach. Fishing enthusiasts and the authorities have been slow to act and generally need to see evidence before taking action.

The way we care (or rather fail to care) for our waterways also demonstrates how we divorce ourselves from the ecosystem that sustains us and which we are dependent on. How many of us recognise that we are literally approximately 60 per cent water? To what extent do we recognise that we are therefore composed of water, that water is constantly cycling through us, and that it might even be reasonable to assert that 'we are water'? So why is that when we look at how we respect and care for watercourses, it would appear that we have ceased to see streams and rivers as part of our extended selves? Our capacity to respect the environment has been eroded, decimated even. It is this capacity to respect and appreciate that we need to nurture.

This special feature on dippers and mountain stream ecology leaves us with challenging questions to ponder. Lead was offered as one potential threat that can lurk under the surface, but there are many others, including detergents, fertilisers and even the sunscreen that may wash off the legs of those who paddle in mountain streams. Our understanding of the complex aspects of the health of upland streams is still very much unfolding, and requires us to pay careful attention to aspects that we have largely remained ignorant of or perhaps conveniently ignored.

Figure 10.12c: With a beak full of larvae, this parent will shortly fly back to the nest to feed the waiting young. Try not to get in the way of the bird's flight path as you may cause some distress and either delay the flight or cause the bird to deviate. And if you notice another flicker of white, it is because when the dipper is blinking the dipper's third eyelid can be seen to be slightly opaque. This structure is likely to provide the eye with some degree of protection when under water whilst still allowing them to locate prey.

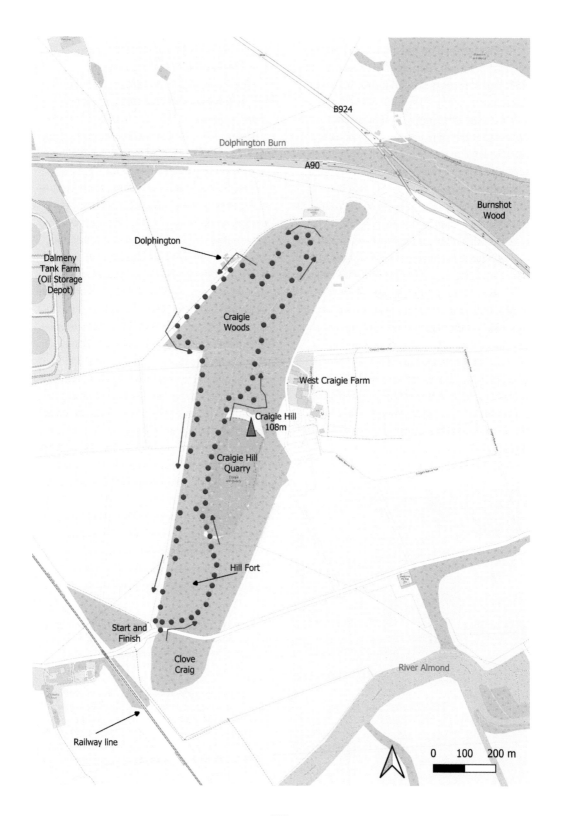

B924

Dolphington Burn

A90

Burnshot
Wood

Dalmeny
Tank Farm
(Oil Storage
Depot)

Dolphington

Craigie
Woods

West Craigie Farm

Craigie Hill
108m

Craigie Hill
Quarry

Hill Fort

Start and
Finish

Clove
Craig

River Almond

Railway line

0   100   200 m

Walk 11

Craigie Hill Wood, Fort and Quarries

This walk explores abandonment and provides us with deep-time insights into what abundance can arise phoenix-like from the embers of human fires of occupation and extraction. The historic visitations of our human ancestors have made of Craigie Hill Fort and, more recently, Craigie Quarry, places where our defensive, trading and economic practices can still be felt. In our abandonment of these places, however, opportunities have arisen for nature to reclaim what is hers and heal the traces and scars left behind.

This walk's highlights include:

- An opportunity to discover and learn about the vestiges of an Iron Age fort

that, sitting atop Craigie Hill, is now a haven for wildlife.

- The birch woodland that has reclaimed much of Craigie Hill and Craigie Quarry; it provides a mesmeric performance of pale colours and dancing leaves.
- An opportunity to glimpse brown hare sprinting through the woodland or out across the surrounding fields.
- The possibility of seeing buzzard and sparrow hawk hunting through the woodland.
- An opportunity to consider the many ways that nature reclaims land that once was occupied and/or exploited by humans.
- Encounters with a number of old oak and beech trees who have borne witness to the comings and goings of countless humans.

Figure 11.1: The view north-west from Craigie Hill Fort to the snow-covered Ochils, the Forth road bridges and the Dalmeny Fuel depot. The latter, visible in the foreground, was built in the 1970s on the site of a disused shale mine and refinery. It stores as much as 4 million barrels of petroleum products in eight floating tanks. The oil is produced by the Grangemouth oil refinery and stored at the depot prior to being piped to two crude oil loading jetties at Hound Point in the Firth of Forth. So much history in one image!

❡ Summary

The walk starts from the small layby (NT 152 757) on Burnshot Road, a short distance before it passes under the railway bridge. There is limited parking here; if there is no room, an alternative starting point is near the junction between the road leading to Dolphington House and that running from the A90 to Craigie Farm (NT 159 769).

From the layby, follow a path up onto the hill fort that occupies the southern half of the long whinstone ridge known as Craigie Hill. Good paths then allow you to keep to the high ground that runs almost south–north, following the ridgeline for a 1.5 kilometres before descending to where the woodland meets the track to Dolphington House. Then follow one of several woodland paths, keeping to the outer edge of this retained area of deciduous woodland, with fine views into the woods to the left and out across fields to the right. This path follows the western foot of Craigie Hill and allows you to regain the car park on Burnshot Road.

🏛 History

Craigie Hill has a rich history, but one that is not particularly easy to fathom and piece together. The OS 6-inch first edition map, published in 1856, contains some interesting hints as to this history, including reference to four wells, one 'old quarry' and three other whinstone quarries. There is also a mysterious reference to a stone coffin, or kistvaen …

The hill fort itself is described by Historic Environment Scotland as being from an 'unassigned period'. It was listed as a Scheduled Monument on 23 July 1935, having first been identified and then excavated by James Y. Simpson, MD, in 1866. This is the Dr Simpson buried in Warriston Cemetery and mentioned in Walk 6, for not only was he an obstetrician, but his interests extended to archaeology; he was a member of the Society of Antiquaries of Scotland, and in 1860 became its president.

> In the Society's Proceedings from their 85th session (1864–65), published in 1867, Simpson writes of how he, with the assistance of Craigie Hill's then owner, a Mr Hope Vere, discovered what he describes as an ancient British city:

The summits of various hills in the Lothians and adjacent districts have remains of ancient strongholds and defences upon them. These fortified hills are not the highest, but those of minor elevation and isolated. Within the walls and oftener below still on the slopes of the hills are frequently the remains of hut circles and other pit-like excavations. Few or none have yet been searched for sculptured stones and rocks. On the middle hill of Craigiewood I found, some time ago, within a few miles of Edinburgh, an ancient British city of this description abutting a steep rock on the eastern side; and on its other sides defended by a triple rampart, and entered by gates placed obliquely. The proprietor, Mr Hope Vere, was so kind as to examine by the spade and mattock, the mode in which the three inclosing valli on the western side were constructed. We found that originally they each consisted of a rude cyclopic wall of uncut stones, now buried under a covering of accumulated soil and turf. The area of the enclosed town extends to about forty acres. In different parts of it are still visible the hollows or pits which formed the flooring of the original houses or huts; and a little digging beneath the turf showed rude circular walls built around several acres. (Simpson, 1867, p.45)

At Craigie Hill you will be able to see that the eastern side is well defended by a set of cliffs. The defensive position was thus made good by three defensive walls on the west side. These are perhaps best appreciated on the 1:25,000 OS map rising from the 75-metre contour interval. The walls themselves were some 5–7 feet thick, and it is inside these walls that the huts were found. At the north end of this hill lies a secondary stone-walled fort.

Simpson (1867, p.28) notes when the road was built in the early 19th century, it uncovered a burial chamber (cist or kistvaen), consisting of two lateral stones and two end stones, with a covering slab that measured 3 feet in width by 5 in length (Figure 11.2). He details how this chamber was 30 × 18 inches in size and lay about 3 feet below the surface of the soil. Once exposed, the slab had projected out over the road; it must have provided an intriguing sight for those passing on the roadway some 8–10 feet below. Gradually, as the surrounding earth fell away, the stones became unstable, whereupon the landowner, Mr Hope Vere, removed them and preserved them.

This history is worth bearing in mind as you arrive at Craigie Hill, for the signs of the history the hill has borne witness to are grown faint. Our ability to read them is also somewhat limited, for this site is being reclaimed by the trees whose centuries-long work is to help build up life-giving soil over the underlying rocks.

The 1856 map shows how the area of Craigie Hill was dotted with old whinstone quarries from the 19th century; these bear testimony to a long-standing extractive relationship between humans and the land hereabouts. A wartime pamphlet was produced to take stock of the mineral resources of the Lothians (MacGregor, 1945), listing whinstone as of particular value in roadmaking. It was for this purpose that the extensive and more recent but now disused quarry at Craigie Hill itself came into operation, carv-

PLATE XV.

KIST-VAEN, AT CRAIGIE-HILL, LINLITHGOWSHIRE.

Figure 11.2: The exposed chamber of the kistvaen is depicted here overhanging the road by as much as 10 feet, where it passes between Clove Craig and the middle hill of Craigie on which sits the fortified settlement. The covering slab was carved on its underside with nine or ten groups of concentric circles. some of which possessed a central cup. The circles varied from 4 to 10 inches in diameter; beyond these measurements, however, their significance and meaning are hard to decipher. So much of the history of our ancients lies buried in this way. One question that we can perhaps usefully ponder, though, is whether the emphasis on circles and of circular interconnected cycles is a form of ancestral wisdom that our high-paced linear ways of thinking have lost sight of.

ing out the bulk – the 'heart, indeed' – of the hill. The igneous rock was quarried for use as road mineral until the 1970s. Since then, the quarry has lain abandoned and has been reclaimed by an assortment of new visitors, ranging from birch trees and wild strawberry plants to deer, brown hare, dog walkers and mountain bikers. Their visitations may grace your own visit and help you try to make sense of this remarkable place, its ancient and contemporary history and the possible futures that will emerge from these remains.

🍃 Habitats

Deciduous woodland, abandoned quarry, edge habitats bordering farmland.

🚌 Transport links

This area is not served by any direct bus routes, but is close to the traffic-free cycle route running from South Queensferry / Dalmeny to Kirkliston.

☕ Refreshments

Craigie Hill is quite isolated, but in its shadow sits Craigie's Farm, which has developed into a thriving soft fruit and vegetable-growing business that now welcomes 260,000 visitors each year. The farm boasts its own café, which can be a great place to call into after your walk. https://craigies.co.uk/cafe/

📖 References and further reading

Daiches, J. (2004). 'Quarry'. Included in *Best Scottish Poems* 2004. https://www.scottish-poetrylibrary.org.uk/poem/quarry/

Fox, R., Dennis, E.B., Brown, A.F. and Curson, J. (2022). 'A Revised Red List of British Butterflies'. *Journal of Insect Conservation and Diversity*. doi.org/10.1111/icad.12582

MacGregor, A.G. (1945). 'The mineral resources of the Lothians'. First issued as *Wartime Pamphlet No. 45* in 1945. Reissued by the British Geological Survey in 2004.

Simpson, J.Y. (1867). 'On ancient sculpturings of cups and concentric rings on stones and rocks in various parts of Scotland'. Proceedings of the Society of Antiquaries of Scotland: Appendix to Volume VI. Edinburgh.

🌐 Weblinks

https://canmore.org.uk/site/50391/craigie-hill.

🚏 Directions

1 Parking layby to the Hill Fort and hillcrest

Pick up the path that initially runs perpendicularly away from the road before turning to the right and rising gently through the trees. There, you pass under some fine old beech trees whose beechmast litters the ground (Figures 11.3a–3b). This is what litter should look like, for it is dropped with purpose and gives back to nature, providing abundant nourishment to the

Figures 11.3a–3b: The path climbs up under a series of old beech trees whose silvery trunks are greened with lichen. On a crisp clear morning there can be frost on the ground, which adds to the crackle as feet move over the bronzed beech leaves and beechmast that carpet the floor.

Figure 11.4a: An early autumn morning sees a dazzling web of jewels festooning the gorse sprigs. The brown stem and thimbles of a once-purple foxglove's flowerhead tell the tale of the imperial jewels of another colour that graced this path earlier in the year.

wider biotic community. Contrast this with the human litter that is thrown away and comes to characterise roadside verges and the layby you have just left. There is no such nourishment in such litter, for it does not give back to, nor enrich, the environment. Such are the lessons trees can teach us.

The path passes among a throng of gorse bushes whose fragrant flowers are always worth appreciating and whose spidery cobwebs are brought to life, or at least rendered visible, by morning dew (Figure 11.4a). The path is also a good place to see foxgloves (Figure 11.4b) whose purples seem to have a great ability to add colour and vibrancy to a woodland scene (Figure 11.4c) and whose trumpets seem designed to amplify the buzzing of visiting bumble bees and other

Figures 11.4b–4c: Foxgloves trumpet a sense of vibrant welcome to passing pollinators and other passers-by.

Figure 11.5: The path through the young birchwood is light and airy, with a rich understorey. The play of light against the birch bark is particularly magical, especially as the light becomes more horizontal in the autumn.

pollinators. Spare, if you will, a moment to stop, close your eyes and listen.

The birch woodland hereabouts can be a great place to spot brown hare, so keep your eyes peeled for a flash of brown careering away from you at speed. These sensitive creatures do not take kindly to dogs and mountain bikers careering along the woodland paths, so if you are not treated to such an encounter please ponder what it takes to provide sanctuary for such creatures and how we can ensure they are not squeezed out. It may be that they have moved out into the surrounding fields or a less-visited part of the woods. It may be that they simply do not feel safe and that we are no longer in tune with notions of

respectful distance and how to minimise the disturbance we create so that we can savour peace without destroying it.

The path allows you to gain the ridge-line upon which the hill fort was located. It provides a fine vantage point from which to enjoy views out in all directions. The view across to the bridges and distant hills is particularly good and appears now and again through the trees. This area of woodland is light and airy, for it is mainly made up of young birch trees (Figure 11.5). There are mature oaks, sycamore, beech, lime and elm too, though, but where the birch dominates the canopy remains airy and the understorey a veritable delight, with plants, including woodland germander and harebell, appreciating the dappled light.

From this hilltop position I often find that I am struck by the contrast between the silence of the woodland and the roar of planes taking off from nearby Edinburgh Airport or the rumbling clatter of a train passing by. The threats and intrusions into this landscape have become so much more human-made than they were for those of our ancestors who chose to dwell on this defensive site. Our ability to discern threats has not evolved in concert with the landscape we face today, for lookouts can no longer warn of us of the advancing hordes of carbon dioxide molecules or of the urge to exploit and consume that has led to our current ecological crisis.

At the same time, in the quiet that floods back after a passing train, we can turn to contemplate life and what we choose to value.

2 From the hillcrest to Dolphington and back to the parking layby

Where the ground starts dropping down with the quarry ahead of you, look out for a path descending steeply to the left, un-

der mature trees. Where this bottoms out, a fainter path can be picked up that leads through gorse, slightly uphill, to emerge at the back of the quarry. This path can be a little hard to find, but once you do, you will have discovered a way to access the quarry floor, where you can get a real sense of how early-colonising plants like silver birch, brambles and wild strawberry (Figures 11.6a–6b) can reclaim a space where heavy machinery once ruled.

Ahead of you, but hidden by a rampart, is a deep human-made pit that you can skirt, taking care to avoid the steep sides and drops to your left. After skirting this part of the quarry, a path to the left can be spied out; this leads into another delightful wooded area. This might not be possible however as work in 2023-24 on the floor of the quarry has obliterated the paths. In this case, the safest thing to do is retrace your steps in order to pick up the path running along the edge of the woodland, with the rim of the quarry on your right. This wonderful woodland strip is a delight to walk through and somewhere where you may hear and encounter wood-

Figures 11.6a–6b: Wild berries can be found growing on the edges of the quarry, and their berries will provide a feast for local wildlife and the appreciative visitor, who may want to consume these mindfully, savouring each sensation, each part of the experience. These wild berries are very different from the bloated commercial varieties to be purchased at shops and supermarkets, and gobbled mindlessly.

land birds, including long-tailed tit, great tit, treecreepers, nuthatch, great spotted woodpecker and song thrush. You may also be treated to the sight of butterflies such as red admiral and the speckled wood (see the special feature) moving through these dappled areas of woodland.

This path skirts the western edge of the quarry, which you will spy at times through the gorse and trees. At one point, you will encounter two large boulders in the middle of the path, but you can easily pass between or around them. A little further on the path turns uphill to the right, to gain the ridgeline at the northernmost tip of the quarry. A range of path options then present themselves. Perhaps the best line is to keep to the high ground and move steadily in a north-north-easterly direction. The ground to the right is more densely forested with conifers, and the lack of understorey reflects the lack of light penetrating this area of wood. All the more reason to enjoy the deciduous woodland with its mix of trees both live and dead; on the dead wood look out for birch bracket fungus and other fungi, including witch's' butter (Figures 11.7a–7b).

The paths all gradually drop towards the private road and track that serves Dolphington House and the ruined farm buildings at Dolphington (Figure 11.8). A little beyond these farm buildings (NT 154 767), pass through a kissing gate and onto a path where you will soon pass an impressive view of the underside of a tree's root system where a tree has fallen away from the path. As you pass through an area of deciduous trees, you get closer to the field edge, reaching a clear junction in the path with a sign pointing three ways: to Dalmeny, West Craigie Farm and Carlowrie. The return route is the Carlowrie one, and it follows the western edge of the wood all the way back to the start.

*Figure 11.7a: Witch's butter (*Tremella mesenterica*) is a parasitic jelly fungus that feeds on fungi that feed on dead wood. It looks like a brain and is often called yellow brain fungus.*

Figure 11.7b: Birch bracket fungus is a sure sign of a dead birch tree, and it can be interesting to notice these on a birch trunk that one might have assumed to be alive, only to then look up and see that the trunk is broken off higher up.

Figure 11.8: The old farm buildings at Dolphington reflect the westering sun as it tries to warm a wintry day with frost on the ground.

★ Special Feature – woodland butterflies

There is something delightful and uplifting about seeing butterflies skipping ahead of you along a woodland path. At Craigie much of the woodland is light and open, and this makes it very well suited to butterflies, who appreciate the warmth of the sun and the availability of food for themselves and their caterpillars. Woodland habitats are essential breeding grounds for up to three quarters of the UK's butterflies – but all is not well in our woodlands and before I provide you with some clues as to where to look and what species to look for, it is worth reminding ourselves of the perilous state of our butterflies.

Butterfly Conservation

The UK Butterfly Monitoring Scheme (BMS), which has been running since 1976, monitors butterfly populations across the country. Its structured approach to surveying allows populations to be monitored year on year, providing an invaluable opportunity to evaluate the impact of climate change, land management (including agri-environment schemes) and local and national biodiversity action plans on the health of the ecosystem. The fast life cycle of butterflies and their sensitivity to a wide range of environmental conditions means that butterflies are particularly well suited to the assessment of ecosystem health.

Sadly, the UK has seen a massive decline in butterfly numbers, pointing to some major concerns about the health of our planetary ecosystems. Of the 62 British species known to have bred in the UK, four are now extinct, and half are on the latest edition of the Red List. This official report was published in May 2022, using data gathered by volunteers through the UK Butterfly Monitoring Scheme and Butterflies for the New Millennium recording scheme.

It is therefore worth contributing to butterfly conservation by recording and reporting any sightings you make on your walks. The British charity, Butterfly Conservation, can provide you with a free app that can help you report any butterflies you see. You can also make your reports online via their Butterflies for the New Millenium online portal. A separate scheme is available for moths: the National Moth Recording Scheme. As the climate continues to warm up, many butterflies currently seen primarily in southern England are likely to spread northwards. One such species with the potential to spread to Scottish woodlands is the white admiral (*Limenitis camilla*); a woodland specialist, this stunning butterfly is partial to the blossoms of brambles, and could easily show up in Craigie one day.

Butterfly watching in Craigie Wood

It may sound counterintuitive to look at butterflies through your binoculars. But the number of times I have caught myself vainly trying to catch up with a flittering butterfly is embarrassing. Viewing them through a pair of binoculars instead is far more rewarding, for you can then follow them without disturbing them, and discover a wealth of colours and hidden details that would otherwise pass un-noticed. Observing them in this way also opens up a whole new world to your imagination. What are they feeding on? Why are they moving off so fast? What are they looking for? Where do they lay their eggs? Where have they come from? These are all good questions to take with you into the woods.

Craigie can be a good place to see the red admiral (*Vanessa atalanta*), a butterfly whose wing-span can reach up to 8 centimetres from tip to tip. These butterflies are strong fliers, and many of our visiting red admirals have migrated from as far away as north Africa. They lay their eggs on nettles, and this done, the adults are thought to migrate south again towards the end of the sum-mer, although some individuals will overwinter in the UK.

Another butterfly you are likely to encounter at Craigie is the speckled wood (*Pararge aegeria*) (Figure 11.9). Male speckled woods are highly territorial, and will engage intruding males in a spi-ralling dance to test each other's fitness. This is just one mating strategy, however. Another is for males to patrol a wider area in search of a mate. The males adopting this latter strategy are darker in colour, so warm up more quickly when basking; this is thought to help them sustain longer flights. The females, once mated, lay their eggs on a number of grasses including false broom and Yorkshire fog. The caterpillars hatch within one to three weeks; they are bright green with faint dark green and yellow stripes. Try searching them out towards the end of the summer, or pause to watch birds seeking them in the grassy understorey of the wood. The caterpillars that survive will either pupate and overwinter as a pupa or, incredibly, do so as a caterpillar.

I had often wondered why I was not seeing these butterflies feeding on nectar-producing flowers. This kind of observation can feed into some helpful reading and research. It turns out that both male and female speckled wood butterflies feed in the treetops, on honeydew, the sugary secretion produced by aphids. When aphid activity is low in the early and later seasons, butterflies may then be seen feeding on flowers.

I would also encourage you to scan the upper realms of the mature trees, especially the oaks. There is a chance that you may be graced by something special such as the purple emperor or purple hairstreak. That would be a memorable sighting and one well worth reporting.

Figure 11.9: A speckled wood butterfly rests on the leaves that even in mid-August cover the woodland floor. The speckles on the upper side of the wing can be discerned even from below, as the four dark spots with their cream-speckled centre draw the eye.

Walk 12

The Water of Leith: from Canonmills to the Gallery of Modern Art

This walk sets out to explore the life of the river running through the heart of Scotland's capital city. It further seeks to make sense of the health of our relationship to this ribbon of blue and green, and to rivers and water more broadly speaking.

The Water of Leith rises in the Pentland Hills, south of Edinburgh, where the West, Mid and East Burns flow across Crow Moss and join to form the Water of Leith, which soon flows into Harperrig Reservoir. The Water of Leith re-emerges from the north-east shore of this reservoir, and continues on its winding way all the way to Balerno, where it is joined by the Bavelaw Burn, bringing water from the Threipmuir and Harlaw reservoirs. From Balerno the Water continues on its journey seaward passing through Curry and Colinton before passing under the Union Canal. It then skirts Murrayfield, the home of Scottish rugby,

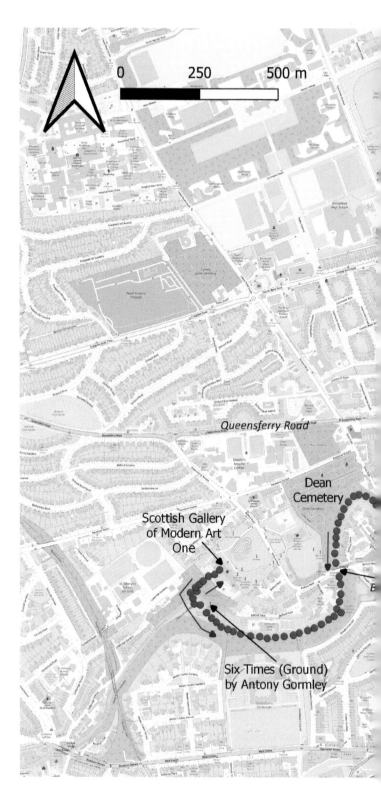

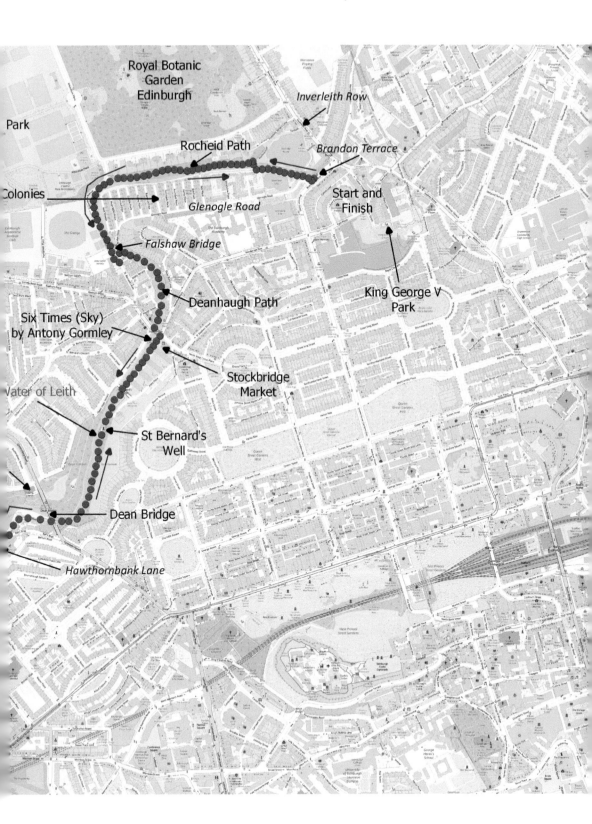

Royal Botanic
Garden
Edinburgh

Park

Inverleith Row

Rocheid Path

Brandon Terrace

Colonies

Glenogle Road

Start and
Finish

Falshaw Bridge

Deanhaugh Path

King George V
Park

Six Times (Sky)
by Antony Gormley

Stockbridge
Market

Water of Leith

St Bernard's
Well

Dean Bridge

Hawthornbank Lane

Figure 12.1: The Antony Gormley statue standing above the weir close to the Gallery of Modern Art stands as erect and as patiently as a heron, monitoring the water closely. The water above the weir is still and tranquil, providing a mirror to the vegetation cascading down the far bank. For a sense of the volume of water flowing down from the hills, pay attention to where the water sits relative to the statue's knees.

before passing through Dean village and Stockbridge on its way to 'empty' into the Firth of Forth, in the heart of Leith.

This journey, from source to sea, is often said to measure 24 miles. This emphasises a form of linear thinking that is decidedly unecological, in the sense that there are no straight lines in nature, and where water is concerned there is a water cycle that ensures that water is constantly moving from clouds to high ground to the sea, searching for a way to return to the heavens sooner or later, one way or another. So much of what has been thrown into our rivers makes its way back to us in the end, although we seem to largely ignore these hidden costs especially when they are shifted onto the environment and future generations. Walking this stretch of river is an opportunity to head upstream in a number of ways: literally, on the ground, historically in terms of our relationship to the river and to water, and in terms of the thinking born of deeper awareness.

This walk's highlights include:

- An opportunity to discover and learn about the history of the Water of Leith as you follow the river upstream and back through time.
- The possibility of encountering grey heron, kingfisher and dipper, and even otter.
- An opportunity to savour the peace and tranquillity that await you in the river bottom, away from the hubbub of the city streets above.
- The possibility of seeing goosander expertly fishing for their dinners.
- An opportunity to consider the many ways that the river is being conserved and restored for the benefit of our collective health and wellbeing.
- Encounters with a number of old willow trees who have borne witness to the comings and goings of floods and droughts and generations of humans.

🪶 Summary

The walk starts from Brandon Terrace in Canonmills, where a flight of steps leads down to the Water of Leith a short distance from the Canonmills Clock. The walk follows the Water of Leith Walkway all the way to the Gallery of Modern Art, emerging briefly onto street level in Stockbridge, but for the most part sticking close to the river. The walkway itself is surfaced for most of its length, although you may want to make forays away from the path to explore short sections of path free from tarmac.

Once you have reached the Gallery of Modern Art, you may want to visit the Gallery and its excellent indoor and outdoor café before retracing your steps back along the walkway to Canonmills. Walking upstream and then following the river back downstream will allow you to experience this wonderful stretch of waterway twice, both against and with the current. Returning with the current, you are perhaps a little more tired, and the quality of attention may change. The return is also likely to be later in the day, so unless you have set out early the path will be busier.

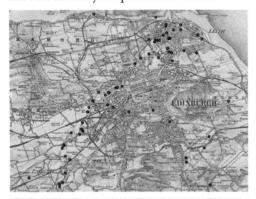

Figure 12.2: The 1896–1911 OS one-inch map is overlain here with red dots representing the location of mills across the Edinburgh area. The Water of Leith can be traced by these red dots for much of its length, until it emerges into the Inner Harbour of Leith. Please do visit the map on the NLS website (see 'Weblinks' below) to explore this history further.

🏛 History

The Water of Leith has a rich and varied history, much of which requires us to look carefully, with a discerning eye, for clues to the industrial past and to the various ways the river is coming back to life. This short historical account pays attention to the various ways the river has been valued and devalued as human livelihoods have ebbed and flowed, entangling themselves with the life force that is the river.

The very name 'Canonmills' reflects the fact that this part of Edinburgh was once a milling village. A plaque on the house that stands on the corner of Eyre Place and Canon Street identifies the building as the Canon Mill. The land hereabouts had been gifted to the Augustinian monks of Holyrood Abbey by King David I after the legendary accident in which he was thrown from his horse. On the night following his escape and accompanying vision of a holy rood (or cross), he is said to have dreamt of a great religious house. The year was 1128, and later that year approval was granted for the founding of the monastery that was to become Holyrood Abbey. The canons of the abbey gave their name to the burgh of Canongate which grew up around the abbey and palace. This burgh remained distinct from Edinburgh until 1865, when it was subsumed into the City of Edinburgh.

Today, it is hard to believe that much of Canonmills and the surrounding area was marshy fen. The area was in many respects distinctly wilder and wetter; what is now King George IV Park was a loch fed by the Water of Leith. Known as Canonmills Loch, it was eventually drained in 1847, as it was no longer needed to power the mills. The Water of Leith's mill sites thus date back to the 12th century, from which point the practice of harnessing the energy of the river grew, peaking in the late 18th century, at which time there were reportedly some 76 mill sites stretching along the 23 miles of river. One of the best ways to appreciate the extent to which mills dotted the banks of the river is to visit the Scottish Mills Project on the National Library of Scotland's website. This fantastic project brings to life this industrial period's footprint, if only in a topographical sense.

During this period of over half a millennium, the river provided power and served as a sluice for evacuating humanity's waste towards the sea. It is fair to say that for generations of our ancestors the river was thus grossly and perhaps even unashamedly exploited and polluted. In the same way that the river was thought to flow from source to sea, humanity's thinking, it could be argued, was linear; there was little awareness of who was paying the cost of such practices, and little way for clues as to the heavy price paid by the ecosystem (and nature's life-sustaining processes) to enter the public consciousness.

As the mills closed down, the river started to recover a little. This was greatly helped by the creation in 1988 of the Water of Leith Conservation Trust, the first river charity to be created in Scotland. Its work to rehabilitate the river's role in the ecosystem and our relationship with the river is quite remarkable.

Over more than 30 years, this small charity has worked hard to raise awareness of the value of this wonderful wildlife corridor and promote community initiatives to care for this ribbon of blue and green as it flows towards the Firth of Forth. A read through its annual reports and newsletters highlights the depth of commitment to conservation, a commitment that this charity can be justifiably proud of. The multiple aspects of facilitating the community's engagement with its community river include a vibrant volunteer programme, guided walks, educational initiatives, river clean-ups and much more. River clean-up operations remain at the heart of the charity's work, with other key areas of work including the control of giant hogweed, Himalayan balsam and

Japanese knotweed. All this work is dependent on and made possible through contributions. In 2017 the charity's funding from Scottish Government (via SNH) was cut, however. For nearly seven years some £12–15,000 had been provided by SNH that had helped to subsidise a wide range of projects. That the charity has gone from strength to strength since then and continues to do is in part due to the support of Edinburgh City Council and various corporate and private supporters, as well as the income generated by the Trust's Visitor Centre and Café. The contribution made by volunteers is, however, enormous with over 10,000 hours of work volunteered annually. In 2021 Paths for All named the charity Community Path Group of the Year, recognising the volunteer hours which amounted to some 126 working days. As part of this volunteers undertook 12 boat-based clean-ups in Leith, preventing human litter from being carried out to sea. This is worth remembering every time you see a plastic bottle or Coke can floating downstream or caught in a logjam. Please do consider contributing to history in the making by volunteering for the charity.

🍃 Habitats
River and riverbank, deciduous parkland and urban streets.

🚌 Transport links
This area is well served by a range of bus services that stop on Brandon Terrace, where the walk starts. For more information please visit the Lothian Buses website. The start point is also close to the cycle network, and bicycles can be locked to bike stands on Brandon Terrace.

🍺 Refreshments
Café Modern One at the Gallery of Modern Art spills out onto a stone terrace surrounded by a beautiful walled garden. It is arguably

one of the calmest and most delightful lunch spots Edinburgh has to offer, and is a veritable highlight of this walk. Throughout the year the café's own kitchen garden supplies the kitchen with a source of fresh produce, including apples, plums, pears, berries, rhubarb, asparagus, salad leaves and herbs and even edible flowers. It is worth looking out for these in the various homemade offerings served up each day by the kitchen. https://www.heritageportfolio. co.uk/cafes/our-cafes/cafe-modern-one/

References and further reading

Brown, H. (2020). *Water of Leith Management Plan 2020–30.* Edinburgh: Water of Leith Action Group.

Freire, P. (1985). *The Politics of Education: Culture, power, and liberation.* Bergin & Garvey.

Nature Scot (2022). *Scotland's Beaver Strategy 2022–2045.* Available from: https://www.nature.scot/doc/ scotlands-beaver-strategy-2022-2045

O'Donohue, J. (2000). *Conamara Blues.* London: Bantam Books.

Priestly, G. (2000). *The Water Mills of the Water of Leith.* Edinburgh: Water of Leith Conservation Trust.

Wall Kimmerer, R. (2001). *Gathering Moss: A natural and cultural history of mosses.* London: Penguin.

Weblinks

https://www.wateroflleith.org.uk/
https://maps.nls.uk/projects/mills/
https://canmore.org.uk/site/120092/ edinburgh-dean-miller-row-lindsays-mill.
https://treesforlife.org.uk/rejecting-extinc- tion-beaver-reintroduction-offers-major- benefits-to-scotland/.
https://www.nationalgalleries.org/art- and-artists/features/visiting-antony- gormley%E2%80%99s-6-times.

Directions

1 Canonmills Clock to Arboretum Avenue

The Canonmills Clock, which stands overlooking the traffic lights and pedestrian crossing on Brandon Terrace, serves as a useful landmark from which to commence this walk. It was gifted to the City of Edinburgh in 1945 by Archibald Bryson, the then session clerk at St Mary's Parish Church, Broughton.

With the clock at your back, walk away from the bridge, along the right-hand side of Brandon Terrace. As you do so, look out for a flight of stone steps dropping down to the river. Descending these steps presents you with a great opportunity to slow down internally, to pay attention to your breathing and to the subtle changes that make themselves felt as you descend the steps. The hubbub of the busy street seems to fade away, and the gurgling of the river draws you into a welcoming embrace. You may also notice the song of the robin or perhaps a wren, then experience a remarkable wave of calmness that seems to sweep over you.

The river was referred to by locals as the Puddocky Burn, reflecting perhaps the presence of frogs in the surrounding wetlands. In old Scots verse, a puddock is a frog, as we are reminded by John M. Caie's poem 'The Puddock' that tells of a frog's realisation of life's finalities.

A puddock sat by the lochan's brim,
An' he thocht there was never a puddock like him.
He sat on his hurdies, he waggled his legs,
An' cockit his heid as he glowered throu' the seggs.
The bigsy wee cratur' was feelin' that prood,
He gapit his mou' an' he croakit oot lood:
'Gin ye'd a' like tae see a richt puddock,' quo' he,
'Ye'll never, I'll sweer, get a better nor me.
I've fem'lies an' wives an' a weel-plenished hame,
Wi' drink for my thrapple an' meat for my wame.
The lasses aye thocht me a fine strappin' chiel,

An' I ken I'm a rale bonny singer as weel.
I'm nae gaun tae blaw, but th' truth I maun tell-
I believe I'm the verra MacPuddock himsel'. …
A heron was hungry an' needin' tae sup,
Sae he nabbit th' puddock and gollup't him up;
Syne runkled his feathers: 'A peer thing,' quo' he,
'But – puddocks is nae fat they eesed tae be.'

John M. Caie (1878-1949(

An alternative explanation proposed for the
naming of this shallower section of river
is from the neighbouring substantial mansion house, Paddock Hall, in what is today
Powderhall. Whether or not one etymology
is more correct than the other is probably a
distraction, for names often hide common origins. The Scots 'Poldre Haw' refers to a marshy
haugh or marshy loch, which is likely to have
been home to frogs; local people familiar
with this habitat may well have encountered
frogspawn, tadpoles and frogs, and heard the
call of frogs as part of the soundscape. The
invitation to you, dropping down from street
to river level, is to immerse yourself in and
become intimate with this soundscape. As you
walk towards the footbridge across the river
(Figure 12.3), you pass several venerable willows whose own sweet music is worth tuning
into and listening to. The wind in the willows
is not just the name of the Kenneth Grahame's
classic – it is a magical part of the riverbank
experience. When was the last time you tuned
in and listened to Radio Willow?

You may want to pause on the bridge, close
your eyes and listen to the music. Opening your
eyes, you may wish to scan the water for signs
of life. Goosander breed on the river, and it
can be a real joy to see the mother teaching her
young to fish. They learn quickly, and can be
seen coming up with fish caught in their bills,
clear evidence that the river is home to a range
of fish including eel, grayling, three-spined
stickleback, stone loach, minnow and flounder.

On the far side of the bridge you find
yourself on the Rocheid Path, named after the
Rocheid family who in 1774 built Inverleith
House, whose extensive grounds are now the
Edinburgh Royal Botanic Gardens. Between
1960 and 1984 Inverleith House was home to
the Scottish National Gallery of Modern Art,
until it moved to the building of the former
John Watson's Institution in west Edinburgh,
where you are heading. As you walk with
the river on your left, look across to the
Stockbridge colonies. These rows of upper and
lower flats were built between 1861 and 1911
by the Edinburgh Building Cooperative. This
organisation was formed by seven stonema-
sons as part an industrial dispute that kicked
off when construction workers were barred

Figure 12.3: The footbridge across from the south to the north bank passes close by a venerable old willow tree before delivering you onto the Rocheid Path.

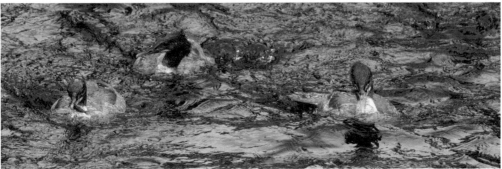

Figures 12.4a–4b: A trio of female goosanders provide their young and any viewers on the bridge with a masterclass in diving for fish. In shallow water it is possible to view them swimming and hunting under water, propelled at speed by their powerful hindlimbs and webbed feet. A healthy river ecosystem is needed to support these apex predators, sitting as they do at the top of the food chain.

from work for striking over the length of their working day. They came up with a scheme that successfully raised funds for the building work that was to provide low-cost housing for skilled workers and artisans. This remarkable initiative, reproduced in nine further locations across the city, demonstrates the ability of cooperative societies to ignite social change in the face of poverty and of political refusal to address issues of social injustice.

In 2000 this area of the Water of Leith experienced some severe flooding. It is estimated that some 500 properties were affected

when the river burst its banks at Stockbridge, Canonmills and Bonnington, causing some £25 million in damages. The Irish firm Lagan Construction successfully bid for the flood prevention contract in January 2011, and began work in March that year to create a flood defence scheme. On the far side of river you can see evidence of the defences, including walls and sealed gates. Edinburgh City Council's flood team liaise with the Scottish Environment Protection Agency (SEPA) in deciding when to close flood gates. Decisions are based around the predicted flows and rainfall forecasts accompanying any specific event; when the water flow exceeds 10m3/s, SEPA notifies the council of the rising water and the accompanying weather forecast. When the flow passes 18m3/s, the reservoir outflows upstream are automatically closed and standby staff notified. At this point, with the alarm raised, SEPA communicates the estimated peak flow and time to the council. At 30m3/s, the first gates are closed (at Ettrickdale Place and Veitch's Place) and barriers erected (at Glenogle Place and Avondale Place). If flow levels continue to rise, further measures are put in place.

Whilst these measures are massively reassuring for local residents, it should also be recognised that the river's natural flood plain has been destroyed and that our hard surfaces ensure that water is funnelled at speed into the river, when before it would have been absorbed by the land to a much greater extent. This is not intended to criticise the decisions of our ancestors, who were contending and wrestling with their own challenges. It is, however, important to recognise the extent to which we are affected by what is termed a 'shifting baseline syndrome'; our awareness of what a healthy river might look like has been distorted by centuries of ecological devastation and environmental injustice. Not only have the marshes and fens that bordered the river and served as flood plains been lost; we have also lost the engineers who maintained these floodplains.

'Engineers?' you ask ... I am of course speaking of the beaver, whose last remaining ancestors were exterminated from Scotland in the 16th century by being hunted to extinction. The beaver has recently made a successful return to Scottish rivers, including the Tay, but it may be a while before we see them on the Water of Leith. There is cause for hope, however, following the September 2022 release of the Scottish Government's Beaver Strategy for 2022–45, which means that a course has been charted in the direction of a healthy river ecosystem. Where the beaver's return is much anticipated, that of the otter is much celebrated, for they have made a successful return to the river, although signs of their presence are much less obvious than those of beavers.

All this to provide the walker with food for thought on how we humans relate to the river, to water, to the water cycle, to nature, to the provision of affordable housing (for humans and the more-than-human world). Much of our recent history has been characterised by an exploitative relationship in which we sought to dominate and profit by nature. Slowly, there is a dawning realisation that we have an alternative, that we can evolve to live with nature, adapting to her in a more dynamic and responsive way. We don't have to fight, subjugate or control her. Indeed, when we take this option, we are guaranteed to lose sooner or later. We need to learn to hop responsively like a puddock, or – better still, perhaps – to flow like water.

As you continue your walk, you may want to consider how we can learn from water and walk like water. As you walk, marvel at the waters flowing past, how they can take any shape and thus stay close to reality. Water stays focused and consistent. Whilst soft, it is strong enough to sculpt rocks. Paying attention to the wisdom of water, we can find inspiration to effectively engage with the challenges we face. The eighth verse of the Tao Te Ching reads:

> The supreme good is like water,
> which nourishes all things without trying to.
> It is content with the low places that people disdain.
> Thus it is like the Tao.
> In dwelling, live close to the ground.

In thinking, keep to the simple.
In conflict, be fair and generous.
In governing, don't try to control.
In work, do what you enjoy.
In family life, be completely present.
When you are content to be simply yourself
and don't compare or compete,
everybody will respect you.

The Rocheid Path emerges on Arboretum Avenue, where you turn left to follow the river towards Glenogle Road and Stockbridge. A black gate on the left before you reach the pavement allows you to avoid the pavement and follow a path beside the river.

2 Arboretum Avenue to Saunders Street

After following the path beside the river towards the Falshaw Bridge that carries Glenogle Road over the river, you will emerge briefly onto Arboretum Avenue, and follow this round to the bridge, where you can pick up the walkway (Figure 12.5) without crossing the river. This next section of the walk follows the walkway along the Deanhaugh Path to reach Deanhaugh Street, where you

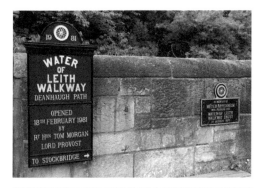

Figure 12.5: The Deanhaugh Path was opened in 1981 as part of the Water of Leith Walkway. The walkway itself was only completed in its entirety in 2002, with funding from the Millennium Project. The walkway is now managed by the City of Edinburgh Council Parks, Greenspace and Cemeteries Department.

Figure 12.6a: A handsome feral pigeon emerges from his nesting site and looks out over the river. This is a perfect example of a bird of cliffs exploiting the ledges and recesses provided by our urban environment. How we live together in urban spaces can teach us a lot about co-existence and mutuality.

cross back over the river to reach Saunders Street, where on a Sunday morning the square occupying the corner between Kerr and Saunders streets plays host to a vibrant local farmer's market.

As you walk this section pay attention: stay open to any surprises that may present themselves to you. There have been times when, on walking along the Deanhaugh Path I have watched a handsome pigeon emerge from the narrow nesting spaces (Figure 12.6a) on the far wall that towers above the river. I have enjoyed watching the way the sun gleams on their plumage, listened carefully to their gentle reassuring murmurs as they communicate with a mate. When they have flown from the nest site, I have been gifted a sight of the smooth white curving shape of a pigeon egg in the darkest recesses of the wall. Sometimes my attention is drawn to the flowers that appear on my path (Figure 12.6b) or to the sounds of the river as it rolls over a particularly rocky section. One such flower is ivy-leaved toadflax (*Cymbalaria muralis*); this is not a plant native to the UK, but was introduced several hundred years ago and is now considered to be naturalised and unproblematic.

Figure 12.6b: The ivy-leaved toadflax
(Cymbalaria muralis) *can be found growing
on the stonework between the iron railings that
line Saunders Street. Here, the river flows far
below street level, and this section of the river is
well vegetated.*

It is worth considering how our approach
to dealing with the three so-called 'invasive'
plants' mentioned in the introduction to
this walk will evolve over the years ahead.
Currently, work groups are treating Japanese
knotweed and giant hogweed on the Water of
Leith with the herbicide glyphosate. Across
Scotland, however, there is growing awareness of the harm that herbicides and pesti-
cides cause to the environment, to human
and ecosystem health. What will it take for us
to work with nature rather than against it? If
we were to value volunteering and outdoor
work more, it is quite possible that we would
refuse quick fixes and invest in ecological
restoration more comprehensively.

3 Saunders Street to the Old Dean Bridge

Continue along Saunders Street with the river
on your right, to pass through an archway and
onto a wide gravelly path that follows the riverbank towards a circular temple whose Doric
columns surround a statue of Hygeia, the Greek
goddess of health and cleanliness (Figure 12.7).
This is St Bernard's Well, named after the 12th-
century monastic St Bernard of Clairvaux, who
is said to have lived in a nearby cave. The spring

may well have been known to St Bernard, but
its discovery is credited to a group of Heriot's
schoolboys out fishing on the river in the
1760s. Such is the way that stories become folk-
lore. We should of course remember that as the
educator and philosopher Paolo Freire (1985,
p.73) pointed out: 'the relationships between
the dominator and the dominated reflect the
greater social context. … Such relationships
imply the introjection by the dominated of the
cultural myths of the dominator'.

So I find it gratifying to be able to share
with you the links between this well and the
abolition of slavery through the purchase
of the well', in 1789, by Lord Gardenstone,
an Edinburgh advocate, philanthropist and

*Figure 12.7: The statue of Hygeia is not the
original. This one was cut from Carrara marble
by David Watson Stevenson as part of the major
renovation work conducted in 1888 and paid for
by the Edinburgh publisher William Nelson.*

staunch anti-slavery campaigner. Gardenstone had played a key role in a landmark case that oversaw the overturning of the subjugation of a slave named Joseph Knight. Eleven years earlier, in 1778, long before any official campaign for abolition had come into being, judges at the Edinburgh Court of Session had ruled eight to four in favour of an African who had been purchased at a Jamaican slave market by Sir John Wedderburn of Ballindean and brought to Scotland to work in Wedderburn's household. Gardenstone was one of the eight judges who ruled in Knight's favour, declaring that Scots law 'could not in principle uphold the institution of slavery'. Gardenstone went on to lead the Edinburgh Committee for the Abolition of the Slave Trade, and his work contributed to the passing of the 1833 Abolition of Slavery Act.

The temple itself was designed by the Scottish painter Alexander Nasmyth in 1789, and became a popular attraction, drawing people who wanted to take the waters. For nearly two centuries it was commonly believed that the mineral-rich waters that sprang from the ground could cure a variety of ailments including muscle pain, arthritis and blindness. These beliefs are reinforced by the inscription above the entrance doorway to the room under the temple: '*Bibendo Valeris*', or 'Drink, and you will be well'.

The room can be visited on certain days of the year (including Sundays through August) so it is always worth checking in case your passage coincides with such an opening. Inside, you can admire the mosaic on the ceiling, the pump with its Grecian vase, and the fireplace that allowed hot water to be dispensed. The temple has been gifted to the City of Edinburgh, but in 1956 it was closed by city health officials, concerned that the water was unfit for consumption and contaminated with, among other things, arsenic.

Figure 12.8: The tree's desire to thrive has led it to push through the railings and absorb them into the trunk. At ground level the tree's roots can also be seen to have lifted the slabs on which some boundary-marking human had chosen to erect this fence.

A viewing platform between the temple and the river is worth exploring for the views it provides of the river. A little beyond the temple a set of steps drop down to the river and provide a further excellent viewing point, with opportunities to watch grey wagtail and dipper as they move up and down the river. Moving on up the main walkway, always with the river on your right, you will soon encounter another example of healing properties. This time, though, it is provided not by taking the waters but by a tree's wrestling match with a set of iron railings (Figure 12.8).

The path then passes under the impressive soaring arches of Dean Bridge, designed by Thomas Telford and built in 1830. There are plenty of opportunities to admire the depth of the gorge through which the river flows, and the wooded banks (Figure 12.9) that were unsuitable for human development. As you approach Miller's Row, look out for a small gateway that allows you to drop down to the riverbed for a view upstream towards World End Weir. This is particularly impressive: the roar of the water cascading down the drop

Figure 12.9: Looking upstream towards the World End Weir; the mature woodland on the far bank provides a beautiful spectacle in autumn as the leaves start to colour up and catch the angled light.

against each other in a monumental heap. These stones are made of French quartz so heavy that they had to be transported in sections. The quartz, particularly resistant, was imported to grind the cheap American grain, which was much drier than Scottish grain, and harder to grind.

The next bridge you reach is Old Dean Bridge, built in 1643 by the Baxter family. From the bridge, you have excellent views both upstream and downstream and this can be a great vantage point to watch birds such as dippers and grey wagtails moving up and

Figure 12.10a: The plaque and inscription on the tollbooth beside Old Dean Bridge can just about be deciphered. It reads: 'God bless the Baxters of Edinburgh who built this house', and shows a crossed pair of wooden shovels (or 'peels') that were used to move the loaves in and out of the ovens.

can be quite deafening – yet surprisingly calming, for it drowns the hubbub of traffic and chatter. Many of the mills downstream of this weir used to be powered by its waters passing into a mill lade. The Great Lade, as it was called, ran for 2 miles, including sections consisting of wooden trough, providing power for a total of eight mills. In 1881 a landslide destroyed the lade, and this fateful accident led to the closure of the mills, as they were no longer able to operate.

Whilst the mills may have closed, there is plenty of evidence of their existence, from street names to the inscriptions on local buildings. As you approach Miller's Row, look out for three iron-bound millstones resting

Figure 12.10b: A bushel of wheat is clearly seen on the plaque high up on the wall of the West Mill buildings.

Figure 12.11a: A rose bush in flower, with the cottages of Hawthornbank Lane curving away above the river.

Figure 12.11b: When the river is flowing slowly, the surface can be calm enough to pick up the reflections of the cottages.

down river. The yellow ochre building you pass before setting foot on the bridge was both a granary and a tollbooth for the river crossing. The inscription on the building is quite weathered and takes some deciphering (Figure 12.10a).

Looking downstream towards the weir you have just passed, you will see the building of West Mills, which was converted into flats some nearly half a century ago. This still bears clear signs of its history (Figure 12.10b). Upstream, the curving cottages running along Hawthornbank Lane draw the eye. and are sometimes reflected in the river itself (Figures 12.11a–11b).

4 Old Dean Bridge to the Gallery of Modern Art

The walkway briefly moves away from the river to skirt an impressive red stone building known as Well Court. This social housing complex, with its community hall and clock tower, was commissioned in 1884 by J.R. Finlay, the owner of *The Scotsman* newspaper, and a philanthropist. Skirting Well Court, you will find yourself rediscovering the river at an old ford, where the riverbed shallows out; this is where northbound traffic leaving Edinburgh would have crossed the river. Today it is a great place to watch dippers immersing themselves to hunt for food on the riverbed.

Pass under the footbridge and follow the walkway up to another plunging weir, known as Damhead Weir. This used to power all the mills on the north bank of the river, and you have to cast your imagination back a long way to picture how polluted this area was with its chemical works, distillery, skin factory and eight mills. A coincidental but no less ironic reminder of how environmentally poisoned this area was can be found in the nightshade encountered along this part of the walkway (Figure 12.12). The properties of this poisonous plant's better-known relative, deadly nightshade, are widely revered; in

Figure 12.12: The flowers of this relative of belladonna, more commonly known as bittersweet (or woody nightshade (Solanum dulcamara), are easily recognisable from their purple and yellow colours.

Figure 12.13: The wall offers support for several specialist plant forms, including ivy and mosses. There is something magical about the prospecting investigations of the ivy tendrils reaching out into the universe. Beyond the ivy we see an established carpet of moss that is all too easily dismissed as an uninteresting green carpet.

Renaissance Italy it was used by women to enlarge their pupils, rendering the women more alluring, and thus earning the common name belladonna. The plant's active ingredients of atropine and scopolamine are still widely used in medicine, allowing detailed eye examinations to be performed. Atropine is also used as an antidote to certain intoxications from chemical warfare agents and insecticides, and can be used as part of a treatment regimen for conditions characterised by muscle spasms, including irritable bowel syndrome, spastic colon, diverticulitis and Parkinson's disease.

Continue on along the walkway to pass under another bridge and past another weir. You then cross over a footbridge to the other bank, whereupon you encounter an impressive stretch of wall running above the river (Figure 12.13). It would be easy to allow this linear feature, which seems to put distance between you and the river whilst blocking out light and creating shade, to affect your mood. It often seems that this area is less appealing, deprived of light and more sterile – lifeless even – as a result. In such habitats life is possible, but colonising such spaces calls for specialists. This is a place to slow down and pay attention to the life that flourishes within the boundary level (or microhabitat) that extends upwards for a few centimetres along the top of the wall. It is for such moments that I encourage you to carry a hand lens (see the special feature).

Continue beyond the wall to find the ground opening out ahead of you and the river coming back into view. You will hear, then see, another weir at the river bend ahead of you. This can be a reliable place to see and watch herons fishing. Another statuesque presence that can reliably be met here is a second Antony Gormley statue, standing calf-deep and sometimes knee- or even thigh-deep in water. A little further upstream, a bridge crosses the river and provides you with access to the back entrance of the Gallery of Modern Art.

★ Special Feature – *Gathering Moss*

Figure 12.14a: Bending down, attending with curiosity and an openness to wondrous discoveries, we come to realise that the green carpet we have dismissed all this time is more than green and mossy; it is rich and beautiful, pulsating with lively forms and lively questions.

Gathering Moss is the title of Robin Wall Kimmerer's exquisitely beautiful cultural and natural history of mosses, a small volume that has done much to promote our appreciation of one of the most overlooked and underestimated life forms – mosses. I cannot recommend it enough as a piece of nature writing, with the potential to heal the disconnections from the natural world, and perhaps even from life itself, that our species is slowly waking up to.

Kimmerer encourages us to slow down and patiently attend to these wonders of nature: 'Attentiveness,' she says, 'can rival the most powerful magnifying lens,' (2003, p.8) – so imagine the extent to which we can find ourselves suddenly transported into a mysterious world (Figure 12.14a) when we are both attentive and armed with a hand lens. Mosses are small, and have evolved to inhabit the small space where earth and air meet, and where air movement is slowed down by the friction of the surface across which it flows. They are beautifully adapted for life in miniature … which is also why we overlook them.

How is it that we dismiss the small and the simple so easily? Kimmerer writes (2003, p.13) that 'mosses are small because they lack any support system to hold them upright'. They also lack vascular tissue, so are unable to conduct water from the ground to the parts of the plant where water is needed. But they have turned these limitations into advantages, and it is their ability to live in micro-communities where being large would be a disadvantage that allows them to grow where many other plants cannot thrive.

Mosses are almost always identified by their scientific names, as we humans, with few exceptions, have paid so little attention to these members of the plant kingdom that few of them have been given common names. One exception to this is the aptly named swan's-neck thyme moss (*Mnium hornum*) also known as the forest star moss (Figures 12.14a–14b). This is one of our commonest mosses in the UK, a lifeform whose leaves stand erect when wet, becoming contorted when dry. Close inspection will show the stems supporting the leaves to be a dark red-brown, paling to a yellowish-green towards the tip. These leafed stems can be 2–4 centimetres tall, and yet these are not the most prominent part, for the spore-bearing part of the moss pushes into the airstream above the boundary layer. This allows its spores to catch a breeze and set off in search of new surfaces to colonise – necessary, because the spores cannot germinate in the leafy carpet provided by their parents. So they are raised on tall stems called setae (Figure 14b) allowing the passing airstreams to draw out and lift the powdery spores. When the spores eventually land on a suitable moist surface they absorb moisture, swelling up before sending out a green thread that spreads and branches, much like the moss's algal ancestors. This resemblance to algae is soon lost, however, as leafy shoots emerge from buds and a new cushion of moss establishes itself.

Figure 12.14b: The red setae of the swan's-neck thyme moss support the maturing green sporophytes, and allow them to stand free of the still air within the boundary layer. The sporophytes have been produced as a result of the eggs carried by the female moss being fertilised by sperm carried through the moisture coating the moss itself.

5 Arriving at the Gallery of Modern Art

Hopefully your encounters will have allowed you to slow down and gather a little of your own moss. The Antony Gormley exhibit (titled 6 Times) is an invitation to slow down and become more contemplative. its six life-size cast-iron sculptures of the Turner Prize-winning artist's own body invite us to consider the natural and the human interconnections this world is woven of. This, one of the six Gormley statues, stands above the weir below the Gallery of Modern Art.

The surrounding trees are favoured hunting grounds for the colourful local kingfisher. In autumn the colours of the surrounding trees are also a feast for sore eyes, perhaps best feasted upon by adopting the pose and attitude of the statue, calmly absorbing the magic of each and every moment.

The first of the Gormley statues stands buried to the neck in the concrete at the front entrance of the Gallery of Modern Art, and is worth a visit even if it is to contemplate how trapped we ourselves are by our controlling, unhealthy relationship with the natural world. After visiting the gallery's excellent café and refreshing yourself, you could take the walk back along the river. This allows you to experience the river as it flows towards the sea. But whether you choose to end your walk at the gallery or retrace your steps, there is a sense of freedom associated with flowing water that you can perhaps carry with you. John O'Donohue famously wrote how he 'wished that he could live life like a river, constantly surprised by its own unfolding' (2000, p.41).

Walk 13

River Esk, Levenhall Links and Musselburgh Lagoons

A visit to Musselburgh and the mouth of the River Esk might not on the face of it be as inspiring as a visit to the long sweep of unspoilt coastline between Aberlady and North Berwick. The coastal stretch around Musselburgh has a long industrial past, and the Esk powered several mills and industries. More recently, the area was overshadowed for 40 years by the Cockenzie Power Station, until it finally closed in 2013. This, however, is a true birdwatcher's walk! How so?

You get to explore a diversity of habitats capable of drawing in a rich variety of species, bringing them into view at different points and times, depending on the tides and the weather. This area provides rich feeding grounds as well as resting and roosting areas. It has benefited immensely from the work undertaken by Scottish Power to restore the 120-acre site where, whilst the coal-powered station was still operational, fly ash from

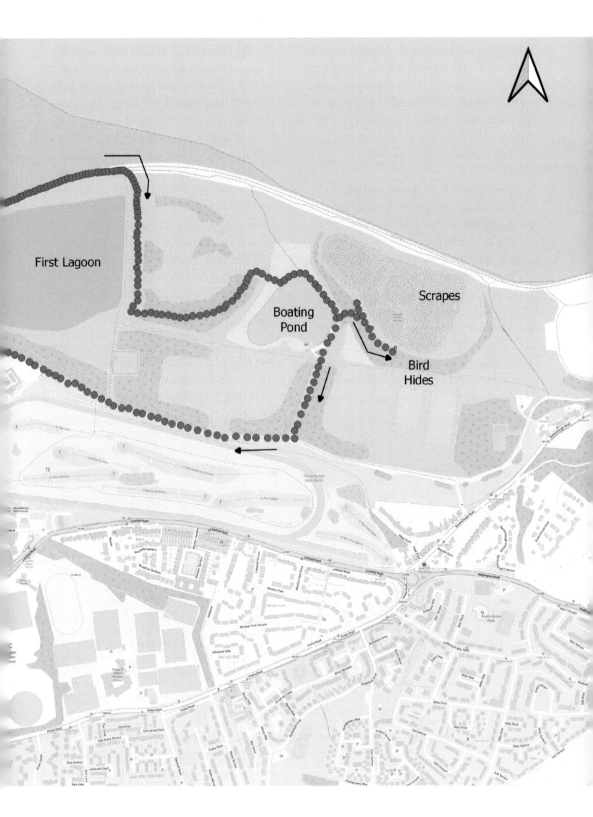

First Lagoon

Boating
Pond

Scrapes

Bird
Hides

it was dumped into four large lagoons extending between the sea wall and the Musselburgh racecourse. The area is now an important part of the Firth of Forth Special Protection Area[5] (SPA) and SSSI, and is recognised as one of the best birdwatching sites in Scotland.

This walk's highlights include:

- An opportunity to observe and study the birds gathering to feed and amuse themselves on the banks, shoreline and food-rich mudflats where the River Esk opens up and enters the Firth of Forth. This area can be a hot spot for wintering waders including curlew, redshank and bar-tailed godwit, as well as sea ducks, grebes and divers.
- An opportunity to see and watch one of our most attractive ducks, the goldeneye, who are partial to visiting the river upstream from the mouth and can easily be viewed from the riverbank and bridges.
- The opportunity to scan flocks of gulls for unusual species including Iceland, little, glaucous and Mediterranean gulls, with the possibility of Sabine's, laughing, Franklin's and ring-billed gulls keeping gull enthusiasts on their toes, whilst challenging the identification skills of non-gull enthusiasts.
- A walk along the sea wall which, in winter, will often reward you with sightings of sizeable groups of Slavonian grebe.
- An exploration of how an industrial site has been restored for wildlife and how this contributes to both wildlife conservation and the local economy.

❧ Summary

The walk starts in the heart of Musselburgh, where parking is available beside the river, at the junction of Shorthope Street and Millhill (NT 344 727). From the footbridge cross-

Figure 13.1: The mouth of the River Esk is full of contradictions, highlighting humanity's troubled and troubling relationship with the natural world. Here, two shopping trolleys lie resting in the mud at low tide as a sweep of water winds its way seaward. A car tyre has similarly found a temporary resting place in the mud, which also supports visiting birds who come to feed in vast numbers twice a day, when the mud is exposed. What we don't see is the wealth of invertebrate life, including worms and molluscs, thriving within the mud. Many of the visiting birds possess long bills perfectly designed to probe the mud and seek out the food that is nature's harvest. The birdlife on view at the mouth of the Esk lives in close reciprocal relationship with nature, a relationship that our dysfunctional human civilisation has become disconnected from. Rebuilding those connections is one of the challenges we now face.

5 https://sitelink.nature.scot/site/8163

ing over the Esk upstream of a small island, follow the right bank of the river down to its mouth, where it empties into the firth. The route then skirts the Air Training Corps (ATC) buildings to reach the sea wall. Follow this until the opportunity arises to explore an area of grassland and young woodland, then emerge beside the boating lake. Walk around this in order to visit the hides overlooking the sheltered collection of shallow ponds or scrapes where the third lagoon used to be. On the way back, follow a path to reach the racecourse, where a right turn brings you back towards the ATC building and the Esk, and follow it to regain your starting point.

🏛 History

This section focuses primarily on the history of the coastal strip explored on this walk, and so touches only briefly on the history of Musselburgh itself.

Construction of the Cockenzie Power Station began in 1959 on the site of the Preston Links Colliery. The building was designed by RMJM, one of the largest architecture and design networks in the world. The firm was founded in 1956 as a partnership between Sir Robert Matthew (Professor of Architecture at the University of Edinburgh 1953–68) and Sir Stirrat Johnson-Marshall. Their website[6] boasts a photograph of the power station's twin chimneys soaring nearly 150 metres into the sky, belching out smoke and occupying a major part of the Edinburgh and East Lothian skyline for over half a century. The accompanying text nostalgically celebrates the heritage value of the power station, which was listed as one of the 'top 100 modern Scottish buildings' and lamenting the fact that the demolition of the chimneys was not more widely opposed.

Historic Scotland did not stand in the way of its destruction. Further, Scottish Natural Heritage was unequivocally clear when it stated that the iconic chimneys 'serve no functional purpose' and demolition 'presents an improvement to the visual amenity of the area'. Almost a year after the power station's demolition it's clear that there are many who don't agree. Cities are now gripped with talk of sustainability, space and new technologies. Yet for all that, cities are their skylines. If nothing is added, as in the case of Cockenzie, then something is irrevocably lost.

And yet, as we shall see, by not forcing something human-made to remain on the skyline, by letting go and embracing loss, a space was created for nature to co-create her own gift to this place. Nature is and will remain the 'largest architecture and design network in the world', and our challenge as a species arguably lies in respecting this and working with rather than against her.

When Cockenzie came into operation in 1967 for the then South of Scotland Electricity Board, it was the UK's largest coal-powered fire station. Initially it was supplied with coal from the deep mines of the Midlothian coal fields, but when these closed coal from the Lothians, Fife, Lanarkshire and Ayrshire was ferried to the power station by train. This was at a time when public awareness of the damage wreaked on the environment by coal power was only just starting to emerge. Such awareness only emerged over time, and it took a while for knowledge of the impact of the power station on air quality, on human health and on the ecosystem's health to filter through.

Some of the waste products produced by the power station were visible, others much

---

6   https://rmjm.com/cockenzie-power-station-history-and-memory/

less so. One of the most visible was the pulverised fuel ash (PFA) and dust arising from the burning of coal. Fly ash from the flue gases was captured by the station's electrostatic precipitators. Together with bottom ash, this was sold to the construction industry for use in products such as cement. Large quantities of remaining ash needed to be disposed of locally, and these were piped to the four large lagoons that had been constructed on reclaimed land north of Musselburgh's racecourse. So far so good, perhaps. A less visible waste product were the oxides of nitrogen (NOx). A report prepared by Entec consultants for the European Commission assessed the emissions of NOx together with sulphur dioxide from large industrial plants across 27 European countries between 2004 and 2006. It found Cockenzie to be the worst offender by far, emitting 50 per cent more NOx than the next-worst plant, in Middlesbrough, and nearly 100 per cent more than the most polluting Italian plants. These emissions contribute to the formation of acid rain and to the air pollution that exacerbates the symptoms of people living with asthma, emphysema and other lung conditions.

In 2001, in recognition of these concerns, the EU Large Combustion Plant Directive was issued, setting out to control the emissions of sulphur dioxide, oxides of nitrogen and dust from such plants. As well as setting standards for new plants, this directive required older plants to either comply with strict emissions limits or opt out, in which case they were limited to a maximum of 20,000 hours of operation from 2008, and had to close completely by the end of 2015. Cockenzie opted out, and between 1991 and its closure in 2013 the station was run as a marginal station, meeting seasonal and peak increases in

energy demand and covering for other power stations when needed.

The reclaiming of the land for the ash lagoons and the subsequent filling and redevelopment of the four lagoons has had a range of implications for wildlife. According to Andrews (2021, p.2) the area between the mouth of the Esk and the harbour at Prestonpans had been used as a rubbish dump for some 40 years, and the coastline ran close to the racecourse. The creation of a 2.7 km-long stretch of sea wall allowed land to be reclaimed for the construction of the lagoons, and this area soon came to the attention of waders and other birds in search of a safe place to roost and rest up at high tide. The lagoons were gradually filled by ash, starting with the easternmost lagoon closest to the power station. For many years, the westernmost lagoon remained full of water, but by 1985 this too had been filled in. Raised bunds were then created to form four higher-level lagoons. During this time, the value of the land for birds was becoming recognised, offering as it does the only major roost on the south shore of the Forth between Cramond and Aberlady. In 1993 a series of scrapes were created, and the overlooking hides built in 1998/99. The scrapes consist of a series of freshwater pools lined with clay, which are particularly attractive to waders, ducks and other birdlife, providing further feeding opportunities throughout the tidal cycle. Their inclusion within the Firth of Forth SSSI[7] further recognises their value to birds.

In 2004 Scottish Power, the then owners of the site, launched a Biodiversity Action Plan (BAP) that outlined a series of ecological enhancement objectives and a timescale for their implementation. As part of this plan, the lagoons have been planted with native trees

---

7   The lagoons also form a component in the Firth of Forth Special Protection Area and Ramsar site designation.

including alder, ash, birch, hawthorn, rowan, white poplar, whitebeam and willow. This restoration work has attracted several UK BAP breeding birds, including bullfinch, dunnock, house and tree sparrow, grasshopper warbler, grey partridge, linnet, reed bunting, skylark, song thrush, skylark and yellowhammer.

Despite the site's well-established value for nature and therefore for people, there is an ongoing need to defend this when other values and visions of the future threaten the site. In January 2021 local papers reported that a draft proposal had been developed and put forward for an international Formula 1 racetrack at Musselburgh Lagoons. This led over 6,000 people to sign a petition demanding the lagoons be protected from developments that would be to the detriment of the site. The *East Lothian Courier* reported on a war of words that erupted on social media, with the businessman proposing the scheme 'accusing those supporting the wildlife sanctuary of putting the welfare of "cannibal seagulls" ahead of the local economy'. The article[8] went on to quote him as saying:

> It is scandalous that this valuable site will not generate any local income from bird-watchers, butterflies and seagulls.

The *Courier* offered an alternative perspective from Laura Moodie, Scottish Green Party candidate for the South Scotland region:

> This is a horrendous proposition and deserves to be opposed every step of the way. … The developer's claim that the lagoon's wildlife is a 'wasted opportunity' is an insult to the hundreds of people who use the area for rec-

reation every day. … Rather than hear about hare-brained schemes like this, what we need to do is ensure that the proposals for the wider redevelopment of the Cockenzie Power Station area are sustainable and balance the creation of jobs with improving the natural environment of this beautiful coastline.

In 2018 the former site of the power station, which lies between the villages of Prestonpans and Cockenzie, was acquired by East Lothian Council with a view to supporting its ambitions to promote economic growth in the area and create opportunities. The intervening years have seen the development of a Masterplan[9] that seeks to redevelop the area in consultation with the local community and other stakeholders. It is striking that these plans pay limited attention to the ecology of the area. They highlight that 'there are several protected species and habitat designations within close proximity of the site, including the adjacent SPA' and that 'works within the Firth of Forth could impact on these' – but there is no attempt made to integrate biodiversity explicitly into the planning process. This is alarming. It reflects perhaps the ongoing concern that there is less awareness of the biodiversity crisis facing the planet than to the climate crisis that scientists, politicians and the general public are awake to and seeking to address. The United Nations has held a Conference of the Parties (COP) to address the biodiversity crisis and establish agreements as to how we address these. In December 2022, the 15th COP meeting on biodiversity was held in Montreal, Canada, bringing together government representatives and other official organisations from across

8 https://www.eastlothiancourier.com/news/19002187.
   formula-1-track-musselburgh-lagoons-thousands-oppose-plans-petition/
9 The masterplan can be consulted on the East Lothian Council website: https://www.eastlothian.gov.uk/info/210547/
   planning_and_building_standards/12312/former_cockenzie_power_station/3

the world to discuss a pledge to bring 30 per cent of the planet's terrestrial and marine habitat into conservation for nature by 2030.

The so-called '30 by 30' target is the equivalent of that set by the climate COP to limit planetary temperature rise to 1.5°C. What does this look like in practice, and how might it be relevant to the Musselburgh Lagoons? To answer that question, it is helpful to return to the challenge of balancing sustainable development with ensuring that our environment is healthy and sustains life.

The quotes reported on the previous pages highlight the challenges we still face in shifting the conversation about nature conservation. There are those who – blinded, perhaps, by their short-term obsession on making money and on profit – fail to appreciate how we undervalue at our peril the health of the ecosystem on which we all depend. It is important that we find ways to guard against such myopic views, for they shift the burden of costs onto the environment, onto future generations, and onto the health and wellbeing of the wider population, who have become disconnected from the natural world but who are increasingly looking for ways to reconnect because they appreciate that healing nature is synonymous with healing ourselves.

The contribution made by wildlife tourism to regional economies was recognised in a 2016 report by Visit Scotland, highlighting the extent to which visiting nature lovers make a significant financial contribution to local establishments such as cafés, restaurants, B&Bs and hotels. It can be argued, however, that such accounting fails to capture the immeasurable value made by such places to human health and wellbeing. Fortunately, the recent pandemic helped develop an appreciation for how interdependent our health is with that of nature. A shift towards a wellbeing economy that recognises the many ways of valuing nature is long overdue.

🍃 Habitats

River and riverbank, urban streets, tidal estuary mudflats, grassland, deciduous woodland, lagoons and boating pond.

🚌 Transport links

This area is well served by a range of bus services that stop on Musselburgh's High Street (Stop B) a short distance beyond the junction with Shorthope Street. If you are cycling from Edinburgh, National Route 76 links Edinburgh with Musselburgh and provides a quiet route out of town via the Innocent Railway Tunnel and the John Muir Way.

☕ Refreshments

Musselburgh has a range of cafés and establishments where you can seek warmth and refreshment after your walk. These include the Coffee Gallery on the High Street and, if you are willing to walk back across the Esk, the East Lothian Bistro at the Brunton Theatre. https://www.bistroatbruntonhall.co.uk/.

🔖 References and further reading

Andrews, I.J. (2021). *Birds in Musselburgh 2020*. Available from: https://tinyurl.com/mc2ub2cd.

Visit Scotland (2017). Insight department: 'Wildlife tourism'. Available from: https://tinyurl.com/yt8du4py, https://tinyurl.com/3tetp4tp.

🌐 Weblinks

https://rmjm.com/cockenzie-power-station-history-and-memory/.

A film of the demolition of Cockenzie Power Station: https://www.youtube.com/watch?v=hSZEIZ9eFtY.

Figure 13.2a: A flock of pigeons gather to enjoy the sun and some pigeon conviviality on a rooftop overlooking the Esk. Their feathers dance in the sunlight, and their eyes are constantly surveying the world for their next meal and the potential threat of a sparrowhawk that they need to remain alert to.

⚑ Directions

1 Millhill car park to Goose Green Place

From the car park, head across to the river-bank immediately downstream of the Store Footbridge, which crosses the Esk above a small island. This, one of seven bridges connecting the town of Musselburgh with Fisherrow on the opposite bank, is located at the historic ford. The islands, with their willow trees, are much favoured by the local waterfowl, and there is usually plenty of interaction between people and the swans and ducks who gather to be fed. I would encourage you, however, to observe rather than take part, and to gradually immerse yourself in the theatre of bird activity that the Esk offers up.

The first section of the walk follows the east bank of the Esk towards the mouth of the river; this gentle stroll provides an excellent opportunity to slow down and become more fully present to the unfolding experience. There is always something going on, whether it be the sight of grazing geese on the far bank,

the fascinating comings and goings of the local feral pigeons (Figures 13.2a–2b) or the choral performance of the starlings (Figure 13.2c) who provide a musical score to accompany the narrative of your walk as it unfolds. Slowing down is a way to ease yourself into the walk,

Figure 13.2b: When gathering in such numbers, there is a good chance that you may see them take off in a flurry of confusing activity. This is a true spectacle to observe and enjoy, as each bird traces a path in the sky that seems designed to add to the confusion of a predator, before the flock settles again.

Figure 13.2c: The local starlings like to gather on the aerial masts of the Cadet Centre. One can imagine them listening in to the many radio messages and transmitting them on in their own unique and very cheeky way.

to find a gentle rhythm, to make those little adjustments that allow you to tune into the seasonal rhythms of place.

With the river on your left, follow the bank, passing a further bridge and noting any debris caught by the pillars of the bridge after any recent stormy weather. The route finding is easy for you need only follow the river, choosing between the pavement or the grassy sward (much favoured by geese) until you reach the ATC hut, home to 297 Musselburgh Squadron of the Air Cadets, at the end of the very aptly named Goose Green Place. This can be a particularly good place to observe the local starlings if you haven't already been treated to a singing performance when passing under the trees that line the riverbank.

A careful scanning of the river, especially during the winter months, is likely to throw up a good number of goldeneye, who many consider to be one of our most majestic ducks; see the Special Feature dedicated to them. Other birds that you can expect to see before reaching the mouth of the river include grey heron and oystercatcher, but there are often surprises too.

★ Special Feature – goldeneye

The word 'goldeneye' alone in an internet search engine will produce several pages of links to the 1995 Bond film starring Pierce Brosnan, so to avoid this you may want to add Bucephala clangula to your search term. This medium-sized diving duck is particularly handsome and very athletic with its large domed black head, which carries a green sheen. The face is broken up by a jewel of an eye that sparkles golden in the sun. Between this eye and the bill there is a delightful white patch that sets off the blackness of the bill and looks intriguing when the bird is viewed face on; the rest of the body is an exquisite interplay of black and white.

During the winter months we see an influx of goldeneye from northern Europe, and it is these birds who most probably show up on the Esk. Whilst not gathering in large numbers

Figure 13.3a: When the sun sparkles on the waters of the Esk, creating a magical silver blanket, the only bird capable of gracing the scene is the goldeneye. Here a female is flanked by two males, resplendent in their finery.

Figures 13.3b–3c: The male goldeneye above (left) is throwing his head back, bringing it to rest on the middle of his back. This fore-and-aft movement creates a pumping action that is itself impressive and worth watching for. It is part of the bird's communal display, which is further enhanced when a kick from the bird's feet pushes its rear end upwards, causing its front to dip into the water. At the same time the bird thrusts his head and neck up vertically whilst emitting a loud double whistle that carries well across the water. A very different sound is produced when the birds explode forwards, running on the water and pumping their wings to take off.

like other duck species, they do appear in small groups and it can be a real joy watching them interact (Figures 13.3a–3c). They are reputed to be shy birds, and so I always feel privileged when getting to observe them at close hand on the Esk.

Scotland has historically been at the very limit of the goldeneye's breeding range, and the story of how they were first encouraged to stay and breed here is worth sharing. It had been known for some time that this duck had a well-established habit of nesting in trees. Yes, indeed: trees! In Scandinavia, they often took over the large cavities excavated by black woodpeckers and raised their young within the shelter provided by these hollowed-out trees. In Lapland over the last two centuries, locals had taken to harvesting their eggs by encouraging the birds to use nest boxes. It was this knowledge that inspired Roy Dennis, when he was working for the RSPB in the Cairngorms during the 1970s, to erect nest boxes among the Scots pine forests fringing the lochans on which wintering ducks were regular visitors. These boxes may have helped persuade a small number of pioneering ducks to stay on in Scotland and refuse the migratory call; in 1973, of six nesting pairs of goldeneyes five were using nest boxes. A quarter of a century later, in 1998, some 58 pairs were nesting at the RSPB's Insh Marshes Reserve, near Kingussie. Of these only five were in natural sites, reflecting the importance of the black woodpecker's contribution to this story.

How do we make sense of this? Perhaps by recognising that we are part of nature and can contribute in positive ways to her unfolding. We can co-create healthy futures by realising the potential that a healthy ecosystem is ripe with. In this case, we had to compensate for the missing piece of the jigsaw – a giant woodpecker. This does not mean all our contributions have merit, for as a species we have a tendency toward arrogance combined with a real dearth of humility. With sufficient humility we can learn to partner nature and evolve with her in a respectful reciprocal sense. This is about mutuality and partnership. We have much to unlearn, however, for our default is to seek to exert power over and to control things; this is characteristic of the domination system we have been enculturated into. Our own survival on this planet may require us to develop power literacy and to abandon the domination system in favour of partnering. Power *with* is nature's way; it is a characteristic of open systems, and of openness to feedback and to evolving together as part of nature rather than apart from her.

Albert Einstein is quoted as saying that the most important question any of us can ever ask ourselves is: 'Is this universe a friendly place?' It's a powerful question, and one worth considering as you walk along the riverbank and then the sea wall. It is a question that shapes the way we view and react to the world. If we assume the world is threatening, we adopt a fear-based way of seeing the world. If we believe that the universe is an unfriendly place, there is a strong chance we will use our sciences, our technology and the natural resources to create bigger walls to exclude the unfriendliness, and weapons to destroy it. So, as you ponder the goldeneye who has befriended Scottish lochs and forests and who visits the Esk in winter, please give a thought to how we as a species befriend and find our home in nature.

2 Goose Green Place to path running from sea wall alongside first lagoon

Skirting to the right of the cadet centre, you reach the sea wall and a broad track running alongside it. As you do so, it can pay to take a moment to look at the trees to your right; many of these are alder (*Alnus glutinosa*), and early in the season their cones and catkins are a real delight to contemplate. The brown, woody cones you may see on the tree will be from last year; these are the remnants of the female flower. Alders are monecious, however, which means they have both male and female flowers. The long pendulous catkins that appear every spring are the tree's male flowers, preparing the way for the year to come. They gradually elongate and drop to a length of 2–6 centimetres, revealing a delightful yellow-green colour. Their pollen is released to the wind, to pollinate the green oval-shaped female flowers. These gradually become woody, and will eventually release their seeds, which are dispersed by wind and water during the last quarter of the year. The path along the sea wall offers a remarkable series – a plethora even – of opportunities to observe birds feeding either on the shore below the wall or on the mudflats on the far bank. Look out for curlew, redshank, oystercatcher, turnstone (Figures 13.4a–4b) and other waders as well as a range of other less common species, including wood sandpiper, curlew sandpiper, ruff and little stint. The walk that traces the sea wall also typically

Figures 13.4a–4b: It is remarkable how well turnstone (Arenaria interpres) blend into the environment. If it weren't for their give-away orange legs and foraging behaviour, they might mass totally unnoticed. An ability to notice such colours is born of attentiveness, providing an opportunity to distinguish different shades of colouration. In doing so, you come to appreciate and learn the differences in colour between the oranges of the turnstone's legs and the oystercatcher's bill, the reds of the redshank's legs and the oystercatcher's ruby red eye and their pinkish legs. The various hues can slowly become a meaningful visual code.

provides excellent views of divers, grebes and sea-going ducks, including eiders, goosanders and various scoters, including the rare surf scoter. Other birds to look out for include rock and meadow pipit as well as pied wagtail. In recent winters there have been over 40 Slavonian grebes sighted here, and it would not be unusual to see red-throated diver. If you are keen to record new species, it is worth scanning through the flocks of gulls, as you may find yourself looking at regular species such as little, Mediterranean, Iceland and glaucous gulls, but you may less commonly see Franklin's, Sabine's and ring-billed gulls cropping up. All this to show how easy it can be to succumb to the bird-twitching virus! There is nothing wrong in ticking off new species, but it is important for the experience to be much more than a tick-box exercise.

As you walk eastwards, look out for a track coming in from the right (NT 352 739). This runs along the side of the raised bank that has been built up around the first lagoon. The lagoon itself was designated a Special Protection

Figure 13.5a: Hunkered down and hidden from view in the grasses, it is possible to view a kestrel hovering in the pursuit of a bank or field vole. Picking your spot and quietly observing the grassland area requires patience, but the rewards, when they come, are of inestimable value.

Area (SPA) for its value as a roosting site. At this point the walk moves away from the sea wall, to explore the grassland and wooded areas between the sea wall and the boating pond.

3 Sea wall to boating pond

This next section explores an area of unmown and therefore tussocky grassland that is a great habitat for voles. The tunnels of these fast-breeding small mammals can be seen when you look closely at what appears to be an impenetrable mass of grassy stems and leaves. Hunting for voles challenges the predator to detect their movement and pounce in from above with a long snout (if a fox) or a pair of talons. Unsurprisingly, this area is much favoured and visited by short-eared owls, kestrels (Figures 13.5a–5b) and other birds of prey who have developed a specialism in hunting over such grasslands. The area, however, is also open to dog walk-

ers, and a network of paths have built up that give rise to a lot of disturbance. So your best chance of seeing birds hunting across this area is likely to be in the early hours of the day and, to a lesser extent, the late evening. The surrounding strips of woodland provide good cover from which to watch, and are themselves worth pausing and resting in for a while, rewarding yourself with a slow, contemplative moment (Figure 13.6), listening to the woodwind section of the orchestra. Both meadow pipit and skylark are recorded as breeding here, as are grey partridge. In winter, the grassland may well play host to groups of foraging twite and linnet.

Two possibilities present themselves for wending your way to the boating pond. Both are described here as prompts to encourage you to explore the area and discover different vantage points from which to observe the grassland areas.

Figure 13.5b: The black arrow-tipped triple buds of the ash tree frame this young kestrel, who is content to survey things from this high, bouncing vantage point and wait for the next hunting opportunity. The ash branches rattling together when free of their leaves in autumn provide a very different experience from that of the delicate sounds produced by the fine-branched birch trees.

Figure 13.6: The birch trees of the new woodland stretching between the boating pond and the first lagoon have a magical allure, especially if you pause for a moment and contemplate the soaring trunks as they reach for the sky and allow themselves to explore new frontiers and horizons. The music of such trees has its own unique character, which reveals itself when we close our eyes, and open our ears to the sounds floating through the air.

Option 1 involves following the track with the high bank of the first lagoon immediately on your right. As you near the end of this bank look out for a small path heading off to your left and disappearing into the area of woodland; if you reach a junction of tracks (NT 325 726) you have gone too far and need to backtrack a little. Once in the area of woodland, follow a path winding through the birch trees. This emerges in one of several points at the far edge of the copse. You then turn right, to work your way towards the pond.

Option 2 involves picking your way round the northern edge of the open area and then swinging round to meet the edge of the copse, beyond which you glimpse the pond.

Approaching the pond, keep an eye out for the more confident species who may be making use of the pond despite its human frequentation. You can usually expect to see a grey heron hunting the shallows, and kingfishers are often seen. Looking out across the water, it is worth scanning the ducks for more unusual species such as scaup, whilst in winter the visitors may include some Mediterranean gulls.

Move left to follow the northern edge of the pond, with the water on your right. The willows and alder lining the edge of the pond help to provide shelter and a little habitat which hopefully will be encouraged to develop further, to help overcome the sterility we humans impose on green spaces by tidying them up and chasing out the wild. A good example of this chasing out can be seen when large groups of humans descend on the place with their barbecues, boats and paraphernalia. The birds who do choose to stay can be seen putting distance between themselves and the source of the disturbance. Observing such interactions provides a shop window on the uneasy relationship that exists and the disconnection that has arisen between many urban humans and the natural world. From the air this pond is close to heart-shaped – yet it is loved as an amenity rather than as nature in all its wondrous glory.

4 Boating pond to the Scrapes

Following the northern edge of the boating pond, heading towards the car park at its south-eastern corner, you arrive at a grassy area with an East Lothian Council sign for the bird reserve. A small path heads into the trees, and can be followed as it winds its way to two observation hides. These are cold concrete structures open to the skies, so if you plan to spend any time scanning the scrapes with your binoculars or telescope, it is worth taking an extra layer of clothing and an insulated sit mat. A warm flask of tea might not go amiss, either.

The extent to which birds value these scrapes is clear, for they can be seen gathering in large numbers, and the conviviality is very apparent. At any one time there is no knowing who you might see; a good variety of waders may be there, especially when the birds are on passage to their breeding or wintering grounds. Those recorded include black- tailed godwit, ruff, snipe and wood sandpiper. Rarities on the scrapes can reward the observant birdwatcher and have, in the past, included red-necked phalarope, spoonbill and avocet and various sandpipers including marsh, pectoral and western sandpiper. One of my favourite sights though is that of groups of lapwing wheeling above the water, their black and white colouring providing a birding

spectacle of sorts. There is something magical about the alternating interchange of black and white as lapwings' broad wings are drawn through the air in a flapping liquorice spectacle. The spectacle is often accompanied by the' characteristic *pee-wit* call that this bird emits. When the bird settles and the sun catches their backs, the black of colouration is seen to be a sparkling emerald green, which is why the lapwing is also referred to as the green plover.

5 The Scrapes to Musselburgh Racecourse, and back to the Cadet Hut and Millhill car park

After visiting one or both hides, retrace your steps to the boating pond and cross the car park area to reach the far end of the pond. Carry on straight ahead along a tree-lined avenue to reach the edge of Musselburgh Racecourse (NT 356 732). Turn right here to follow the edge of the racecourse, with areas of woodland on your right (Figure 13.7).

Figure 13.7: Many of the trees lining the path near the racecourse are poplars. They too have their own sound, produced when the wind catches and twirls their small, delicate leaves. The underside of the leaves is a silvery white due to the presence of woolly hairs. This white contrasts with the green of the upper side, which yellows in the autumn, and this contrasting colouration creates a spectacle similar to that of the lapwing in flight, described earlier. At its best, the shaking leaves of the poplar can give the impression that the trees are trembling and murmuring some mysterious message to the wind.

The path eventually passes behind the racecourse pavilion and past a biking area to emerge in front of a playground in a large grassed area. Follow its right-hand edge back to the Cadet Hut, where you pick up the outward route along the river, and follow the river back to the Millhill car park.

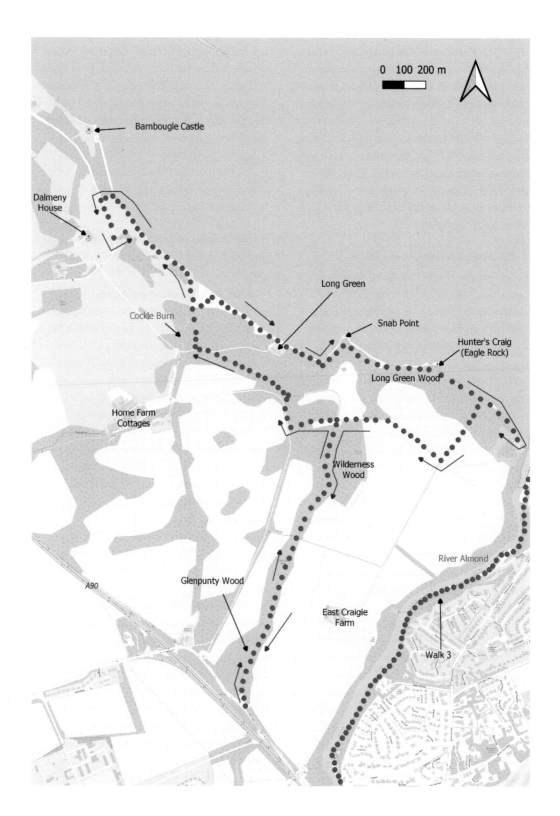

Walk 14

The woods, shore and parkland of Dalmeny Estate

Dalmeny Estate lies on the southern shores of the Firth of Forth between South Queensferry and the River Almond. It is an example of an aristocratic estate, with at its heart the imposing Gothic Revival mansion Dalmeny House, home to the Earl and Countess of Rosebery. The estate is extensive, and the woods, parkland and shore are well served with a range of paths that can be explored in a variety of ways, including a one-way route from Cramond to South Queensferry via Old Cramond Brig (linking to Walk 3). The walk described here is a circular one that provides a flavour of the estate's various habitats, whilst staying off the beaten path.

This walk's highlights include:

- An opportunity to bathe in the soothing majesty of long leafy treelined paths and rides, and to enjoy their changing colours and moods through the seasons.
- A good opportunity to hear, and perhaps even spot and observe, one of our shyest and most elusive corvids, the jay.
- The movement of shorebirds, coupled with inspiring views, up and down the Firth of Forth's Special Protection Area (SPA) and SSSI.
- The sounds of the wind in the reed beds beside the Cockle Burn, and of the cockle shells crunching as you walk along the cockle-rich shoreline.
- A quiet section of the John Muir Way, which may inspire you to walk more of the route that stretches between Muir's birthplace, Dunbar, to Helensburgh.

- A chance to consider what role large estates and landowners have in addressing the biodiversity crisis we face.

⚲ Summary

The walk starts from a small layby (NT 173 671) opposite one of the lesser-known gates into the Dalmeny Estate. A wooded track passes through Edinburgh Gate and heads through an area of mixed mature woodland known as Glenpunty Wood. After crossing two more tracks, you will swing west before cutting down through Long Green to reach the John Muir Way, beside the Cockle Burn. At this point make a detour to explore the coastline between here and Barnbougle Castle, with views across the parkland to Dalmeny House.

Regain the burn, and walk along the shoreline then the John Muir Way towards the River Almond. The way leaves the coast to head inland. After a short distance take a turn to the right to rejoin the outward path.

🏛 History

The Dalmeny Estate has a long history. It was acquired in 1662 by Sir Archibald Primrose (1616–1679), whose fourth and youngest son (1664–1724) was created Earl of Rosebery in 1703. He, like his father before him, was called Archibald. Over the intervening years there have been a further six earls of Rosebery and ten countesses, with the eldest son usually taking the courtesy title Viscount Dalmeny. When the 1st earl's father acquired the estate in 1662 from Sir Thomas Hamilton, afterwards Earl of Haddington, it included Barnbougle Castle, which became the family seat and was to remain so for several generations. The 4th earl (1783–1868), however, realising that the

Figure 14.1: A collection of wood pigeon and two jackdaws occupy the upper branches of a tree and contemplate the frozen ground below, safe in the knowledge that eight pairs of eyes are better than one and that any approaching buzzard or sparrowhawk will easily be spotted.

castle needed replacing, commissioned plans for a new house, which was eventually built in 1817. This is the Dalmeny House you see before you today. It was much more comfortable than Barnbougle, which was abandoned and used to store explosives. An accidental explosion damaged it, and it was left as a ruin, but was rebuilt in 1881 by the 5th earl (1847–1929), to house his library. He too was called Archibald, and was to become perhaps the best-known inhabitant of Dalmeny House, for he enjoyed a remarkable political career, serving as undersecretary to the Home Office, and foreign secretary in William Gladstone's cabinet, before becoming prime minister briefly in 1894.

It is remarkable how so much of recorded history is dominated by the accounts of the ruling and landed classes. There is barely enough room for those living on and from the land, even in the narrow margins. As for natural history, this is something that has been largely presented through the world-view of the privileged, with the worldview of the barely human and other-than-human relegated to footnotes. There is clearly a need for a more-than-humanhistory, but this is one that makes itself known slowly and in subtle, perhaps even mysterious, ways. All this, to invite you to hold the history of Dalmeny House at a distance and to suggest instead that we make room for nature's nameless and awe-inspiring creativity to manifest itself.

⬬ Habitats

Mixed deciduous woodland, parkland, tidal estuary and farmland.

⬛ Transport Links

The slip road off the A90, which passes the Burnshot and Edinburgh gates into the Dalmeny Estate and is served by Lothian Buses service 43. If cycling to the start, this is well served by National Cycle Route 76. This route runs from Dunbar to Kirkcaldy and is often referred to as the Round of the Forth.10

☕ Refreshments

There are options for a coffee or food stop in both Cramond village and South Queensferry. But I know of no options within walking distance of the start and finish of the walk.

---

10 https://www.sustrans.org.uk/find-a-route-on-the-national-cycle-network/
national-cycle-network-routes-in-edinburgh-the-lothians-and-scottish-borders/

🔖 References and further reading

Aebischer, N.J. (2019). 'Fifty-year trends in UK hunting bags of birds and mammals, and calibrated estimation of national bag size, using GWCT's National Gamebag Census'. *European Journal of Wildlife Research*, 65, p.64. https://doi.org/10.1007/s10344-019-1299-x.

Carss, D.N., Brito, A.C., Chainho, P., Ciutat, A., de Montaudouin, X., Fernández Otero, R.M., Filgueira, M.I., Garbutt, A., Goedknegt, M.A., Lynch, S.A., Mahony, K.E., Maire, O., Malham, S.K., Orvain, F., van der Schatte, A. and Laurence Jones, O.L. (2020). 'Ecosystem services provided by a non-cultured shellfish species: The common cockle, *Cerastoderma edule*', *Marine Environmental Research*, 158, 104931, https://doi.org/10.1016/j.marenvres.2020.104931.

Feber, R.E., Johnson, P.J. and Macdonald, D.W. (2020). 'Shooting pheasants for sport: What does the death of Cecil tell us?' *People and Nature* 2, pp.82–95. https://doi.org/10.1002/pan3.10068

Mustin, K., Arroyo, B., Beja, P., Newey, S., Irvine, R.J., Kestler, J. and Redpath, S.M. (2018). 'Consequences of game bird management for non-game species in Europe'. *Journal of Applied Ecology*, 55, pp.2285–2295. https://doi.org/10.1111/1365-2664.13131

Parrott, D. (2015). 'Impacts and management of common buzzards *Buteo buteo* at pheasant *Phasianus colchicus* release pens in the UK: A review'. *European Journal of Wildlife Research*, 61, pp.181–197. https://doi.org/10.1007/s10344-014-0893-1

Rackham, O. (1986). *The History of the Countryside*. London: Dent.

Tebble, N. (1976). *British Bivalve Seashell: A handbook for identification*, 2nd ed. Edinburgh: British Museum (Natural History), Her Majesty's Stationery Office.

🌐 Weblinks

Further information about Dalmeny House and the other estates making up the Rosebery family's estate can be found on their website: https://roseberyestates.co.uk/dalmeny-house.

Directions

1 Edinburgh Gate to the Cockle Burn

Cross over to the north side of the slip road and through an open gate, respectfully passing the house without disturbing the residents. You emerge on a broad track running through an area of mature mixed woodland, with larch, beech, sycamore, and chestnut dominating. The silvery beech trunks lining the path draw your eye onwards down the leafy alleyway (Figure 14.2). The OS 25-inch map for 1892–1914 identifies the house as East Main Lodge, and this long strip of woodland as Glenpunty Wood. Below you, to your right, the fields drop away and provide hunting grounds for the local buzzards who you may hear mewing as they circle over the fields and woodland (Figure 14.3a). The woodland is a great place to listen for tits calling, too, and to learn to distinguish the calls of blue and great tit (Figures 14.3b–3c) from those of coal and long-tailed tit. The great tit is a great imitator, and many are the times I have searched the canopy overhead to identify what I thought was a new call, only to spy that characteristic belly stripe and white cheek patch. The mix of trees presents you with opportunities to recognise the various features that can help you distinguish the lime from the elm and the sycamore from the chestnut. A good starting point is to observe the buds in autumn and then revisit these same buds in spring as the leaves emerge, appreciating their shape and then watching them as their colour evolves through the year. Before you know it lime yellow has taken on a whole new meaning for you, and you can identify

Figure 14.2 (above): The beech trees flanking the path beyond East Main Lodge are reassuring and welcoming somehow, and help you ease into a gentle rhythm.

Figure 14.3a (below): A buzzard takes flight from the vantage point from which it has been surveying the fields below. Note the barring of the flight feathers and how these bars become stronger, finishing in the brown tips. This gives the impression of a shift from white to dark brown on the wing's underside.

Figures 14.3b–3c: The discerning eye may notice how the thin black mask of the blue tit (14.3c) is very different from the black cap, chin and collar of the great tit (14.3b). The blue headpiece of the blue tit is also an exquisite feature.

a lime tree at a distance just by the colour it contributes to the canopy.

Progressing along the path, you pass through a set of gates as you cross a track. Glenpunty Wood continues ahead of you. Follow this until you reach a second track (NT 179 771). The pile of wood shavings and other materials on your right is often full of foraging finches. Turn left onto the track and follow this westward to reach a more significant estate road. This is the old coach road shown on the aforementioned map. The area is often alive with pheasants as the estate rears and releases pheasants for sport shooting (see the special feature).

Upon reaching the estate road, take in the vista ahead of you that stretches across Galow

Law, where you can expect to see some of the estate's in-hand flock of Texel and Lleyn sheep grazing on the parkland. According to the estate website, some 1,270 ewes produce 1,930 fat lambs per annum on the sweeping pasture that runs between the wooded copses.

Turn right and look out for a metal gate a short distance along the road on your right. Pass through this and take the track to descend to another estate track, where you turn left (NT 177 773) onto a broad road with woodland on either side. Ignore a track coming up at an acute angle on your right, and look out instead for a footpath heading down towards Cockle Burn on the right. This takes you down to a footbridge over the burn itself.

★ Special Feature – pheasant shooting and conservative conservation

A wander through woodland estates in Great Britain, including the Dalmeny Estate, is likely to include a brush with a pheasant (*Phasianus colchicus*) – or, rather, a great many pheasants. The overdressed cock pheasants running rampant in British woodlands may impress with their bright vermilion wattles, emerald green necks, white collar and jewelled bronzes … but those who can see past all this flashiness (Figure 14.4a), may see the bird as a symptom of an at once decadent and decaying society. The pheasant offers us a vital clue in decrypting and understanding why the UK

Figure 14.4a: Two cock pheasants square up to each other among the leaf litter on the forest floor. The dominant bird can expect to go on to attract a harem of females with his showy territorial display.

is one of the most nature-depleted countries in the world, and why unquestioning members of the general public are oblivious to the centuries of exploitation that have devastated our wilderness.

The pheasant, originating from Asia, was first brought to Europe by the Greeks and subsequently introduced to the UK by the Romans. As such, pheasants can claim to having been part of the UK's fauna and flora for over 1,000 years. But the story of the pheasant's appropriation of British woodlands cannot be attributed to the Romans, for it was the advent of organised covert shoots and gamekeeping during the 19th century that allowed the pheasant's harsh gokk gokk and clattering wingbeat to become one of the dominant sounds of this country's woods and our countryside.

From the mid-19th century onwards, pheasant shooting became a major pastime and a feature of the social calendar for the landed classes. This blood sport often involves a line of beaters startling the birds so that they fly as high as possible over a line of guns and can be blasted from the sky. Given the carnage involved and the numbers of pheasants that have to be buried at the end of each shoot, it is probably fair to say that this activity is a form of entertainment. As such, it is widely recognised as one of the few cruel sports still legal in the UK, a country where animal welfare legislation has seen cockfighting, bear baiting, badger baiting, hare coursing and fox hunting recognised as inhumane, and banned. Setting aside the significant animal welfare concerns that have led to growing calls for such hunting to be banned, there are ecological considerations that need careful consideration if we are to understand how pheasant shooting may or may not be contributing to nature conservation.

It could be argued that many large estates have only managed to preserve their woodlands because they can derive income from this land through such lucrative activities as pheasant shooting. The environmental historian Oliver Rackham has studied the consequences of the pheasant's domination of the landscape and has highlighted the role they may have played in staying the excesses of prairie farming and the way fields have grown at the expense of woodland. Certainly, at Dalmeny the maintenance of strips of unfragmented woodland over the last two centuries is what makes it such a delightful estate to explore. But this hides a more sinister truth, for current generations have completely lost sight of what the land is capable of sustaining. We are suffering from shifting baseline syndrome. To understand this better we must consider what goes into packing pheasants into UK woodlands on an industrial scale.

The numbers: According to a 2014 report by PACEC,[11] there are about 23,000 providers of driven game shooting in the UK, the majority of whom shoot pheasants. Such is the demand for shooting that most of these are almost entirely dependent on releasing captive-bred birds. These are generally first reared indoors after hatching from eggs that are incubated artificially. At six weeks of age, the birds are moved outdoors and reared in open-topped woodland pens. You may spy examples of such pens in the woodlands at Dalmeny. Aebischer (2019) reports that in 2016 some 47 million pheasants were released into the UK countryside; this represents an increase of almost 600 per cent over the last 50 years, and the biomass represented by this release exceeds that that of the entire breeding avifauna of these islands. This provides some indication of the extent to which this activity can impact on the health of our ecosystems.

The impact: it is likely that in conserving pheasants, in ensuring that their needs are met and they can be shot in their millions, other species who rely on the same habitat and living condi-

---

11 The report was produced by Cambridge-based Public and Corporate Economic Consultants (PACEC) and assessed the economic, environmental and social benefits of shooting sports. It is available from http://www.shootingfacts.co.uk/

Figure 14.4b: The tensions between the shooting and anti-shooting lobbies can themselves feel like a cock fight. Transcending such differences and moving beyond the ideologies of those lining up on either side of the debate will require us to explore the uncommon ground we share. This will require us to consider in a radically open way how the health of our woodlands is inextricably entangled with our own health and wellbeing.

tions as pheasants will benefit. This is the umbrella effect, with those gathered in the shelter of the umbrella being clear beneficiaries. Feber et al (2020) provide an account of the many beneficiaries, including insectivorous birds such as warblers, butterflies and moths, and other species who value the shrubby woodland and open glades that a pheasant-focused management system prioritises. They refer to a literature review by Mustin et al (2018) that reported that 85 per cent of the effects of habitat management for game birds in lowland agricultural landscapes were positive.

On the surface this all sounds encouraging … But, as ever, the devil is in the detail, and this devil makes worrying reading for the members of the wider ecosystem who are not covered by the umbrella. In order to maintain industrial concentrations of pheasants in the coverts, game-keepers are employed to kill the predators who are likely to feed on this free source of food. Foxes and mustelids take the brunt of their ire and exterminatory efforts, for they have little in the way of legal protection. Buzzards are also killed under licence (Parrot, 2015) – the only way a protected species can legally be killed.[12] There are, however, ongoing and growing concerns about illegal raptor persecution on estates managed for shooting. A primary concern here is that we are a long way from managing the land for biodiversity, and are only just waking up to the authoritative smokescreen put out by landowners as a way of justifying their traditions and privileges. Holding these up to scrutiny is essential if we are to address exploitation of any kind, and it is significant that the right to roam provided by the Scottish Countryside Access Code means that woodlands

12 For further information on the licensing schemes in Scotland that permit activities that would otherwise contra-vene the important legislation we have to protect our wildlife, see the Nature Scot website: https://www.nature.scot/professional-advice/protected-areas-and-species/licensing

can be accessed and explored. This is not, however, the case south of the border, as highlighted by Oliver Rackham (1986, p.93):

> [gamekeepers] took it upon themselves to persecute beasts and birds of prey and to exclude the public from woods. This need not have been so. France, Germany and Switzerland are equally good shooting countries, and yet ancient woods are everyone's heritage; in Britain alone we have lost that birthright, and with it our knowledge and love of woods. A generation of people grew up who, except in such fortunate areas as south Essex, had never been in a wood and could easily be persuaded that woods had merely economic function. People who have been rudely expelled from a lime wood are unlikely to oppose its destruction.

So we in Scotland do have much to be grateful for. We have areas of woodland that have survived, and we are entitled to access them, as here in Dalmeny. We also have the surge of global pandemics to thank for as a disruptive element in this story. What do I mean? Well, at the time of writing the woods are relatively free from pheasants because the Highly Pathogenic Avian Influenza outbreak in 2022 hit the supply of pheasant eggs from the Vendée and Loire Atlantique departments of western France. It is estimated that some 16 million farmed birds, including poultry, were culled as authorities tried to control the outbreak. The subsequent controls on exports meant that the import of pheasant eggs and poults from France dried up overnight. The disease highlighted the failings in a pathologically sick human-made system of exploitation that failed to acknowledge and respect the rules of nature. Struan Stevenson, writing in the *Herald* on 4 October 2022,[13] bemoans the impact of a perfect storm of disasters that will hit the pheasant shooting season hard as it opens on 1 October:

> Scotland's fragile rural economy, struggling to recover from two years of coronavirus shutdowns when game shooting ground to a halt, is now facing the catastrophic impact of avian flu, a shortage of pheasant and partridge poults and soaring feed and energy costs. The additional expense of a looming government ban on lead shot for shotgun cartridges has added to the sense of despair descending like a black cloud over the industry.

The perfect storm hitting this traditional industry could easily be compared to the peppering of shotgun pellets thudding into a poor pheasant and either wounding them mortally or causing untold suffering. It beggars belief, however, that someone should write such a piece without recognising the impact of polluting the ecosystem with lead, a highly toxic metal that has caused untold neurological damage to all animals, humans included, with a nervous system that can be poisoned by lead. There is also a failure to recognise the damage caused by polluting the ecosystem with large quantities of drugs to control the diseases that intensively farmed birds are vulnerable to, and the ecological disturbance arising from the supplementary feeding of pheasants once released. This is an issue that reflects the tensions (Figure 14.4b) between a conservative landowning élite who think they own and understand the countryside and a majority who are learning to care for the planet and are willing to ask challenging questions of the ruling and shooting classes.

---

13 https://www.heraldscotland.com/sport/23015404.struan-stevenson-perfect-storm-game-shooting-will-hit-scotland-hard/

2 Across the Cockle Burn to Dalmeny House

The reedbed flanking the sides of the burn can be quite a magical place to watch, especially when it is moving in a stiff breeze or kissed by a rainbow over the waters of the Firth of Forth (Figure 14.5a). Crossing over the footbridge, pick up a path that hugs the shore and runs towards the restored pile that is Barnbougle Castle, which occupies the obvious promontory jutting into the firth. The building you see today was created in 1881, when the previous castle was entirely reconstructed and extended – primarily, it is said, to house the private library of Archibald, 5th Earl of Rosebery (1847–1929), a collection that specialised in Napoleonica. Rosebery became prime minister in 1894, and practised his parliamentary speeches here, in a purpose-built gallery hall.

Refocusing on the ground underfoot and the present moment, the walk along the beach is a delight, for it is regularly resupplied with cockle shells that crunch under foot as you move over them. This is sand in the making. I always try to direct my attention towards and into the sound rising from beneath my feet as I walk this stretch. Can you savour the crackle? Can you feel it vibrating through the roll of your foot?

Other sounds may summon your attention. The piping calls of oystercatchers foraging over the lawns around Dalmeny House or along the shoreline are very much part of the local soundscape. The lawns are part of Dalmeny Golf Course, although it is rare to see a golfer playing this course, which perhaps explains why the windows are all intact! I would invite you to walk as far as the woodland surround-

Figure 14.5a: The reedbeds flanking the west bank of Cockle Burn glow golden in the autumn sunshine. Reedbeds are wetlands dominated by stands of a single plant, the common reed (Phragmites australis). Whilst primarily found in freshwater habitats, they can, as in this case, be found in brackish and tidal waters. They are threatened by land drainage, water abstraction and conversion to intensive agriculture.

Figure 14.5b: Dalmeny House was built in 1817 after the son of the 3rd Earl of Rosebery succeeded his father in 1814. Today, the house is home to the 7th Earl and Countess of Rosebery.

Figure 14.5c: Exploring the lawns between the shore and Dalmeny House can be rewarding in many ways.

ing Barnbougle Castle and, turning left, follow the fence line as it runs alongside the woodland as far as the Leuchold Drive, the main road running through the estate. You can then explore the grassed area surrounding the house (Figures 14.5b–5c) and you may wish to walk up to the impressive bronze statue of King Tom (1851–1878) a thoroughbred racehorse and famous sire. It would be very easy to write of his pedigree and all the famous racehorses he sired – but I feel it more appropriate to draw your attention to the sad fact that after winning races as a two-year-old, although he had suffered an injury he was put in for the 1854 Epsom Derby, and finished second.

After that he was dead lame, and the injury curtailed his racing during the rest of the year; it was only in his fourth year that he returned to racing, winning one further race before breaking down. Such are the depravities of what in humans would be recognised as child labour but in the horse racing world passes as standard practice. After his retirement from racing, King Tom continued working, becoming the foundation stallion for Baron Mayer de Rothschild's Mentmore and Crafton Studs. King Tom died in 1878, at the age 27, and was buried in the grounds of Mentmore Towers beneath a life-size bronze statue, which now stands in the grounds of Dalmeny House.[14]

14 You might wonder why the move to Dalmeny: the answer may lie in the fact that in 1878 Hannah, Rothschild's only daughter, married the 5th Earl of Rosebery.

3 Cockle Burn to the Long Green Cottages

After regaining the banks of the Cockle
Burn, take a moment to absorb its thoughtful meanderings and the way it converses
with the land. This area is full of life, both
deep to the surface and above ground
(Figure 14.6). Every time I contemplate this
scene and try to make sense of the rippling
waters of the burn, flowing toward the sea, I
think of Khalil Gibran's (1883–1931) tribute
to fear:

It is said that before entering the sea
a river trembles with fear.
She looks back at the path she has travelled,
from the peaks of the mountains,

the long winding road crossing forests and villages.
And in front of her,
she sees an ocean so vast,
that to enter
there seems nothing more than to disappear
      forever.
But there is no other way.
The river can not go back.
Nobody can go back.
To go back is impossible in existence.
The river needs to take the risk
of entering the ocean
because only then will fear disappear,
because that's where the river will know
it's not about disappearing into the ocean,
but of becoming the ocean.

Figure 14.6: The Cockle Burn swings first one way then the next after passing the reedbeds and getting a first good smell of the sea. The sandy banks can be a good place to look for animal tracks. Ahead, the beach exposed at low tide is often well frequented by a variety of feeding birds, including oystercatcher, redshank and curlew as well as crows, all of whom are experts in finding delicate morsels in this twice-daily banquet.

Figure 14.7: The beaches of the Forth estuary between Barnbougle coast and the Forth bridges can appear almost Caribbean thanks to the presence of a rich population of molluscs. How we care for such places will determine whether future generations are able to enjoy nature's bounty and beauty.

After crossing the footbridge over the Cockle urn, pick up a path that heads fearlessly seaward through the back of the beach. There is evidence of Scots pine and a range of shrubs colonising this habitat. Ahead of you, you may be able to hear the tidal surge of the Forth in conversation with the cockle beach. This section of coastline is a delight, and I invite you to pay attention to the sounds of a water-kissed and caressed beach to encourage you to slow down and savour the experience. One of the principal delights of this bit of coastline are the cockles, and the special feature below is offered as a tribute to these amazing crustaceans.

Continuing along the water's edge, you get a sense of the extent to which this shoreline is appreciated by waders, ducks and other birds, and why the Firth of Forth is a Special Protection Area. The shore is both restaurant and dormitory, for its mud and cockle beds offer rich pickings to those with probing bills and inquisitive intellects, whilst the water lying in the lee of the headland ahead of you provides shelter from easterly winds pushing up the Forth.

Sadly, our human species' lack of respect and appreciation for the marine environment is also very much in evidence. It can be sobering to see the amount of marine plastic and other human refuse deposited by each receding tide. Some items, such as fishing nets, plastic bottles and plastic ropes, are very obvious; other items, such as plastic cotton buds less so. A more insidious plastic is also to be seen in the sand itself, for much of the plastic pellets produced in plastic recycling make their way into the marine environment when ships carrying this recycled plastic flush out their holds. FIDRA, a Scottish charity based in East Lothian, has taken a particular interest in these pellets, called nurdles. This has resulted in the creation of a citizen science project called the Great Nurdle Hunt. According to FIDRA,[15] an estimated 230,000 tonnes of nurdles, equating to 15 billion plastic bottles, escape from the plastics supply chain into the environment every year. This plastic pollutes every part of the ecosystem and of the food chain, including our own bodies. This fact should help us appreciate the direct relationship between choosing to buy a bottle of Coca Cola in a plastic bottle and plastic getting into our food and therefore our bodies and bloodstream.

The United Nation's Environment Programme (UNEP) does not mince its words when it states:

> The oceans are under attack from the same patterns of unsustainable consumption and production patterns that are causing such problems on land. They have become a dumping ground for all matter of pollution, from plastics to toxic chemicals. Plastics represent the largest, most harmful and most persistent proportion of marine litter. The cumulative hazards and direct impacts of marine plastics already contribute to an estimated loss of USD 500 to USD 2,500 billion in marine ecosystem services per year.

The uplifting and reviving wind that brings colour to our cheeks as we walk along the beach can help to sweep away many of our concerns. It can also embolden us to embrace the challenge of enquiring into our ecological footprint – the extent to which the impact of our choices in life weighs on nature. Curiosity can help us become better informed and make better choices. How to refuse plastic then becomes a game we can engage with playfully and creatively. Many companies, including the University of Edinburgh, now offer their staff a paid volunteering day every year. One excellent way to use such a day is a beach clean. These can feed into citizen science projects as well as cleaning the beach. Wouldn't it be nice to see beach-clean stations on all our beaches? These would allow visitors to conduct impromptu clean-ups and deposit the rubbish they collect on a walk. At the time of writing, this is not, however, available on the beaches visited in this walk. What you will find, though, are a few artistic sculptures where driftwood and debris have been co-opted and erected so they stand surveying the incoming tide and watching over visitors to the beach.

If you are motivated to help, please visit the websites below for ideas and advice on how to conduct a nurdle hunt or a beach clean-up. Nurdle hunts involve (a) visiting a beach (b) searching for nurdles, and (c) reporting your results online. For more information see: https://www.nurdlehunt.org.uk/take-part.html.

The Million Mile Clean was initiated by Surfers Against Sewage (SAS) in 2021, and provides support for those wanting to organise a beach clean or who are looking to take part in a clean near them. You are encouraged to report your findings on their website, thereby helping to improve our understanding of the scale of the problem. For more information see: https://sas.org.uk/plastic-pollution/million-mile-clean/

15 https://www.fidra.org.uk/projects/nurdle/

★ Special Feature – the common cockle

Figure 14.8: The winter sun kisses the cockle shells and razor shells that have been cast up on the beach below Cockle Burn Wood. These shells, or valves, tell us a lot about the health of the marine ecosystem, for they are a clue as to the hard work being done deep under the sand of the intertidal area – work to clean the water, produce food for countless predators, sequestrate carbon (11.7 per cent of the shell is carbon), and to make contributions, too, to human culture and wellbeing. We have much to thank the cockle for … they truly warm the cockles of our hearts when we open our hearts to them and feel grateful for the life they contribute to sustaining.

The common cockle (*Cerastoderma edule*) whose presence on this stretch of coast has led the stream and neighbouring wood to be named Cockle Burn, is a bivalve mollusc whose geographical distribution along the coast of the north-eastern Atlantic coastline extends from the Baltic and the western parts of the Barents Sea down along the coast of Europe to the Iberian peninsula, into the Mediterranean, the Black and Caspian seas and onwards, south, along the coast of West Africa as far as Senegal (Tebble, 1976). Bivalves are so called because they have two hard, typically bowl-shaped, shells, referred to as 'valves', which protect the soft body inside. The shell provides protection against the predation and dehydration that are a feature of life in the intertidal zone. Where mussels and oysters attach to rocky surfaces, the common or edible cockles live freely, unattached. This is why they prefer flat, sheltered areas where they are less likely to be swept away by the currents and can bury themselves a few inches under the surface of the seabed in clean sand, muddy sand, mud or muddy gravel. This means that they are commonly found in coastal areas characterised by intertidal flats, estuaries, coastal lagoons and sheltered coastline bays.

From their sandy, muddy refuges, cockles feed by filtering water through their shells and extracting tiny creatures, plankton and other organic matter. When on the surface of the seabed, they can move along by thrusting out their muscular foot and kicking themselves along. This allows them to evade predators, and this foot also helps them to dig themselves in again. But this free-living lifestyle means that they can easily be thrown up the beach. High winds and heavy stormy seas can tear up the seabed with all its cockles, and scatter them high up the beach. This is partly why you can see so many shells on the beach at Dalmeny. There are other reasons too, for, amazingly, cockles can reach densities of up to 10,000 individuals per square metre! And here, at least, they are not exploited by humans. Elsewhere across its geographical range, *Cerastoderma edule* is widely exploited by commercial bivalve fisheries as well as by individuals collecting for their own consumption. The exploitation of cockles at scale and for profit by commercial operations also involved human exploitation ; this was evidenced in 2004 when a group of Chinese immigrants were cut off by the incoming tide while cockle-picking in Morecambe Bay; 23 members of the group lost their lives. This serves to remind us that those who set out to pillage nature are likely to bring the same attitude to the way they fail to respect and safeguard the welfare of the workers who are sent out to collect the cockles at low tide. In many areas of the cockles' range, cockle beds are suffering under the combined pressures of illegal cockle picking, overcollection by commercial operations, and environmental factors. This has led to cockle-picking being banned completely in some areas, to allow stocks to recover and maximise the chances of the future sustainability of the cockle beds.

A recent paper by Carss et al (2020) highlighted the many ways that cockles contribute to sustaining life on earth. Their study recognised the common cockle as Europe's most important wild-harvested bivalve species, and demonstrated the substantial role played by this mollusc, by assessing the ecosystem services that cockles provide. Ecosystem services are typically defined as services provided by the natural environment that benefit people. They are an increasingly common way of considering the contributions, and therefore the value, of nature. Whilst very anthropocentric and therefore selfish, they do help put things in perspective, as illustrated by the list of five key contributions:

(i)   Cockles support ecosystems through water filtration and biogeochemical cycling.
(ii) Cockles protect sediments, create habitats and support biodiversity within food webs.
(iii) Cockles provide meat and shell by-products with potential value of €11.3 million per annum.
(iv) Cockles remove nitrogen, phosphorus and carbon from the marine/estuarine environment.
(v)   In coastal places, cockles are a bridge between ecosystem function and cultural values.

They conclude that the cockle is an ecosystem engineer who works very effectively to promote the productivity of sedimentary habitats, providing a food source for predators such as the oystercatchers you can expect to see on this walk. The cockle also plays a key role in filtering and purifying water and in controlling algal blooms and eutrophication; and in addition its role in human culture is both significant and easily underestimated. Looking ahead to the future, and conscious of the extent to which we are polluting the marine environment with plastics and other pollutants, it is ironic that we are still so unaware of the cockle's uncomplaining efforts to clean the waters around our coasts, of the plastics that find their way into their bodies and that we in turn consume when ordering a plate of shellfish.

If you are partial to eating shellfish, this represents an opportunity to be unselfish and to care for the environment. Firstly, you can start to think of the connection between your own choices as a consumer and how these choices find their way into your food and into your body. And, secondly, you can choose food that has been produced as sustainably as possible. Suction dredging and other industrial-scale harvesting collect indiscriminately and cause damage to the seabed, so I would encourage you to always choose hand-gathered cockles. Look for Marine Stewardship Council (MSC) certified cockles, and find out how a sustainable industry is being encouraged. In Wales, the cockle pickers working on the Burry Inlet in Carmarthenshire and the Dee Estuary in North Wales have both earnt MSC certification.[16] This reflects the respect of nature shown by a highly selective harvesting process in which individual pickers gather cockles by hand, using a small hand-rake, sieving the cockles on the beach to ensure that any undersized cockles are returned unharmed to the wild.

---

16 https://stories.msc.org/uk/burry-inlet-cockles/ . https://stories.msc.org/uk/dee-estuary-cockle/

Figure 14.9a: The evening colours often filter through the trees and hedgerow plants, including these cow parsley stems, rewarding the tired walker with some encouragement and reminding them to keep wandering in wonder.

4 Long Green Cottages to Cobble Cottage and the Mouth of the Almond

The cottages set back from the beach used to house estate workers and are now available for rent. They nestle into the surrounding woodland of Long Green Wood and have a tranquil feel about them. You can leave the beach here (NT 177 775) and skirt the left-hand edge of the cottages to gain the John Muir Way. Alternatively, continue along the beach and climb a steep (and often slippery) section of bank under a large tree. The John Muir Way follows the rocky edge of the promontory round to Snab Point before continuing on to Hunter's Craig, also known as Eagle Rock. Snab Point provides a great vantage point from which to look up and down the estuary, with fine views up to Barnbougle Castle.

Eagle Rock is so called because it is said to have a Roman eagle carved into it. A Historic Scotland sign explains that the Roman legionnaires garrisoned at Cramond may have been responsible for carving the eagle, but that there is no conclusive proof for this. To view the rock, you have to descend to the beach, from where you can gain a closer view of the rock and the early piece of graffiti that still has people trying to make sense of it almost 2,000 years after it was carved.

Continue on along the John Muir Way until it swings inland. At this point, you may want to continue along the path ahead towards Cobble Cottage and the River Almond. This extension of the walk brings you to the mouth of the Almond where it joins the Forth, and rewards you with views across the estuary, out to Cramond Island and across to the village of Cramond itself. A quiet spot in the trees can allow you to survey the birds feeding on the mud flats or on the water. There is something peaceful about this place that the birds appreciate and that the discreet visitor will observe in turn. The trick is to stay discreet and respect the tranquillity that reigns on this bank of the river.

5 The Mouth of the Almond to Edinburgh Gate

Retrace your steps to the John Muir Way and turn left up a track that emerges from the trees, rising gently to pass between two fields that are often a good place to watch for foraging birds, including thrushes, starlings and corvids. If walking this way into the evening sun, you may be spoilt with sunset colours (Figure 14.9a).

At the next track juncture, turn right and head up to meet the track through Glenpunty Wood that you came in on (NT 179 771). Turn left up this track and retrace your steps to Edinburgh Gate, enjoying the low westering light of the sun in autumn (Figure 14.9b) as it drops through the trees. Don't forget to listen to the leaves underfoot, and to reflect on the day you have just enjoyed, whilst remaining attentive for the calls of great spotted woodpecker, jay and buzzard.

Figure 14.9b: walking back through Glenpunty Woods in autumn, the low-angled light of the setting sun can create a delightful atmosphere, a gentle play of light and shadow.

Conclusion

As this book draws to a close, I very much hope, dear reader, that you feel inspired to look beyond these pages to an unfolding world of beckoning wild places and wild encounters.

So this is, I am hoping, not so much an end as a new beginning, for once nature has touched our hearts and awoken us to her wondrous beauty and – dare I say it? – sacredness, we cannot but encounter her wherever we venture. And such encounters can move us profoundly and leave us feeling grateful and keen to enter into a more reciprocal relationship. There are so many ways we can reciprocate, as I have tried to share with you in these pages. Reciprocity involves seeing life as a gift and paying that gift forwards. We can share our passion with others and, going forth, we can explore ways to care for nature much as she cares for us.

I therefore hope you feel inspired to venture forth, learn more and volunteer in the work that reconnects us to the wild. Many of the local and national wildlife conservation organisations mentioned in this book offer talks guided walks, short courses and volunteering opportunities. Please support them in whatever ways you can. I particularly recommend the events programmes offered by the Scottish Ornithologists Club (SOC),[17] the Scottish Wildlife Trust (SWT)[18] and the Water of Leith Conservation Trust,[19] but there are a growing number of small charities doing excellent work. Wherever you choose to join the conservation community you will find yourself part of a growing network of like-minded people seeking to make a really significant contribution.

At the time of writing, we are approaching the halfway point in this the UN Decade of Ecosystem Restoration. There is so much still to do, and we all need to raise our game. Here in Scotland, there is a decent chance that we could soon declare ourselves the world's first rewilding nation. Please do therefore support the work of Scotland: The Big Picture,[20] who are championing this vision. Here in Scotland's capital, it would be wonderful to see conservation of biodiversity and habitat restoration on a collaborative landscape scale. Local communities have a really important role to play in this. That is my hope and vision. Let's see if we can make it happen for nature and for future generations.

17 https://www.the-soc.org.uk/
18 https://scottishwildlifetrust.org.uk/
19 https://www.waterofleith.org.uk/
20 https://www.scotlandbigpicture.com/